European Sovereignty

Gavin Barrett · Peter-Christian Müller-Graff ·
Jean-Philippe Rageade · Viktor Vadász
Editors

European Sovereignty

The Legal Dimension

Springer

Editors
Gavin Barrett
University College Dublin
Dublin, Ireland

Peter-Christian Müller-Graff
Heidelberg University
Heidelberg, Germany

Jean-Philippe Rageade
Academy of European Law
Trier, Germany

Viktor Vadász
Academy of European Law
Trier, Germany

ISBN 978-3-031-71850-2 ISBN 978-3-031-71851-9 (eBook)
https://doi.org/10.1007/978-3-031-71851-9

This Springer imprint is published by the registered company Springer Nature Switzerland AG
The registered company address is: Gewerbestrasse 11, 6330 Cham, Switzerland

Foreword

European Sovereignty: A Union Seeking to Control its Own Destiny

Since its inception, the EU integration project has had an internal focus, seeking to ensure peaceful relations between its Member States by relying on the rule of law. In a hostile and chaotic world, one in which the EU and its States are losing their relative weight, this focus is gradually changing to an external one. If the Member States want to limit this decline and to control their destiny, they must cooperate in an increasing number of subject fields, including security and defence issues. This collective power has a price: Member States may have to forego sovereignty in internal matters to gain sovereignty in external affairs, not only *vis-à-vis* third countries, but also in respect of strong private players that operate mainly in the digital sphere. This balancing exercise is an ongoing one and, implies, in legal terms, that the European Union and its Member States must continually seek to define the limits of EU law in relation to national law. This is the task and responsibility of the constitutional courts of the Member States and the Court of Justice, which must define together the contours of the EU legal order and, hence of the collective pool of sovereignty-enhancing power. This cooperation relies on a constant dialogue, but uniformity and efficiency in a Union of 27 States requires that one court must have the final say and that court is the Court of Justice.

The European integration project is hard to conceive without crises. That is not very surprising, since it finds its roots in the aftermath of the Second World War, probably the biggest crisis that Europe and humanity, as a whole, has had to face. It is also true that many, smaller, crises that have hit the European continent since then have created a sense of urgency or need that impelled Europeans to find a common answer, often obtained after endless discussions or during negotiation marathons. Even so, it would be too simplistic and too negative to characterise the European integration project as merely a reaction to threats or problems. The project also has a dynamic of its own. In many respects, each step towards integration raises new needs and demands. Europe is not only known for its wars, but also for its buildings, cities and arts. It is not without reason that the integration project is often referred to as "*la construction européenne*".

Thirty years ago, when the Academy of European Law Trier was founded, these positive integration dynamics had the upper hand. It was the time of the internal market project. After years of sclerosis and stagnation, European leaders realised that the free circulation rules of the European Economic Community Treaty, as interpreted by the Court of Justice, did not suffice to transform the common market into a truly internal market. Positive harmonisation measures were needed to achieve a common space for European not only for workers, goods, services and entrepreneurs, but also for citizens. The European Commission under the inspiring leadership of Jacques Delors developed an ambitious legislative programme that, alongside the implementation of the European Single Act, would give rise to the world's biggest internal market in terms of revenues by the end of 1992.[1] A large display at the top of the Commission's headquarters in Brussels showed the countdown. It was a relatively joyful period.

The same cannot be said of the present period. At present, war is raging again on our old continent. As already experienced shortly before in the context of the COVID-19 crisis, Europeans are increasingly aware of their relative weakness, their dependency on foreign supply lines and their lack of geopolitical influence. The question arises as to whether the EU and its Member States are still players or mere pawns in world politics. This time, a real crisis and a genuine sense of urgency have activated the integration process, which in a relatively short time span has led to an impressive set of legislative, budgetary and political measures, that within or outside the context of the Treaties, must ensure that the EU remains a geopolitical subject.

Despite the real progress that the EU made in terms of self-assertion, this author would submit that it is too soon to claim that the EU is sovereign and in control of its destiny. In my perception, it is a work in progress, as the European project always was and is. During that continuum, the key issue has always been sovereignty. Unlike classic international cooperation agreements, the Union project is based on the idea that the Member States pool parts of their sovereign powers in a common legal order and that they have an interest in doing so because the pool yields more power and influence than the sum of its constituent parts. By being in the pool, Member States have more to gain than to lose.

Obviously, there is a balance to strike between the advantages and disadvantages of pooling sovereignty. This is a complex exercise in itself, because the pros and cons in pooling sovereignty can be direct or indirect, concrete or diffuse, in nature. The balancing exercise becomes even more complex in its temporal dimension: participating in the pool by a transfer of powers implies an immediate loss of sovereignty, whereas the benefits may take time to materialise. Moreover, the outcome may differ from one Member State to another. The smaller Member States may have more to gain than the bigger ones, especially the bigger States that believe that they are still serious actors on the world scene. Finally, as the Brexit drama has shown, when

[1] Commission White Paper on completing the internal market, COM(85) 310, Brussels, 14 June 1985.

it comes to sovereignty, sentiment may get the upper hand over rational equations, bearing in mind that sentiments are often volatile. It cannot be excluded that the outcome of the referendum on the United Kingdom's membership to the EU would have been different if it had been held today.

Emotions and sentiments set aside, the European integration project is a sovereignty-increasing mechanism. Even if Member States resent transferring powers to the pool, their participation in the institutions that govern it, gives them a say over issues that would have been beyond reach in the absence of such transfers. Collectively, the EU Member States punch well above their weight. An example of this is the field of digital services, which involves an issue that transcends the classic question of state sovereignty. Whereas energy, trade and defence questions most often concern international relations between public players, such as States, blocs of States or international organisations, the digital services industry is controlled by private actors that possess powers and means equivalent or superior to those of many Member States. Whereas these actors may try to defy an individual State, they will have to comply with the common European rules if they do not want to forego the benefits of the EU's internal market. These common rules yield an influence which goes well beyond the European Union, because they become a *de facto* trading standard with which third States and private actors align themselves by virtue of the "Brussels effect", so well described by Anu Bradford in her writings.[2]

The European Union, thanks to this soft but real power of its common legal order, regroups the parts of sovereignty that the Member States have transferred to it. Over time, this common legal order has evolved into a comprehensive set of complex rules that affect nearly every aspect of the EU citizen's life. These rules may sometimes amaze or irritate by their length, degree of detail and woolly language, but they are the price to pay for European Union's autonomy and, hence, its sovereignty. Apart from the size and density of this legal thicket, the EU legal order also has its own dynamics. The EU legal order is not necessarily a consistent whole and has not been conceived like that. It grows organically in a way the authors of the Treaty or the legislator did not necessarily foresee when they made the rules. Moreover, Member States, institutions, companies and citizens may disagree as to the precise delimitation of the EU's competences or on the way in which European Union rules should be applied.

As in any other legal order, the EU legal order provides for conflict settlement mechanisms to deal with such issues. However, unlike other legal orders, the EU legal order relies on other legal orders—those of the Member States. The first port of call for those who seek to enforce the rights which they derive from European Union law, are national administrations and courts. Moreover, the Court of Justice is not the only constitutional court in the Union. It interacts with its national counterparts to define the boundaries of the EU legal order. However, for this legal order to be truly common to all Member States and to ensure that all EU citizens enjoy equal rights throughout the Union, one court must necessarily have the final say. That

---

[2] See Anu Bradford, *The Brussels Effect: How the European Union Rules the World* (Oxford University Press 2020).

court is—the Court of Justice. Without a uniform interpretation of the law, the EU legal order and the integration project simply cannot exist. Even so, finding the right divide between the national and Union sphere of competencies is a delicate task. As European Union law has grown exponentially over the years, the probability that it will conflict with national rules has increased considerably. The rules of direct effect and primacy may be harder to accept when EU law starts to interact with national law in nearly all its dimensions. The Court of Justice and national constitutional courts must closely work together to ensure the best possible symbiosis between the European and national legal orders. It is hard to say whether the relationship between national and European sovereignty will involve an unsolvable conflict, but it certainly is–and will be–a recurring one. As already noted in the text above, the European project is never finished. It will always be a work in progress. Frictions between the national constitutional orders and the European legal order will continue to exist but this is not problematic as such as long as the courts of the Member States and the Court of Justice are willing to cooperate to find workable solutions. Even if these solutions might not always square with the orthodoxy professed by legal purists, the importance is that they reflect a common commitment to the European project as a project that it is on balance sovereignty-enhancing both for the Member States and for the Union. This common commitment requires an open mindset from both national and EU courts. This openness is testified to in the chapter in this volume by the President of the Court of Justice of the European Union, Koen Lenaerts, in which he rejects the submission that the Court of Justice will always side with the institutions to the detriment of Member States. The Union is not a legal Pac-Man that gradually eats up national competencies. It is interesting to note that a few weeks after the delivery of the 2022 speech on which that chapter is based, the Court of Justice delivered an interesting judgment that significantly reduced the scope for the Commission to rely on State aid rules to control national tax advantages.[3]

Issues concerning the democratic organisation of European sovereignty also underline the idea that the European project continues to be work in progress. Although this project yields concrete benefits for many, it remains by its very nature a relatively abstract intellectual construction to which it is not so easy to adhere to for those who do not have or do not want to take the time to reflect upon it. Paraphrasing Rousseau, Lincoln or Article 3 of the French constitution, sovereignty belongs in the end to the peoples of Europe. There is still quite some work to do before the European Union will be seen as a project of these peoples, by these peoples and for these peoples.

[3] Joined cases C-885/19 P and C-898/19 P *Fiat Chrysler Finance Europe v Commission* EU:C:2022:859 (judgment of 8 November 2022). See Koen Lenaerts, "The extension of the competences of the Union through the jurisprudence of the Court of Justice: myth or reality?", keynote speech delivered to *European Sovereignty: The Legal Dimension—A Union in Control of its own Destiny* (30th Anniversary Congress of the Academy of European Law Trier), 13 October 2022.

As noted in the text above, European integration is a continuum. It will always remain a work in progress. This also applies to work of the Academy of European Law Trier, which through its own activities has become part of the integration project itself.

Luxembourg

Marc van der Woude
President of the General Court
of the European Union
Marc.Van_der_Woude@curia.europa.eu

Preface

In October 2022, the Academy of European Law (ERA) in Trier celebrated its 30th anniversary by organising a Congress devoted to the legal dimension of European sovereignty.

1992 was not only the year in which ERA was founded, but also a key moment in the history of European integration, as it saw the signing of the founding treaty of the European Union, the Treaty of Maastricht. While sovereignty was a highly controversial issue even then, the (geo)political and economic challenges facing the Union in recent years have brought it back to the centre of debate.

The chapters in this book are based on papers presented at the Jubilee Congress and explore aspects of the sovereignty debate that have attracted recent attention, such as the notions of strategic sovereignty, digital sovereignty and budgetary sovereignty.

The contributions reflect ERA's vocation to provide an interface and a forum for the exchange of views between legal practitioners, judges, policy-makers and academics. We would like to thank the contributors and all those institutions and individuals who have enabled the Academy of European Law to fulfil its mission over the past 30 years and whom we trust will continue to support it in the years to come.

Gavin Barrett
Professor, Sutherland School of Law
University College
Dublin, Ireland

Peter-Christian Müller-Graff
Senior Professor
Heidelberg University
Heidelberg, Germany

Jean-Philippe Rageade
Director
Academy of European Law
Trier, Germany

Viktor Vadász
Deputy Director
Academy of European Law
Trier, Germany

Contents

European Sovereignty in Specific Areas

The European Union as a Sovereign Global Player?

Democratic Organisation of European Sovereignty

Contributors

Gavin Barrett Dublin, Ireland

Anu Bradford New York City, USA

Julia Laffranque Tartu, Estonia

Christine Landfried Hamburg, Germany

Iris Goldner Lang Zagreb, Croatia

Koen Lenaerts Luxembourg, Luxembourg

Margarida Marques Brussels, Belgium

Peter-Christian Müller-Graff Heidelberg, Germany

Ulla Neergaard Copenhagen, Denmark

Cătălin Predoiu Bucharest, Romania

Daniel Sarmiento Madrid, Spain

Nathalie A. Smuha Leuven, Belgium

Elena Simina Tănăsescu Bucharest, Romania

Sabine Verheyen Brussels, Belgium

Jiří Zemánek Brno, Czechia

Extract from Opening Speech at the Thirtieth Anniversary Congress of the Academy of European Law

Sabine Verheyen

I am honoured to open with you the Thirtieth Anniversary Congress of the Academy of European Law (ERA) here in Trier.

It has been thirty years since the Academy of European Law was founded. It has been just as long since the European Community became a real Union with the Treaty of Maastricht. Significant events have transpired since that time, and the world we live in today is certainly different from that of 1992. Over the last thirty years, the European Union itself has developed from an economically–focused association of states, the European Economic Community, the predecessor of the European Union, into a value-based community of states encompassing the majority of European states. Today, it is not only a serious global player in economic terms, but also stands on the world stage as a democratic community of values.

The EU's thirty-year history as a Union and its preceding history as a European Community brought with it a host of European legal norms in the form of European secondary law. The Treaty on the Functioning of the European Union provides for many different legal acts, including regulations, directives, decisions, recommendations and opinions. There are about 2000 directives alone, so it takes some expertise to keep track of them all.

And so today, European law is more than just a new subject area in the curricula of European law students. European law harmonises the various legal systems of the Member States, thus contributing to the realisation of the internal market and, not least, strengthening the sovereignty of the European Union itself, in that the European Union is increasingly engaging in uniform action in the most diverse sub-areas and thus appears as a unit both internally and externally.

Sabine Verheyen—Member of the European Parliament, Chair of the Committee on Culture and Education (2019–2024).

S. Verheyen (✉)
Brussels, Belgium
e-mail: sabine.verheyen@europarl.europa.eu

G. Barrett et al. (eds.), *European Sovereignty*,
https://doi.org/10.1007/978-3-031-71851-9_1

ERA has made a significant contribution to the legal 'unification' of the Union. The Academy of European Law's goal of helping individuals and institutions to work closely together in the implementation and application of European law and of actively providing a forum for legal discourse has enabled comprehensive mutual exchanges of experience and thus contributed significantly to the further development of European law. For this, I would like to thank today with sincere gratitude all members of ERA and all of those who have been responsible.

Without you, European law would not be at the level it is today, and we would perhaps be a long way from 'unity in diversity' in today's Europe. This unity, as the last years and months in constant crisis mode have shown us, is more necessary today than ever.

Today, the European Union operates in the complex political and economic web of our globalised world. This has given rise to numerous new challenges, both external and internal, which we must face, starting with the growing together of Western and Eastern Europe after the fall of the Soviet Union and the end of the Cold War—which also made possible a massive increase in the number of EU member states—and continuing with the attacks of 11 September 2001 and the beginning of the war against terror. The EU's more recent history is characterised by several events: the attacks of 11 September 2001 and the start of the war on terror, the financial and economic crisis of 2008–2009 and the refugee crisis of 2015, the shock of Brexit, the shifting balance of power in the world and the rise of the People's Republic of China as a dominant economic power in many key areas, as well as what is currently probably the worst threat on European soil, the Russian war of aggression against Ukraine, with the ensuing explosion in energy prices, which has also brought with it a high potential for social conflict, and a resurgence in refugee numbers.

Although some such events have always challenged the EU, sometimes shaken it, and (rarely) thrown it off course, it has always survived them and emerged stronger and more united than before. Understanding crises as an opportunity for learning processes, for change and for strengthening our own sovereignty is the great strength of our Union.

And so, for some years now, the demand for genuine European sovereignty has been reiterated. Jean-Claude Juncker has been an initiator and source of ideas, and one who started the recent process of debating how we imagine our Europe and of what vision we have of Europe. Charles Michel called European sovereignty "the task of our generation" in 2020, and Commission President Ursula von der Leyen called for technological sovereignty in her 2021 State of the Union address. The call for genuine European sovereignty, meanwhile was also advanced by some national governments such as those of Germany, Finland, Denmark and Estonia, culminating in 2022 with a call for European autonomy in foreign and security policy. Thus, the ambition of a strategic European sovereignty has become a dominant objective.

The reasons for the call for European sovereignty were numerous even before the war; in particular, the pandemic and the subsequent health crisis, the challenges of the digital transformation, the need for joint action in the climate crisis and, last but not least, the shifting global balance of power in general make joint, strong, independent action indispensable.

Since 24 February 2022, when war once again broke out on European soil, the call for European sovereignty has taken on a whole new dimension. We are witnessing a country that aspires to our European values and ideals of democracy, to the rule of law and to freedom being subjected to a brutal war of aggression by Russia which is contrary to international law.

But this war also confirms our values. Never before in the history of European unification have we been shown so forcefully what an enormous achievement the European Union is—and, above all, how fragile our peace, our prosperity and our cohesion are, and how worthwhile it is to stand up for them and to defend and develop this, our common Union.

With its unprecedented sanctions against Russia, the EU demonstrated that it sticks together in times of crisis and acts in unity. It reacted immediately and thereby massively weakened Russia. This was a collective success on the part of the EU. But the war also revealed our vulnerabilities: our dependence on fossil fuels leaves us vulnerable in many respects. This needed to change urgently. That is why Commission President Ursula von der Leyen announced a whole package of measures with the REPowerEU plan, so that Europe could become more independent as quickly as possible.

On the one hand, the Ukraine war has united Europe strongly again. On the other hand, it has also shown us that in order to be able to keep up with the global showdown of the great powers and not to become dependent on states like Russia or China, Europe must become more independent in many areas—namely, in terms of energy policy, technology, intellectual property and political strategy. In order to be able to conduct a mutual dialogue at eye level, it is essential to act as the EU from a self-confident, strong and thus sovereign position.

ERA could therefore hardly have chosen a more topical theme for its Thirtieth Anniversary Congress. I very much welcome the fact that you, the Academy of European Law, are using this occasion of your thirtieth anniversary to enter into dialogue and exchange on precisely this topic. I am sure that you will once again contribute significantly to the further development of this objective.

European Sovereignty: Some General Reflections

European Union Membership: A Loss or Gain of Sovereignty?

Iris Goldner Lang

1 Introduction

There is a common understanding that by joining the European Union, an acceding state loses a significant part of its sovereignty by transferring many of its national competences to the European Union institutions. Even though this is true, this chapter argues that the transfer of national sovereignty—albeit significant, both qualitatively and quantitatively—is, at the same time, a huge political, economic and social gain on the side of both the acceding Member State and the EU. Additionally, the transfer of sovereignty does not imply its complete loss at the national level, as the new Member State participates in the EU decision-making process in the Council of Ministers and it becomes one of the "masters of the Treaties", jointly with all the other Member States. For these reasons, this chapter suggests that European Union membership is a two-way win–win process, which strengthens both EU sovereignty and national sovereignty, while changing both of them conceptually.

The chapter will address this topic by analysing the accession process of the newest European Union Member State, Croatia, and by examining the reasons why both Croatia and the EU were so keen for this enlargement to take place, despite the considerable decrease of sovereignty it involved at the national level. Following this introduction, the second section will give a short overview of the Croatian accession process to the European Union, while outlining the main challenges on the way to membership. The third section will try to answer the question of why young, independent states aspire to join the European Union, despite the inevitable transfer of sovereignty which this involves. It will show that accession was a top political priority in Croatia, despite the fact that, on the break-up of Yugoslavia, Croatia

Jean Monnet Professor of EU Law, Vice Dean and Head of the Department of European Public Law, Faculty of Law, University of Zagreb.

I. Goldner Lang (✉)
Zagreb, Croatia
e-mail: igoldner@pravo.hr

G. Barrett et al. (eds.), *European Sovereignty*,
https://doi.org/10.1007/978-3-031-71851-9_2

strongly fought for its sovereignty and that it existed as an independent state for only fifteen years before starting European Union membership negotiations. The concluding section will summarise the main findings and point out that the transfer of national sovereignty to the European Union should be viewed as a gain both at the national and at the European Union level.

2 The Croatian Accession Process

Croatia acceded to the European Union on 1 July 2013. The act of accession was preceded by a lengthy and difficult process of accession negotiations. One of the first milestones in the Croatian path towards European Union membership was the conclusion of the Stabilisation and Association Agreement with the EU in 2001.[1] Croatia applied for European Union membership on 21 February 2003 and was granted candidate status in 2004. After the initial postponement of the starting date of accession negotiations until the date on which the Chief Prosecutor of the International Criminal Tribunal for the Former Yugoslavia (ICTY) gave a positive assessment of Croatia's full cooperation with the ICTY, the accession negotiations were subsequently officially launched on 3 October 2005. However, in December 2008, the accession negotiations were stalled as Slovenia blocked the opening and closing of a number of negotiating chapters due to a border dispute with Croatia. Upon mediation by the European Commission and political pressure from a number of Member States, Slovenia agreed to detach the border dispute from Croatia's accession negotiations and resolve it as a bilateral issue by means of international arbitration.[2] Accession negotiations continued in September 2009 and were concluded on 30 June 2011 when the last of the 35 negotiating chapters was closed.

Croatia's accession negotiations were among the longest in the Union's history, similar in length to the six-year-long accession negotiations with Portugal and Spain. Most difficulties were encountered in implementing the *acquis* in the areas of the judiciary and fundamental rights (Chapter 23) and of justice, freedom, and security

---

[1] As a mixed agreement concluded before the Treaty of Lisbon, the Stabilisation and Association Agreement was concluded with the European Community and all its Member States.

[2] The Arbitration Agreement between the Government of the Republic of Slovenia and the Government of the Republic of Croatia (dated 4 November 2009) is available at <https://narodne-novine.nn.hr/clanci/medunarodni/2009_11_12_140.html> (*Official Gazette* 12/2009, 27 November 2009, last accessed on 15 March 2023). The important role played by the European Commission is visible from a number of elements contained within the Arbitration Agreement. First, the parties "welcome the facilitation offered by the European Commission" (Preamble). Secondly, the parties are required to appoint the Arbitral Tribunal from a list established by the President of the European Commission and the Commissioner for Enlargement (see Article 2(1) of the Arbitration Agreement). Finally, the place of arbitration is required to be Brussels and the parties invite the European Commission to provide secretarial support to the Arbitral Tribunal (Article 6(7) of the Arbitration Agreement). On the discussion of the European Union's role in the Croatia-Slovenia border dispute, see F Hoffmeister, "The European Union and the Peaceful Settlement of International Disputes" (2012) 11 *Chinese JIL* 77.

(Chapter 24). Both chapters were opened rather late in the negotiating process. This was to cause difficulties as they were among the most burdensome to negotiate. Chapter 24 was opened on 21 October 2009 and closed late in the negotiating process, on 22 December 2010, while Chapter 23 was opened on 30 June 2010 and was the last to be closed, on 30 June 2011.[3] This experience will be applied in future accession negotiations, which will no longer allow it to be possible for the most difficult chapters to stay closed until late in the negotiating process.

The Croatian Accession Treaty was signed on 9 December 2011 and the ratification process in Croatia successfully completed, with a national referendum held on 22 January 2012. Sixty-six percent of voters voted in favour of accession, and the Croatian Parliament unanimously ratified the Accession Treaty on 9 March 2012. Upon completion of the ratification process in all of the then 27 Member States of the European Union, Croatia became the twenty-eighth Member State on 1 July 2013.

Croatia joined the European Union at the moment when the EU constitutional order, to a large extent, had already been designed not only by the Treaties, but also in European Union constitutional practice. Likewise, the Member States' constitutional practices and, often, the text of their constitutions had been adjusted to European Union membership. It is therefore not surprising, that ahead of its accession to the European Union, Croatia adopted a constitutional amendment.[4]

The 2010 constitutional amendment followed the stipulated amendment procedure. Generally, amendments to the Croatian Constitution may be proposed by a minimum of one-fifth of the members of the Croatian Parliament, by the Croatian President or by the Croatian Government.[5] Accordingly, on 1 October 2009, the Croatian Government proposed the 2010 constitutional amendment. Based on this proposal and the proposal submitted by members of the Croatian Parliament on 16 October 2009, the Croatian Parliament adopted, on 30 April 2010, the Decision on the Commencement of the Amendment of the Constitution of the Republic of Croatia.[6] Based on Article 148(1) of the Constitution, such a decision must be adopted by a

---

[3] Out of thirty-five chapters that were negotiated with Croatia, the final four, which were closed on 30 June 2012, were: Chap. 8 (on competition policy), Chapter 23 (on the judiciary and fundamental rights), Chapter 33 (on financial and budgetary provisions), and Chapters 35 (on other issues).

[4] Readers who are interested in a more detailed elaboration of the topic of the Croatian constitutional amendment, which was effected so as to enable accession to the EU, may consult the following chapter co-authored by the present author, which was used as the basis for this section of this chapter: Iris Goldner Lang, Zlata Durdevic and Mislav Mataija, "The Constitution of Croatia in the Perspective of European and Global Governance", in Anneli Albi and Samo Bardutzky (eds.), *National Constitutions in European and Global Governance: Democracy, Rights, the Rule of Law* (Springer 2019) 1139.

On Croatian constitutional limitations to European Union integration, see Tamara Ćapeta and Iris Goldner Lang "Croatian Constitution and Economic and Monetary Integration in the EU: Report on Croatia for the Horizon 2020 Project 'EMU Choices: The Choice for Europe since Maastricht", in Stefan Griller and Elisabeth Lentsch *EMU Integration and Member States' Constitutions* (Hart 2021).

[5] Article 147 of the Constitution (Article 142 of the pre-2010 version of the Constitution).

[6] *Official Gazette of the Republic of Croatia* 56/10.

majority of all Members of Parliament.[7] The decision to amend the Constitution has to be made by a two-thirds majority of all deputies.[8] With the 2010 constitutional amendment, the relevant decision was made on 16 June 2010, when 133 deputies voted for the amendment, four deputies voted against it and one abstained.

The constitutional amendment had a threefold role. First, it inserted a separate Chapter VIII entitled 'European Union', and comprising four articles, into the Croatian Constitution. The purpose of this chapter was to provide the legal basis for Croatian membership in the European Union and to regulate the status of European Union law in the national legal order. The provisions of Chapter VIII thus regulate the legal grounds for membership and the transfer of constitutional powers (in Article 143)[9]; the representation of Croatian citizens and institutions in the European Union institutions and decision-making process (in Article 144)[10]; and the relationship between national and EU law (in Article 145).[11] Further, they reiterate the rights of

---

[7] Article 143(1) of the pre-2010 version of the Constitution.

[8] Article 149 of the Constitution (Article 144 of the pre-2010 version of the Constitution).

[9] Article 143 of the Croatian Constitution, entitled 'Legal Grounds for Membership and Transfer of Constitutional Powers' provides:

> Pursuant to Article 142 of the Constitution, the Republic of Croatia shall, as a Member State of the European Union, participate in the creation of European unity in order to ensure, together with other European states, lasting peace, liberty, security and prosperity, and to attain other common objectives in keeping with the founding principles and values of the European Union. Pursuant to Articles 140 and 141 of the Constitution, the Republic of Croatia shall confer upon the institutions of the European Union the powers necessary for the enjoyment of rights and fulfilment of obligations ensuing from membership.

[10] Article 144 of the Croatian Constitution, entitled 'Participation in European Union Institutions', stipulates:

> The citizens of the Republic of Croatia shall be directly represented in the European Parliament where they shall, through their elected representatives, decide upon matters falling within their purview. The Croatian Parliament shall participate in the European legislative process as regulated in the founding treaties of the European Union.
>
> The Government of the Republic of Croatia shall report to the Croatian Parliament on the draft regulations and decisions in the adoption of which it participates in the institutions of the European Union. In respect of such draft regulations and decisions, the Croatian Parliament may adopt conclusions which shall provide the basis on for the Government's actions in European Union institutions. Parliamentary oversight by the Croatian Parliament of the actions of the Government of the Republic of Croatia in European Union institutions shall be regulated by law. The Republic of Croatia shall be represented in the Council and the European Council by the Government and the President of the Republic of Croatia in accordance with their respective constitutional powers.

[11] Article 145 of the Croatian Constitution provides:

> The exercise of the rights ensuing from the European Union acquis communautaire shall be made equal to the exercise of rights under Croatian law. All the legal acts and decisions accepted by the Republic of Croatia in European Union institutions shall be applied in the Republic of Croatia in accordance with the European Union acquis communautaire. Croatian courts shall protect subjective rights based on the European Union acquis communautaire.

EU citizens (in Article 146).[12] The amendment came into force on 1 July 2013, the date of Croatian accession to the European Union.

The 2010 constitutional amendment was also necessary in order to satisfy certain European Union membership requirements, and a number of constitutional provisions were amended for this purpose.[13] Finally, a crucial amendment, which facilitated (if not enabled) Croatian accession to the European Union, was the rule requiring a referendum, which had to take place as a legally necessary part of the accession procedure. Specifically, in order for there to be a positive outcome to a referendum, Article 141 of the pre-2010 version of the Constitution–the legal basis of accession[14]–required a majority vote of all voters in Croatia. This strict rule was toned

> Governmental agencies, bodies of local and regional self-government and legal persons vested with public authority shall apply European Union law directly.

On the application of European Union law, in accordance with EU principles of direct effect and supremacy, by the Croatian judiciary, see Tamara Ćapeta, Nika Bačić Selanec, Iris Goldner Lang and Davor Petrić, "Croatia—National Report" (FIDE Report), in Marleen Botman and Jurian Langer (eds.), *National Courts and the Enforcement of EU Law—the pivotal role of national courts in the EU legal order* (Eleven International Publishing 2020) 115.

[12] Article 146, entitled 'Rights of European Union Citizens' stipulates:

> Citizens of the Republic of Croatia shall be European Union citizens and shall enjoy the rights guaranteed by the European Union acquis communautaire, and in particular:
>
> – freedom of movement and residence in the territory of all Member States,
> – active and passive voting rights in European parliamentary elections and in local elections in another member State, in accordance with that Member State's law,
> – the right to the diplomatic and consular protection of any Member State which is equal to the protection provided to own citizens when present in a third country where the Republic of Croatia has no diplomatic-consular representation,
> – the right to submit petitions to the European Parliament, complaints to the European Ombudsman and the right to apply to European Union institutions and advisory bodies in the Croatian language, as well as in all the other official languages of the European Union, and to receive a reply in the same language.
>
> All rights shall be exercised in compliance with the conditions and limitations laid down in the founding treaties of the European Union and the measures undertaken pursuant to such treaties.
>
> In the Republic of Croatia, all rights guaranteed by the European Union acquis communautaire shall be enjoyed by all citizens of the European Union".

[13] Amendments included the provisions on the position of the Croatian National Bank (Article 53) and the State Audit Office (Article 54), as well as the abandonment of the previous rule requiring a complete ban on the extradition of Croatian nationals: extradition of Croatian nationals was now made possible in order to be able to comply with European Arrest Warrants (Article 9).

[14] There was no consensus on the question of whether Croatian accession should take place on the basis of Article 141 of the pre-2010 version of the Constitution (which regulated Croatia's association in and dissociation from international alliances with other states) or based on the general provision of Article 139 of the pre-2010 version of the Constitution (which regulated the conclusion of international treaties and which, together with the then Article 86, contained a more lenient referendum rule requiring a majority vote of all voters who took part in the referendum). In the end, Article 141 was used as the legal basis for accession.

down in order to prevent the possible failure of the referendum. The wording 'the majority vote of all voters in the state' was thus changed to 'the majority vote of all voters voting in the referendum'. The low turnout of only about 44% of eligible voters in Croatia for the referendum which took place on 22 January 2012 testified to the fact that the fear of not fulfilling the strict referendum requirement contained in the then Article 141 had been reasonable. Of the total number of voters who took part in the referendum, more than 66% voted in favour of accession, which sufficed for a positive outcome.

3 Why Accede (Despite a Considerable Loss of Sovereignty)?

The aim of the following paragraphs is to consider the reasons why states like Croatia decide to accede to the European Union, despite a significant quantitative and qualitative loss of sovereignty. Three main incentives for the acceding states will be outlined below: first, political stability and security, secondly, the transition to a market economy and, finally, freedom and prosperity.[15] This section of the present chapter will use Croatia as a case study to analyse these three incentives to European Union membership.

At the outset, it is important to emphasise that the Republic of Croatia is a rather young state. Its establishment as a sovereign and independent state dates back only to 25 June 1991, when the Croatian Parliament passed a Constitutional Decision on the Sovereignty and Independence of Croatia[16]–thus initiating the process of dissociation from the other former Yugoslav republics and from the Socialist Federal Republic of Yugoslavia–and also adopted the Declaration on the Establishment of the Sovereign and Independent Republic of Croatia.[17] Considering the fact that Croatia acquired candidate status for membership of the European Union in 2004 and started accession negotiations in 2005, less than twenty-two years therefore passed in its transition from limited sovereignty (as a constituent republic of the former Yugoslavia) to complete sovereignty (as an independent state) to, once again, only limited sovereignty (this time as a European Union Member State).

However, Croatian transition is not unique. The Baltic States, Czechia and Slovakia underwent similar processes. One might wonder why a state like Croatia–which had fought for its sovereignty and undergone a war and huge human, economic and infrastructural losses–would give up a significant part of its sovereignty to another

[15] For a detailed analysis of the positive impacts of the EU on the acceding states, see the following article by the author, which was used as the basis for this section: Iris Goldner Lang, "The Impact of Enlargement(s) on the EU Institutions and Decision-Making", (2012) 31(1) Yearbook of European Law 473.

[16] *Official Gazette of the Republic of Croatia* 31/91.

[17] *Official Gazette of the Republic of Croatia* 31/91. On 22 December 1990, the Croatian Parliament passed the Constitution of the Republic of Croatia, which has since undergone several revisions and amendments, and is still in force today (*Official Gazette of the Republic of Croatia* 56/90).

supranational entity only a few years after its establishment as an independent state. There were two main reasons for such a decision. First, the position of Croatia (and any other EU Member State) in the European Union's constitutional structure is not the same as it was in former Yugoslavia. Secondly, there was–and still is–a political and social consensus in Croatia that European Union membership is highly beneficial, or even essential, for its viability and prosperity. As a consequence, accession to the European Union (as well as Croatian accession to the eurozone and Schengen in 2023), was its main national policy goal.

The main incentives for an aspiring state—like Croatia in early 2002—to join the European Union, despite the considerable reduction of sovereignty which this involved, could be grouped into three categories: political stability and security; transition to a market economy; and freedom and prosperity. These incentives were, at the same time, used by EU institutions as criteria that had to be fulfilled by a candidate country before joining the European Union. European Union enlargement policy has often been proclaimed as the European Union's most successful foreign policy.[18] The Union's gravitational force has enabled it to stimulate positive changes in countries aspiring to accede. Through its enlargement policy, the European Union deeply affects and alters candidate countries. In this process, the Union takes on a number of important roles in relation to candidate countries. The first of its roles is to act as a promoter of political stability and security. This role manifests itself in a number of ways. First, political stability is contained within the Copenhagen criteria, which have to be fulfilled in order for a country to become eligible for accession. Thus a Copenhagen political criterion requires a candidate country to ensure the stability of its institutions guaranteeing democracy, the rule of law, human rights and respect for and protection of minorities.[19]

[18] Marise Cremona, "Enlargement: A Successful Instrument of EU Foreign Policy?" in Takis Tridimas (ed), *European Union Law for the Twenty-First Century: Volume 1, Rethinking the New Legal Order,* Hart Publishing, 2004, 317; Graham Avery, Anne Faber and Anne Schmidt, *Enlarging the European Union: Effects on the new member states and the EU* (TEPSA 2009) 1. See also the speech of the former EU Commissioner for Enlargement Olli Rehn "Enlargement as an instrument of the EU's soft power" at Anna Lindh Award Ceremony on 19 October 2007 (available at: http://europa.eu/rapid/pressReleasesAction.do?reference=SPEECH/07/642&format=PDF&aged=1&language=EN&guiLanguage=en—last accessed on 15 March 2023).

[19] The Copenhagen criteria were laid down at the June 1993 European Council in Copenhagen. Only upon successful fulfilment of all the Copenhagen criteria is a candidate country eligible for accession. These criteria are: stability of institutions guaranteeing democracy, the rule of law, human rights and respect for and protection of minorities (political criterion); a functioning market economy (the economic criterion); and the ability to take on the obligations of membership including adherence to the aims of political, economic and monetary union (the institutional criterion). The last criterion requires legislative alignment of the candidate country with the *acquis comunautaire*. The membership criteria defined in 1993 in Copenhagen, were later elaborated upon and extended by the 1995 Madrid European Council so as to include the requirement to adjust the candidate country's administrative structures. Finally, the EU must be capable to absorb the new states, while continuing to function effectively (see the EU Enlargement Strategy, COM (2006) 649 final). On the evolution of EU membership criteria, see Frank Hoffmeister, "Changing Requirements for Membership", in Andrea Ott and Kristyn Inglis (eds), *Handbook on European Enlargement—A Commentary on the Enlargement Process* (T.M.C. Asser Press 2002) 90; Christophe Hillion, "The Copenhagen criteria

In the early 2000s, peace and security were high on the agenda for Croatia, as a state still recovering from the devastating impact of war. For this reason, the Union's role as a promoter of political stability and security and as the embodiment of peace, were perceived as a welcome and much needed goal. On the other hand, the European Union insisted on ensuring that Croatia and other countries in the region, would put in place efficient mechanisms to prevent future conflicts. The importance of preserving peace and stability in the Western Balkans[20] led to the creation of an additional accession criterion entitled "regional cooperation" which became an essential element of the Stabilisation and Association Process (SAP) and was included in all of the Stabilisation and Association Agreements signed with Western Balkan countries.[21] All of the Agreements contained a regional cooperation clause, the aim of which was to foster good neighbourly relations among the Stabilisation and Association Process countries and to prevent any further armed conflict in the region.[22] The importance of regional cooperation has been constantly emphasised in numerous Commission and Council documents, including the *Commission's Enlargement Strategy and Main Challenges 2011–2012*,[23] in which the Commission stated.

> regional cooperation and good neighbourly relations are essential elements of the Stabilisation and Association process and, as such, are closely monitored by the Commission at all stages of the accession process. Regional cooperation underpins and enhances reconciliation in a region that suffered major conflicts in the recent past. Regional cooperation and trade can bring further economic benefits to the region. It is also an integral part of the process of integration into the European Union, which often necessitates regional approaches and measures.

The Union thus used its gravitational effect on Croatia during the process of accession negotiations. It continues to do so with other Stabilisation and Association Process countries, in order to enhance regional cooperation and consequently secure peace and stability in the region. Regional cooperation is an important requirement that needs to be met both for the opening of accession negotiations to happen, and

---

and their progeny", in Christophe Hillion (ed), *EU Enlargement: a legal approach* (Hart publishing 2004) 1.

[20] The name "Western Balkans" is a political rather than a geographical designation coined by the European Union institutions for the countries of the South-Eastern Europe, comprising Albania and all the countries of former Yugoslavia apart from Slovenia—Croatia, Bosnia and Herzegovina, Kosovo, the Former Yugoslav Republic of Macedonia, Montenegro and Serbia.

For more on the Western Balkans, see Siniša Rodin, "The European Union and the Western Balkans: Does the Lisbon Treaty Matter?" in Federiga Bindi and Irina Angelescu (eds), *The Foreign Policy of the European Union: Assessing Europe's Role in the World* (Brookings Institutional press 2012) 153.

[21] Forms of regional cooperation have also been encouraged in previous association agreements. Thus Article 73(4) of the Europe Agreement with Slovenia required Slovenia to devote special attention to "measures capable of fostering cooperation between Slovenia and the countries of Central and Eastern Europe". Article 2(2) of each of the Europe Agreements with Estonia, Latvia and Lithuania stated that "the Baltic States should maintain and develop cooperation among themselves and will make every effort to enhance this process".

[22] E.g., Article 11 of the Stabilisation and Association Agreement with Croatia.

[23] COM (2011) 666 final, 12 October 2011.

later on, during the negotiating process. Finally, by preserving peace and stability among its own Member States—the crucial motives for European integration in the 1950s—the European Union acts as a role-model and safe haven for the Stabilisation and Association Process countries. Consequently, peace and stability were among the most important reasons why Croatia wanted to accede to the European Union and, at the same time, a requirement imposed by the EU in order for Croatia to join the European Union.

The second reason why Croatia and other states have wanted to accede to the European Union is the fact that the Union is one of the largest economies in the world with a functioning market economy. Consequently, the Union's second role in the enlargement process is to act as a catalyst for a market economy. The existence of a functioning market economy (as well as the capacity to cope with competitive pressures and market forces within the Union) is one of the Copenhagen criteria. The requirement to respect the principles of a free market economy has been emphasised throughout the Stabilisation and Association Process in numerous Commission documents[24] as well as in Stabilisation and Association Agreements.[25]

Finally, acceding states perceive the European Union as the embodiment of freedom and prosperity. Consequently, the EU's role as a model of freedom and prosperity was the third reason and probably the most important incentive for accession. The first part of this role (freedom) is associated with the abolition of internal border controls among European Union Member States and the establishment of the internal market with free movement of goods, persons, services and capital. Most EU citizens nowadays associate the Union with free movement for the purpose of work, study and travel.[26] In this context, the (re-)introduction of any limitations to such movement, like the ones which were imposed as a response to the COVID-19 pandemic,[27] represents a blow to one of the values most frequently identified with the European Union. In this context, the introduction of transitional arrangements for

---

[24] See e.g., the Commission Communication "Enlargement Strategy and Main Challenges 2011–2012" (COM (2011) 666 final, 12 October 2011) and the Commission Occasional Paper 85 "Progress towards meeting the economic criteria for accession: the assessment of the 2011 Progress Reports and the Opinion (Serbia)" (2011) which is based on its 2011 Progress Report.

[25] Preamble and Articles 1 and 2 of the Stabilisation and Association Agreement with Croatia.

[26] In a 2020 Eurobarometer survey, more than 8 out of 10 respondents (84%) were of the view that the free movement of European Union citizens within the EU brings overall benefits to the economy of their country (Flash Eurobarometer 485, 2020, available at: https://www.europarl.europa.eu/cmsdata/214273/Eurobarometer%20Report%20Summary%20_%20EU%20Citizenship%20&%20Democracy%20-%20July%202020.pdf; last accessed on 15 March 2023).

[27] On the challenges of the introduction of restrictions to cross-border movement in the EU during the pandemic and the introduction of COVID certificates, aimed at easing these reductions, see: Iris Goldner Lang, "'Laws of Fear' in the EU: The Precautionary Principle and Public Health Restrictions to Free Movement of Persons in the Time of COVID-19" (2021) 12(1) *European Journal of Risk Regulation* 1; and Iris Goldner Lang, "EU COVID Certificates: A Critical Analysis" (2021) 12(2) *European Journal of Risk Regulation* 298.

workers from the newly acceded states seeking to access the labour markets of the "old" Member States was often perceived as an unnecessary and unfair measure.[28]

The second element of this role (prosperity) seems to have also weakened recently, as, due to the financial and other crises the Union has undergone in the past decade, the incentive to accede is currently not as strong as it used to be. Nevertheless it still plays an important role in the process of enlargement The European Union seems to have recognised the importance of preserving financial stability and fostering growth not only within its Member States, but also in candidate countries and has expressed its intention to employ its enlargement policy to achieve this objective. Along these lines, the *Commission's Enlargement Strategy and Main Challenges 2011–2012* stated that

> the recent global financial crisis and the present difficulties in the Eurozone have highlighted the interdependence of national economies both within and beyond the EU. These events underline the importance of further consolidating economic and financial stability and fostering growth, also in the enlargement countries. The enlargement process is a powerful tool to that end.

The three roles mentioned above are not the only roles that have been taken on by the Union in the context of the enlargement policy. However, these roles seem to stand out as the most important ones, both from the perspective of the European Union and the candidate countries. Through its enlargement policy, especially through the demanding conditionality which is applied and the benchmarking mechanism which is used for the opening and closing of each negotiating chapter,[29] the Union exports its values, norms and institutions to aspirant countries.[30] This export of European Union internal policies and norms to future Member States represents a policy-driven export of the *acquis*. At the same time, the roles that are taken by the Union in the accession process are the main reasons why states aspire to join the European Union, notwithstanding a partial loss of their sovereignty at national level. By joining the EU, Member States become members of a much larger and globally powerful entity to which they would otherwise have no access. Consequently, the transfer of national sovereignty pays back each Member State, as it is reciprocated by a significant increase of that State's global political, economic and social power.

---

[28] For the discussion of the legitimacy of transitional arrangements in the field of free movement of workers, see Iris Goldner Lang, *From Association to Accession: How Free is the Free Movement of Persons in the EU* (Eleven International Publishing 2011) at 229–260.

[29] Karen Smith, "The Evolution and Application of EU Membership Conditionality", in Marise Cremona (ed), *The Enlargement of the European Union* (Oxford University Press 2003) 105; Martina Spernbauer, "Benchmarking, Safeguard Clauses and Verification Mechanisms—What's in a Name? Recent Developments in Pre- and Post-Accession Conditionality and Compliance with EU Law", (2007) 3 *Croatian Yearbook of European Law and Policy* 273.

[30] On the export of EU values and norms, see Marise Cremona, "The Union as a Global Actor: Roles, Models and Identity" (2004) 41 *CMLRev* 553.

4 Concluding Remarks

The European Union enlargement policy is a two-way process which changes sovereignty at both the EU and national levels. Through this interventionist and transformative policy, the Union takes an active role in the candidate state's preparation for membership and changes it internally for the better.[31] At the same time, the roles taken by the Union in the enlargement process are crucial reasons why states want to join the Union, despite a very demanding and lengthy accession process. Consequently, enlargement is a win–win situation in which the acceding state voluntarily accepts to transfer part of its sovereignty to the European Union, but benefits from the accession politically, economically and socially, while taking part in a much larger and more powerful EU sovereignty through the decision-making process in the European Union institutions. At the same time, every new accession increases European Union sovereignty both quantitatively and qualitatively, transforming it from within. Consequently, European Union enlargement is a two-way sovereignty process with significant gains on the side of both the acceding Member State and the European Union as a whole.

[31] On the Union's active engagement with the candidate state's preparation for membership, see Christophe Hillion, "EU Enlargement", in Paul Craig and Gráinne de Burca (eds), *The Evolution of EU Law* (Oxford University Press 2011) 187.

'European Sovereignty' in Times of Poly-Crises: From Original Manifestations to Points of Concern

Ulla Neergaard

Abstract As war rages in Europe, it has become common to enumerate the many simultaneous crises currently occurring, many of them following in the wake of the war. These include crises related to the economy, migration flows, energy, climate, and eventually may possibly include a social and/or solidarity crisis.With that background, this chapter first touches upon some of the original manifestations of the concept of 'European sovereignty'. The focus then turns to Danish developments regarding 'sovereignty' as an example of where at least some barriers to a strengthening of 'European sovereignty' may exist, since at least some Member States may be hesitant to see such a development. Finally, the chapter concludes by raising some other, more general points of concern.

1 Introduction

As war rages in Europe, it has become common to enumerate the many simultaneous crises currently occurring, many of them following in the wake of the war. These include crises related to the economy, migration flows, energy, climate, and eventually possibly may include a social and/or solidarity crisis. But above all, we are currently witnessing a cruel and senseless war, which may eventually even escalate further. Such times of complexity and unpredictability may call for urgent decision-making and for thinking and acting in novel ways. It is therefore not surprising that in response, some would then be tempted to call for 'more' Europe or 'European

Professor in EU Law, Faculty of Law, University of Copenhagen.

This chapter originated as reflections provided for a panel entitled "Prolegomena: The Janus of European Sovereignty—What Does It Mean Within and Without?", part of the 30th Anniversary Congress of the Academy of European Law, "European Sovereignty: The Legal Dimension—A Union in Control of Its Own Destiny" (Trier, 13–14 October 2022). As such, it is intended to constitute neither an exhaustive account of all of the many differing aspects of "European sovereignty", nor an account of developments which may have taken place since the Congress.

U. Neergaard (✉)
Copenhagen, Denmark
e-mail: Ulla.Neergaard@jur.ku.dk

G. Barrett et al. (eds.), *European Sovereignty*,
https://doi.org/10.1007/978-3-031-71851-9_3

sovereignty'. With that background, this chapter is concerned with understanding the concept of 'European sovereignty' (and to some degree also the related concept of 'strategic autonomy'), as well as with bringing to the fore important concerns, which will be of relevance should the notion of 'European sovereignty' gain further ground.

In line with this, the chapter more specifically, first touches upon some of the original manifestations of the concept of 'European sovereignty' (Sect. 2). The focus then turns to Danish developments regarding 'sovereignty' as an example of where at least some barriers to a strengthening of 'European sovereignty' may exist, since at least some Member States may be hesitant to see such a development (Sect. 3). Finally, the chapter concludes by raising some other, more general points of concern (Sect. 4).

2 Original Manifestations

Originally, the concept of 'European sovereignty' was given its contemporary prominence by the French President Emmanuel Macron in his Sorbonne speech in 2017,[1] and subsequently by the President of the European Commission at the time, Jean-Claude Juncker, in his State of the Union speech in 2018.[2] However, the context in which it appears is now rather different as the direct threat to the European Union's stability and security which the war in Ukraine and its eventual aftermath will represent, has called for, in a fundamental way—and still calls for—urgent and unprecedented action.[3] This has been confirmed, for instance, in the Versailles declaration of 10–11 March 2022, in which the Heads of State or Government called for 'European sovereignty', stating that: "confronted with growing instability, strategic competition and security threats, we decided to take more responsibility for our security and take further decisive steps towards building our European sovereignty, reducing our dependencies and designing a new growth and investment model for 2030."[4] Inherent in any crisis of such magnitude is the trend for executive powers to lead the

[1] See President Emmanuel Macron, Speech at Sorbonne University, 26 September 2017, <international.blogs.ouest-france.fr/archive/2017/09/29/macron-sorbonne-verbatim-europe-18583.html> accessed 8 December 2023.

[2] See President Jean-Claude Juncker's State of the Union Address 2018, 12 September 2018, available online at <ec.europa.eu/commission/presscorner/detail/en/SPEECH_18_5808>.

[3] Also see "Editorial Comments: The response to the war in Europe: A more power based European Union and the challenge of ensuring that it remains rule and value based", (2022) 59 Common Market Law Review 623.

[4] Available online at <consilium.europa.eu/media/54773/20220311-versailles-declaration-en.pdf>. It is added that: "In this respect, we addressed today three key dimensions: (a) bolstering our defence capabilities; (b) reducing our energy dependencies; and (c) building a more robust economic base".

action.[5] When feeling weak, one may look for more 'strength'. The rise of a wish for a more resilient European Union in an increasingly complex and unstable world is thus in many respects very understandable.

To understand the concept of 'European sovereignty' better, it is worth paying attention to the above-mentioned speech by President Emmanuel Macron at the Sorbonne, where he spoke of providing a "...clear and firm response to our fellow citizens that... we can protect them and provide a response to this global disorder", and of "...the route of rebuilding a sovereign, united and democratic Europe".[6] It must be stressed that this appears a purely political concept or objective. The same impression may be obtained regarding the speech by the then European Commission President Jean-Claude Juncker in 2018.[7] It may be understood from a connected factsheet published by the Commission that 'European sovereignty' here "... means developing Europe's '*Weltpolitikfähigkeit*'", meaning "...the capacity to play a role, as a Union, in shaping global affairs."[8]

Regarding the related concept, 'strategic autonomy', this also appears a rather vague, political concept or objective. It might seem a slightly less delicate or sensitive term than 'European sovereignty'. According to one definition, it may be understood as the ability of the European Union to secure its citizens a life to the standards of prosperity, safety, health, and general well-being they are used to expect and is thus seen, in principle, as a reflection of the promise of the Union.[9] Another definition

---

[5] Also see "Editorial Comments: The response to the war in Europe: A more power based European Union and the challenge of ensuring that it remains rule and value based" (2022) 59 Common Market Law Review 623.

[6] See President Emmanuel Macron, Speech at Sorbonne University, 26 September 2017, available online at <international.blogs.ouest-france.fr/archive/2017/09/29/macron-sorbonne-verbatim-europe-18583.html>. The same may be said about his six keypoints regarding: 1. security, 2. control of borders and values, 3. foreign policy, 4. the ecological transition, 5. digital technology, and 6. industrial and monetary economic power.

[7] President Jean-Claude Juncker's State of the Union Address 2018, 12 September 2018, available online at <ec.europa.eu/commission/presscorner/detail/en/SPEECH_18_5808>. He said, among other things, that: "Let us together have the audacity to create this route. As I have done at every point in front of the French people, I would today like to say with resolute conviction: the Europe of today is too weak, too slow, too inefficient, but Europe alone can enable us to take action in the world, in the face of the big contemporary challenges".

[8] See "European sovereignty—What does it mean to President Juncker?", available online at <ec.europa.eu/info/sites/default/files/soteu2018-factsheet-sovereignty_en.pdf>. It is added that it: "... emerges from the national sovereignty of our Member States ... is created by the belief that sharing sovereignty makes nation states stronger ... enables us to offer collective solutions to collective problems ... enables all of us to better protect, defend and empower our citizens ... can never be an excuse for withdrawing from the world, but is rather an encouragement for our continent to assume more responsibility—Europe is a continent that can never be an island, but will only prosper if we are connected to the world".

[9] Also see "Editorial Comments: The response to the war in Europe: A more power-based European Union and the challenge of ensuring that it remains rule and value based", Common Market Law Review, 2022, p. 629. According to e.g. Tocci, autonomy may be understood as: "As the Greek etymology of the word suggests, autonomy means the ability of the self—autos—to live by its laws—nomos"; see Nathalie Tocci "European Strategic Autonomy: What It Is, Why We Need It, How to Achieve It", Istituto Affari Internazionali (IAI), 2021. However, according to "Editorial Comments.

sees it as being "… about equipping the European Union to manage interdependence in line with its interests and values."[10]

Thus, in general terms, 'European sovereignty' and 'strategic autonomy' seem to conflate with power.[11] Simply put, they are thus mostly about the European Union getting more powers and becoming more powerful. In that regard, the bundle of policies and measures assembled under them may also be given attention.

One must, under any circumstances, be careful in detaching these concepts completely from legal reality. In this regard, it may be worthwhile turning our eyes to Luxembourg to begin with. A quick search in the judgments database of the Court of Justice reveals that the concept of 'sovereignty' has so far appeared in 221 judgments, which somehow seems not that many, considering its importance.[12] The first judgments that referred to it—and which are still very important today—date from 1962 and 1965, namely the famous *van Gend en Loos* and *Costa v ENEL* rulings.[13] The term 'sovereignty' has thus been present all along and has, from the very beginning, been connected with the principle of conferral in governing European Union action.[14] In accordance with this latter principle, the European Union may only act

---

Keeping Europeanism at bay? Strategic autonomy as a constitutional problem", Common Market Law Review, 2022, p. 315: "Perhaps more fittingly, this concept can therefore be described as the ability of the European Union to secure its citizens a life to the standards of prosperity, safety, health, and general well-being they are used to expect. As this is part of the promise of the Union (Article 2(1), 3(1) TEU), there is nothing inherently wrong with this goal, except that it renders the whole concept somewhat unspecific".

[10] See Commission Joint Research Centre (JRC) Science for Policy Report, "Shaping & securing the EU's Open Strategic Autonomy by 2040 and beyond", 2021, available online at <publications.jrc.ec.europa.eu/repository/handle/JRC125994> (accessed 8 December 2023) at p. 1. See also Communication from the Commission to the European Parliament and the Council "2021 Strategic Foresight Report: The EU's capacity and freedom to act" COM(2021)750 final (8 September 2021).

[11] See Bart M.J. Szewczyk, *European Sovereignty, Legitimacy, and Power* (Routledge 2021) 2.

[12] The search was accomplished about a week before the congress took place. The result could of course have been different had the search been made in other languages. It might be that several of the 221 judgments are not of any relevance here.

[13] The ruling in Case 26/62 *NV Algemene Transport- en Expeditie Onderneming van Gend & Loos v Netherlands Inland Revenue Administration* EU:C:1963:1 was delivered on 5 February 1962. The Court stated, among other things, that: "the conclusion to be drawn…is that the Community constitutes a new legal order of international law for the benefit of which the states have limited their sovereign rights, albeit within limited fields, and the subjects of which comprise not only Member States but also their nationals…" The ruling in Case 6/64 *Costa v ENEL* ECLI:EU:C:1964:66 was delivered on 15 July 1965. It stated that:

> by creating a Community of unlimited duration, having its own institutions, its own personality, its own legal capacity and capacity of representation on the international plane and, more particularly, real powers stemming from a limitation of sovereignty or a transfer of powers from the States to the Community, the Member States have limited their sovereign rights, albeit within limited fields, and have thus created a body of law which binds both their nationals and themselves.

[14] If one instead searches for "European sovereignty", there are no hits at all.

if, and insofar as the Member States have authorised it to do so.[15] To act, the Union needs 'competence'. But 'competence'—and also 'power' can be obscure concepts, and there seems to be a need for a consistent and shared understanding of what they mean.[16] All in all, it is essential to understand that underlying the two concepts of 'European sovereignty' and 'strategic autonomy', a bundle of policies and measures exists, assembled under these headings. It is important to state that in any discussion of sovereignty, this universe of competence and power obviously needs to be fully understood and respected.

3 Danish Developments Regarding 'Sovereignty'

For Denmark, as for the Academy of European Law, the year 2022 was that of a significant anniversary. The reason is that precisely fifty years before this, Danish membership of what is now the European Union was decided upon in a referendum, on 2 October 1972.[17] Membership itself then began on 1 January 1973.[18]

In the campaign of fifty years ago, sovereignty played a huge role. One day after the "yes" vote on joining, on 3 October 1972, the then Prime Minister, Jens Otto Krag of the Social Democrats delivered a significant speech.[19] He stressed the need for common decisions being made slowly and being based on continuously

---

[15] This was demonstrated in a DPhil thesis defended by Ms Hannah Bogaert in the autumn of 2022 at the University of Oxford. (See Hannah Bogaert, *The Common Language of 'Competence'. Or how rediscovering the often-overlooked distinction between competence and power leads to better legal reasoning on whether the European Union may act*, at p. i.) What follows in the text above is based on this DPhil thesis.

[16] It is rightly argued that "competence" is about more than competence alone, as there is also power. Competence is the field in which the Union may act. Power is the European Union's institutions' actual authorisation to act. To fall within a certain field of competence, a measure must pursue the objectives of that competence and relate to its subject matter. Those are the two dimensions of competence. It is also convincingly argued that power, too, has two dimensions. It determines which legal instrument may be adopted through which type of legal act. There are also power modalities. They relate to the procedural side of the exercise of power: which European Union institution(s) may act and through which voting majority.

[17] Nearly 2 million (1.954.054) persons voted "Yes", corresponding to 57 per cent of those having the right to vote, and about 1.1 million (1.126.095) persons voted "No", corresponding to 32.8 per cent.

[18] See further Ulla Neergaard & Karsten Engsig Sørensen (eds.), "Danmark og EU gennem 50 år—en milepæl", 2023.

[19] Available online at <danmarkshistorien.dk/vis/materiale/statsminister-jens-otto-krag-s-meddeler-sin-afgang-3-oktober-1972> accessed 8 December 2023. From the speech it may be understood that he saw the enlargement of the Communities involving Denmark, Ireland and the United Kingdom as an important historical event, one that opened a new chapter in Europe's history, namely a chapter of cooperation. So, in thinking of Janus, he saw it as a new beginning. He also explained about his great expectations for this era. However, Prime Minister Krag, interestingly, did not say anything explicitly about sovereignty, even though this was an issue discussed intensely by everyone in the rough debate leading up to the referendum.

expanded experience, as well as being made in full respect of the will of the people and of each Member State's independence.[20] This would be something which, with a strengthening of 'European sovereignty', might be left behind to a much greater extent.

The year 2022 involved another European Union-Denmark anniversary worth reflecting upon. The reason is that 30 years prior to this–more specifically, on 2 June 1992–another referendum took place, in which the Danes voted 'no' to the Treaty of Maastricht.[21] This eventually led to the so-called four Danish opt-outs.[22] One of these opt-outs was the so-called defence-opt-out, which recently–more specifically, on 1 June 2022–it was decided (in referendum) to abolish.[23]

Again, during the 2022 referendum campaign, debate about a possible further loss of sovereignty played a huge role. Expert knowledge could be observed to have had a significant role in informing and guiding the electorate. At a certain point, even the so-called Irish Protocol came into the discussions.[24] Although Denmark may now be viewed as being 'on board' as regards defence, Denmark is still outside, in particular, both the euro and the European Union's Area of Freedom, Security, and Justice.[25]

---

[20] The wording in Danish is:

> Gennem alt dette og på tværs af de grænser, der så ofte århundrederne igennem har været blødende fronter, skal det nye Europa langsomt og på den stadig udvidede erfaringsbasis i nøje overensstemmelse med folkenes vilje finde sin form i fuld respekt for det enkelte lands – jeg vil gerne sige fædrelands – selvstændighed. Enigheden skal findes ved forhandling. I intet for et land [så] vigtigt anliggende vil det blive overstemt. Vil denne udvikling gå så hastigt, at vi alene på grund af farten bør nære ængstelse? Jeg tror det ikke. Jeg tror snarere, vi får bekymringer, fordi påtrængende fælles opgaver vil blive løst for langsomt, ikke for hurtigt. Mange eksempler fra Fællesskabernes hidtidige udvikling kunne gives på dette. Hvor Danmarks og Nordens interesser i den europæiske helhed tilsiger forhandlinger med hurtigt resultat, vil den danske regering virke herfor.

[21] With 50.7% of voters opting to reject the treaty.

[22] More precisely, it led to the Edinburgh Agreement of 1992, the purpose of which was to assist in securing a 'yes' vote in a second referendum. Four opt-outs were stipulated in the Edinburgh Decision as part of the Edinburgh Agreement. On 18 May 1993, there was a second referendum which led to a 'yes' vote (with, this time, 56.7% voting 'yes' and 43.3% voting 'no'). In Denmark, there have by now been in total nine referendums concerning the European Union. In six of these, the outcome was a'yes'. (See "Hvor mange folkeafstemninger om EU har der været i Danmark?" (Folketingets EU-Oplysning)).

[23] 66.9% of voters cast their votes in favour of abolition of the opt-out and 33.1% of voters voted against this. See further concerning this Ulla Neergaard & Graham Butler, "Denmark's Defence Opt-out, the Forthcoming Referendum, and the Changing Face of EU Defence and Security Arrangements", *EU Law Live*, 26 March 2022, 1.

[24] See the "Protocol on the concerns of the Irish people on the Treaty of Lisbon", available online at. <eur-lex.europa.eu/legal-content/EN/TXT/?uri = uriserv%3AOJ.L_.2013.060.01.0129.01.ENG&toc = OJ%3AL%3A2013%3A060%3ATOC#L_2013060EN.01013101> accessed 8 December 2023.

[25] To forego the remaining opt-outs, Danish "constitutional requirements" would have to be met. It is worth mentioning in this context that Paragraph 20 of the Danish Constitution can be explicitly read as limiting delegation of powers or "sovereignty". It came into force in 1953 to prepare for

All in all, what can be learnt from this 'case study'? One matter to consider is that ever since Denmark entered the European Union, it has somehow been seen as a more reluctant member, and a more disconnected one from the European Union than are most Member States.[26] Within Denmark, the opt-outs have on the one hand been seen as implying that Denmark has less influence in important matters. They have also, on the other hand, been seen as bulwarks against European integration, and as symbolising the preservation of national sovereignty.[27]

Also worth considering is that a 'classical' or 'old-fashioned' perception of 'sovereignty' still seems to dominate. By this is meant that the prevailing view is that sovereignty has to be understood within the framework of a 'zero-sum game', according to which a gain of sovereignty by the European Union is equivalent to a loss of sovereignty by a given Member State, and whereby the net change is thus zero. It seems not always fully understood or accepted that through conferral it is possible to gain even more influence or sovereignty by exercising it together with other countries.[28]

---

a potential membership of international organisations. It stipulates, more precisely, in Paragraph 20(1) that "powers vested in the authorities of the Realm under this Constitutional Act may, to such an extent as shall be provided by statute, be delegated to international authorities set up by mutual agreement with other states for the promotion of international rules of law and cooperation." It is seen as having its roots back in the Inter-Parliamentary Union, which was established in 1889 and which in Article 1 of its statutes actually referred to be working for peace and cooperation among peoples and for the solid establishment of representative institutions. This was envisaged as implying that states would to some degree have to give up sovereignty. (See Jens Hartig Danielsen, "En forudsætning for dansk medlemskab af EU—grundlovens §20" in Ulla Neergaard & Karsten Engsig Sørensen (eds.), "Danmark og EU gennem 50 år—en milepæl", 2023.) One further point of relevance is the role of Danish courts. Important Danish cases about the Danish membership include in particular: *Maastricht* (U 1998.800 H), *Schengen* (U 2001.2065 H), *Lissabon* (U 2013.1451 H), and *Ajos* (U 2017.824 H). In that regard it has been claimed that even fifty years later, the Supreme Court in particular is still guarding classical sovereignty with all of its original jealousy (see Marlene Wind og Tim Knudsen, "Det danske flertalsdemokrati og mødet med Europaretten" in Ulla Neergaard & Karsten Engsig Sørensen (eds.), *Danmark og EU gennem 50 år—en milepæl* (Djøf Forlag, 2023). It has also been claimed that in a country like Denmark, it is still at times difficult to get used to the fact that a supranational court can overrule national legislation (see Marlene Wind og Tim Knudsen, "Det danske flertalsdemokrati og mødet med Europaretten", in Ulla Neergaard & Karsten Engsig Sørensen (eds.), "Danmark og EU gennem 50 år—en milepæl" (Djøf Forlag, 2023)).

[26] Thus, since the UK started taking steps to withdraw itself from the European Union, beginning in 2016, Denmark has become the Member State with the most numerous explicit stand-alone arrangements on particular policy matters.

[27] In other words, Danes did indeed—as was predicted by Prime Minister Jens Otto Krag—need a long time to get used to everything.

[28] See Marlene Wind og Tim Knudsen, "Det danske flertalsdemokrati og mødet med Europaretten", in Ulla Neergaard & Karsten Engsig Sørensen (eds.), "Danmark og EU gennem 50 år—en milepæl", 2023. Rather, the Member States remain independent sovereign nations but they pool their sovereignty in order to gain the strength and world influence none of them could have on their own. See Jens Hartig Danielsen, "En forudsætning for dansk medlemskab af EU—grundlovens §20″, in Ulla Neergaard & Karsten Engsig Sørensen (eds.), "Danmark og EU gennem 50 år—en milepæl", 2023. In Danish the wording is: "Ved markeringen af Danmarks medlemskab af Den Europæiske Union er det vigtigt at fremhæve, at Danmark ved sin overladelse af suverænitet og samtidige indflydelse i unionens myndigheder har fået andel i en samlet set langt større»suverænitet«, en

In addition, it is worth noting that current challenges have changed the minds of many. These include in particular changes that have taken place on the global stage such as, for instance, former US President Donald Trump having made Europe realise that the continent can no longer necessarily rest assured that the United States will still be a sufficiently reliable ally. Other challenges such as Brexit, COVID-19, and the Russian invasion of Ukraine have also altered attitudes towards the European project. An example of a certain degree of paradigm shift could be seen in the opening speech at the Danish Parliament on 4 October 2022 by the present Prime Minister, Social Democrat Mette Frederiksen.[29] In this, she stressed that Denmark cannot solve current challenges alone and that the European Union and NATO are essential. She also stressed that Europe must stand stronger in its own right—which could be seen as a reference to and acceptance of the idea of 'European sovereignty'.[30]

When such a paradigm shift can take place even in a Member State like Denmark–given, in particular, Denmark's unusual history of membership–it might possibly also happen elsewhere. Nevertheless, this account of Danish developments may also be seen as a kind of warning that Member States may–rightly or not–oppose any further strengthening of 'European sovereignty'.

4 Conclusions: Some Further, General Points of Concern

As was noted at the outset of this chapter, with war currently raging in Europe, it has become common to list the many simultaneous crises now erupting–many of them consequent on the Ukraine war–ranging from crises related to the economy, to those related to migration flows, to energy, to the climate, to the possibility of a social or solidarity crisis—and above all of them, this cruel and senseless war itself, with all its potential for further escalation. Again, as already noted, such complex and unpredictable times can call for urgent decision-making and for novel ways of thinking and acting, and unsurprisingly, some are tempted to call in response for 'more' Europe or 'European sovereignty'. In a way, this is all part of a pattern that has been witnessed before, where crises have led to calls for further integration and the like. However, in this regard, the following six points of concern at least—all

---

suverænitetssamling, i en verden, hvor den enkelte stats suverænitet end ikke i Danmarks nærområde anerkendes som selvfølgelig og ukrænkelig." Also see President Jean-Claude Juncker's State of the Union Address 2018, 12 September 2018, available online at <ec.europa.eu/commission/presscorner/detail/en/SPEECH_18_5808>: "European sovereignty is born of Member States' national sovereignty and does not replace it. Sharing sovereignty—when and where neede"d—makes each of our States and nations stronger".

[29] See "Statsminister Mette Frederiksens tale ved Folketingets åbning 4. oktober 2022" (Statsministeriet (stm.dk)). Thus it was fifty years after the referendum that led to Danish membership of the European Union and thirty years after the referendum leading to the four Danish opt-outs when she explicitly addressed the current security crisis.

[30] Just as the then Prime Minister Jens Otto Krag had done fifty years previously, therefore, she spoke, albeit in a different way, about a new chapter of cooperation.

of which relate to these issues from either a conceptual or a constitutional point of view—may be highlighted.

First, the concept 'European sovereignty' may end up not being taken as seriously as intended. In fact it may appear to be nothing more than a fancy slogan, which on the surface sounds smart and sounds as if it may well drive policies forward, when the reality is that there is in actual fact no single competence or straightforward process that will facilitate such a way forward.[31]

Secondly, the concept 'European sovereignty' may not be the best term to operate with, as–putting matters frankly–it is difficult not to notice fairly unsubtle hints in it of European nationalism *i.e.*, a form of 'anti-American or anti-Russian or anti-Chinese Europeanism'. This could end up being just as harmful as nationalism between Member States has been at times.[32]

Thirdly, the idea of striving to become more powerful has to be contrasted with the reality that the European Union traditionally has been a consensus-driven organisation with Member States' consent at the heart of its legitimacy.[33] When overriding national opposition–for example through the operation of qualified majority voting–the European Union comes into tension with traditional forms of state legitimation based on national democracy, as nationalists and populists throughout Europe often make clear.[34]

Fourthly, what could be called a legal "straitjacket"—broadly understood as legal limitations on action—still needs to be respected, because in times like the present, while large amounts of creativity and flexibility may well be seen as the solution, this may possibly come at the cost of compliance with a number of key principles of European Union law.[35]

Fifthly, it has to be ensured that the political and judicial checks and balances that the European Union Treaties entrust, in particular, to the European Parliament, to

---

[31] See "Editorial Comments. Keeping Europeanism at bay? Strategic autonomy as a constitutional problem", (2022) 59 *Common Market Law Review* 313 at 315 and 319.

[32] *Ibid* 313.

[33] See Bart Szewczyk, *European Sovereignty, Legitimacy, and Power* (Routledge 2021) 6.

[34] *Ibid*. In line with this, at p. 16, Szewczyk stresses that:

> decision-making in the EU is of two types: either by unanimity or by QMV in the Council of the EU, in addition to initiative by the Commission and majority approval by the Parliament. When decision-making is unanimous in the Council, questions of European sovereignty of EU legitimacy do not arise: each EU Member State exercises its national sovereignty, which is legitimated by its domestic (presumably democratic) processes. However, when decision-making is by QMV in the Council, the EU can override the decision of a national sovereign – one or more of its Member States – in a true exercise of European sovereignty that needs to be legitimated.

[35] See "Editorial Comments. Keeping Europeanism at bay? Strategic autonomy as a constitutional problem", (2022) 59 *Common Market Law Review* 313 at 320–321. Examples are the principle of conferred powers, the balance of power between institutions, and the principle of proportionality. These must not short-sightedly simply be perceived as obstacles to the effective pursuit of 'strategic autonomy' by the EU, but might rather be thought of as being of value despite all their imperfections.

the European Court of Justice and to the Member States' judiciaries, are sufficiently effective in order to avoid any abuse even now.[36]

Sixthly, the fundamental values which the European Union and the Member States commonly stand for should still be protected without too many compromises.[37]

In sum, 'European sovereignty' constitutes a complex concept in itself. At the same time, much hope has been put into its creation—hopes which however should somehow be 'tamed' by the face of reality. Because without this 'taming', Europe would no longer be what it has been intended to be, for even an angel with a sword still needs to remain an angel.

---

[36] See "Editorial Comments: The response to the war in Europe: A more power based European Union and the challenge of ensuring that it remains rule and value based", (2022) 59 *Common Market Law Review* 623 at 629.

[37] Also see "Editorial Comments. Keeping Europeanism at bay? Strategic autonomy as a constitutional problem", (2022) 59 *Common Market Law Review* 313 at 325:

> Just as we take Hannah Arendt's warning against European nationalism seriously, we do not want an inhumane ideology like the one that drove her out of Europe to prevail again. By putting people and individuals before capricious imperial dreams, the EU takes its role as custodian of its foundational values seriously, and confronts excesses of nationalism that despite all efforts, have never ceased to exist. As can be seen from the first steps taken against the aggressor… there is hope that the EU will rise to this challenge.

The Primacy of Union Law: Fit for Purpose?

Daniel Sarmiento

1 Introduction

Is the principle of primacy of Union law in crisis? Do the recent rulings from several national superior courts confirm that the notion of primacy was only a mirage, an optical illusion created by the enthused case-law of the Court of Justice and a choir of loud supporters, blind to the crude national reality that surrounded the European project and its legal order?

Several developments point in the direction of a constant erosion affecting primacy as a tool that guarantees the uniformity and effectiveness of Union law in the Member States. From rulings of national courts challenging the authority of the Court of Justice, to rule of law backsliding in some Member States, it appears as if the primacy of Union law has lost force, showing its inherent limitations for all to see. However, this narrative contrasts with the growing role of the Union and the expectations that citizens have put in the Union's abilities and powers to solve the most relevant existential challenges of our time: from fighting a global pandemic to supporting a war in a neighbouring country, or overcoming a climate and an energy crisis, it is the Union which is entrusted by its citizens (and national governments) to deal with such matters. An organisation that receives the mandate to save the very existence of its member countries and their way of life can hardly be defined as a failed project.

In this contribution I will argue that the principle of primacy, as a fundamental criterion that ensures the uniformity and effectiveness of Union law, is indeed undergoing significant stress. However, the argument that will be made does not point in the direction of an existential crisis of primacy and the Union legal order, but rather in that of the need to adapt its physiognomy to the current reality of the European

Professor of EU Law, Complutense University of Madrid, Editor–in–Chief of EU Law Live.

D. Sarmiento (✉)
Madrid, Spain
e-mail: daniel.sarmiento@der.ucm.es

G. Barrett et al. (eds.), *European Sovereignty*,
https://doi.org/10.1007/978-3-031-71851-9_4

project. In contrast with the voices that rely on a pragmatic approach towards overcoming the challenges faced by the principle of primacy at the current time, this paper will support a different approach towards primacy, including some proposals of Treaty change for its reinforcement in a way that reflects the specificities of the Union, whilst preserving the federal spirit that underscores the European project.

2 Primacy Thus Far: As Good as It Gets?

The principle of primacy emerged in the 1960's as a corollary of the direct effect of EEC law.[1] The two principles act as the two faces of the same coin, direct effect allowing individuals to invoke Union rules directly before national authorities, and primacy acting as a sword that empowers those authorities to set aside national rules that contradict the Union rules invoked in the case. Both principles are a pragmatic and original construction to empower individuals to strengthen the enforcement of Union law, defending their own individual interests, but indirectly contributing to improve the effectiveness of European rules in the national legal order.[2]

To conceive primacy in a static way, as a sort of "conflict rule" that simply confirms the preference of one legal rule over another, is a shortsighted approach that does not envision the broader complexities that the principle involves. In fact, primacy is a much more complex and multifaceted principle than this, and requires constant development, as the case-law of the Court of Justice has shown since the inception of the principle in the seminal case of *Costa v ENEL* in 1964.[3]

First, the primacy of Union law *vis-à-vis* national law is not a hierarchical criterion that determines validity in accordance with a predetermined rank. In contrast with what the optical impression of the word might convey, primacy does not determine validity based on hierarchy, but on a criterion of *competence*. The reason why national law must give way to Union law is the mere fact that the Union has exercised its competences in a field of Union policy, agreed by the Member States in accordance with the procedures provided in the Treaties.[4] Once the Union holds the competence in an area of policy within its competence, its rules prevail over national law, due to the fact that the Member State has conferred that power on the Union, either through primary or secondary Union law. The primacy of Union law reflects the competence of the Union and, at the same time, the lack of competence of the Member States. If national rules contradict Union rules, their existence undermines the competence of the Union to act in that field. That is the context in which the principle of primacy

[1] See Bruno de Witte, "Direct Effect, Primacy and the Nature of the Legal Order", in Paul Craig and Gráinne de Búrca, *The Evolution of EU Law* (2nd edition, OUP 2009).

[2] Michael Dougan, "When worlds collide: competing visions of the relationship between direct effect and supremacy", (2007) 44(4) *Common Market Law Review* 931.

[3] Case 6/64 *Costa v ENEL* EU:C:1964:66.

[4] Joseph Weiler and Ulrich Haltern, "The Autonomy of the Community Legal Order—Through the Looking Glass", *Harvard International Law Journal*, 37, 1996.

operates, thus guaranteeing the correct allocation of powers between the Union and the Member States, in an arrangement previously consented to by the institutions and Member States involved.

Secondly, there is a dynamic dimension to the principle of primacy. Whilst the principle can be portrayed in strictly static terms, providing a solution to situations of conflict of rules, the reality is rather different. Together with the seminal judgment in *Costa v ENEL*, a broad array of rulings of the Court have paved the way for the applicative dimension of primacy, navigating the way for national judges to deal with the consequences of an incompatibility among Union and national rules. There is no duty to annul a rule of national law if the national court lacks the power to do so, in which case, according to the *Simmenthal* judgment,[5] the national court has a duty to *set aside* the conflicting rule. Situations of parallelism between jurisdictions can appear, as is the case with "double preliminarity", when the national court has a duty to refer the case to the Court of Justice and to its Constitutional Court as well.[6] Even more delicate issues arise when national courts consider that the setting aside or the annulment of the national rule can create significant harm, in which case the national court may be inclined to limit the effects of its judgment in the time prior to the making of the reference to the Court of Justice.[7] In sum, primacy is not only a conflict rule that determines the fate of a provision that clashes with another, but rather is a complex array of criteria guaranteeing accommodation between two legal orders, both of which deploy directly effective rules and grant rights to individuals who have a legitimate claim to justice in a court of law.

Third, in its most straight-forward dimension–what has previously been called the "static" dimension of primacy–the principle is far from having a settled status. The primacy of Union law extends over the entirety of the national legal order, including its constitutional provisions and any decision of a national authority, including its courts. This maximalist understanding of the scope of primacy has been rejected by the majority of constitutional courts of the Member States, refusing to surrender their prerogative to rule in last instance on the proper allocation of competence between the two political entities: the Union and the Member State. In some jurisdictions this scrutiny has extended beyond competence control, entering the terrain of "identity control", in a more substantive and value-oriented type of review of Union action. This tension in determining the exact scope of Union law and its primacy has kept the Court of Justice and constitutional courts busy down through the decades, resulting in a status quo of stable instability, in which any of the players have the ability to destabilise, and even destroy, the coherence and unity of the current terms of cohabitation between Union and national law.

This situation unfortunately evolved into a scenario of open hostilities in 2020, when the German Federal Constitutional Court declared a ruling of the Court of Justice to be "objectively arbitrary" and not applicable in Germany, followed by the

---

[5] Case 106/77 *Amministrazione delle Finanze dello Stato v Simmenthal SpA* EU:C:1978:49.

[6] Cases C-188/10 and C-189/10 *Melki and Abdeli* EU:C:2010:363.

[7] Case C-379/15 *Association France Nature Environnement* EU:C:2016:603.

same outcome in reviewing a decision of the European Central Bank.[8] Shortly after this, the Romanian Constitutional Court followed suit in refusing to enforce rulings of the Court of Justice declaring prior case-law of the Romanian court in breach of Union law.[9] The same path was followed, although in a different context, by the Polish Constitutional Court, in the midst of the rule of law crisis that emerged after 2015.[10] The unravelling of the stable instability that had kept the Union's legal order in peaceful coexistence with national law appeared to have no end.

Following the first shock caused by these rulings, tensions seemed to lower, particularly in relations with the German Federal Constitutional Court and the Romanian Constitutional Court. However, the scars provoked by these conflicts have shown the limits of the principle of primacy and its inherent weaknesses, including the remedial shortcomings of the judicial system.[11] In the absence of a clear and explicit rule imposing the primacy of Union law, constitutional courts feel entitled to guarantee that the Constitution is upheld, even by the Union. The humbling of the principle of primacy has taken place at a time in which other major developments have gradually but constantly changed the face of the Union itself, in an evolution that raises doubts as to whether the principle of primacy, as we know it today, is fit for purpose.

3 The Changing Face of an Evolving Union of Law

The erosion of the principle of primacy stands, however, in sharp contrast with the success of the Union as an integration project. The past twenty years, and particularly following the financial crisis that erupted in 2008, have witnessed an impressive process of transformation of the Union as a political and economic project. Having hardly amended its Treaties, the Union has undergone a process of transformation that equals, and in some respects even surpasses, the reforms of 1992 in the Maastricht Treaty. These changes have taken place through legislative, executive, or international means, but also as a result of social change in the European polity. The result is a stronger and more ambitious Union, having received from its citizens a broad array of tasks to handle, tasks that the Member States are powerless to address on their own. The paradox lies in the fact that a stronger Union comes together with a weaker primacy of its law, questioned and challenged by the same Member States that rely on the Union to protect them from existential challenges. These changes in the Union

---

[8] BVerfG, Judgment of the Second Senate of 5 May 2020—2 BvR 859/15.

[9] See the press release of 23 December 2021, available at https://www.ccr.ro/comunicat-de-presa-23-decembrie-2021/.

[10] Judgment of 7 October 2021 (Case K 3/21).

[11] On 22 December 2021 the European Commission launched infringement proceedings against Poland as a result of the judgment of the Constitutional Court of 7 October 2021. Earlier in the year, the Commission had also launched infringement procedures against Germany as a result of the *Weiss* ruling, but these were withdrawn once the Constitutional Court stated that its judgment had been complied with.

are tectonic shifts, taking place silently or gradually, or both, but transforming the very face of the European project.

First, the transformations are clearly visible in the array of new powers being exercised by the Union. These powers are not necessarily new, but they are fashioned in unprecedented ways that put the Union on course towards an ever-growing line-up up powers that reinforce the Union's role *vis-à-vis* the Member States and its citizens. Most of these new policy approaches are the result of serious crises emerging from external shocks, namely the COVID-19 pandemic, climate change and the invasion of Ukraine by the Russian Federation. These shocks have triggered the development of unprecedented initiatives to use collectively the Union as an instrument to ensure the protection of existential interests of the Member States and its citizens: whether joint purchases of vaccines or gas,[12] the Green New Deal,[13] or an unprecedented stimulus package under a novel fiscal arrangement (Next Generation EU), using the Union as a financial shield and also purveyor of financial stability among the Member States.[14] The trend has continued following the energy crisis ensuing from the invasion of Ukraine, whilst developments in the field of defence, including the use of Union funds to finance the provision of military assistance to a neighbouring country, have transformed the way in which these areas of policy had previously been implemented.[15] The sum of this trend is a considerably stronger Union, receiving a mandate from the Member States and its citizens to ensure their very subsistence in the face of existential challenges. The Union is not only an instrument to ensure peace among the Member States through an internal market and an area without frontiers. It is now an instrument that guarantees the conditions of *subsistence* of its Member States.

Secondly, the institutional design of many of its policies is turning increasingly federal. The traditional division of tasks between a Union that legislates and Member States that take care of the executive and judicial implementation, is fading and evolving towards a more robust and federal-like system of enforcement, in which Union authorities play a growing role in decision-making, as well as Union courts in settling disputes. The case of Banking Union is a telling example, in which a federal-like composite system has been put in place in the field of prudential supervision and bank resolution.[16] The creation of the European Public Prosecutor and its institutional

---

[12] Francesco Saverio Della Corte, "The EU Vaccines Strategy: A Missed Opportunity for EU Public Health?", *European Journal of Risk Regulation* 1-13, 25 January 2023.

[13] Jerzy Jendrośka, Moritz Reese and Lorenzo Squintani, "Towards a new legal framework for sustainability under the European Green Deal", *The Opoloe Studies in Administration and Law* https://doi.org/10.25167/OSAP.4274.

[14] Federico Fabbrini, "Next Generation EU: Legal Structure and Constitutional Consequences", (2022) 24 *Cambridge Yearbook of European Legal Studies* 45 https://doi.org/10.1017/cel.2022.2.

[15] Tomas Hamilton, "Defending Ukraine with EU weapons: arms control law in times of crisis", (2022) 1(3) European Law Open 635. https://doi.org/10.1017/elo.2022.35.

[16] Regulation (EU) No 468/2014 of the European Central Bank of 16 April 2014 establishing the framework for cooperation within the Single Supervisory Mechanism between the European Central Bank and national competent authorities and with national designated authorities (SSM Framework Regulation) (OJ L 141, 14.5.2014), p. 1–50.

design is another example of this trend,[17] as is the case of the latest anti-money-laundering reform, in which new bodies are emerging in line with the same federal-like design.[18] This shift has forced a new approach in the case-law towards the way in which Member States interact with Union authorities, but also to the division of tasks between national and Union courts. The traditional role of national courts as protagonists in the interpretation and enforcement of Union law in the Member States has shifted and become more centralised in favour of the Union's courts, now facing federal-like institutional arrangements in need of strong centralised powers to attain their goals.[19]

Third, fundamental rights and Union citizenship have been altered as a result of the dynamics of integration. In the case of fundamental rights, what used to be a generic array of principles is now enshrined in writing in the Charter of Fundamental Rights of the European Union, with the same rank as primary law. The difference between having fundamental rights recognised in case-law only and enacting them in a written text of primary law has become significant. Since the entry into force of the Charter, the Court of Justice receives a growing number of questions for a preliminary reference on points of fundamental rights, turning it gradually into a fundamental rights court. The importance of the questions referred has forced the Court into developing a more sophisticated approach, thus reinforcing its position as a fundamental rights court. The importance of fundamental rights goes hand in hand with the development of a growing role for Union citizenship, a status that seemed modest at first, but which is now destined to become the "fundamental status of nationals of the Member States". The status of Union citizenship is not only reflected in a succinct list of rights enumerated in Article 20 TFEU, but also in the overall protection granted by the "substance of the rights attached to the status" of Union citizenship.[20] This evolution has put Union law closer to the very core of nationality law, to the extent of setting limits to Member State decisions on the withdrawal of nationality,[21] and even to the conditions of access and recognition.[22]

Fourth, the Union is not an economic project only, but also a project based on values. Article 2 TEU enumerates the values on which the project is based, in terms that set the core identity of the Union. The terms in which the values are expressed seemed to be declarative, but in the course of time, and because of several regressions in rule of law standards in some Member States, the values now stand as normative tools that also merit protection through law.[23] This transformation of the function of

[17] Council Regulation (EU) 2017/1939 of 12 October 2017 implementing enhanced cooperation on the establishment of the European Public Prosecutor's Office ('the EPPO') (OJ L 283, 31.10.2017), p. 1–71.

[18] Proposal for a Regulation of the European Parliament and the Council establishing the Authority for Anti-Money Laundering and Countering the Financing of Terrorism and amending Regulations (EU) No 1093/2010, (EU) (094/2010, (EU) 1095/2010) (COM/2021/421 final).

[19] Case C-414/18 *Iccrea Banca* EU:C:2019:574 and Case C-219/17 *Berlusconi* EU:C:2018:502.

[20] Case C-34/09 *Ruiz Zambrano* EU:C:2010:560.

[21] Case C-135/08 *Rottmann* EU:C:2009:588.

[22] Case C-369/90 *Micheletti* EU:C:1992:295.

[23] Case C-157/21 *Poland v Parliament and Council* EU:C:2022:98.

Union values stands behind the development of an "identity" of the Union, a set of normative benchmarks that act as limits to Member State action, but also to international law. The introduction of an "identity" of the Union based on values, provides tools with practical implications. For example, the Member States cannot invoke their national identities when their actions compromise the Union's "identity".[24] In symbolic terms, the Union's "identity" is the countermeasure of the Member State's "constitutional cores" or "constitutional identities", as defined in the case-law of the higher national courts. This new approach towards Union values has produced surprising outcomes, as is the case of the Court of Justice becoming an active defender of the independence of national courts, including supreme or constitutional courts.[25] Judicial dialogue in Europe is not only a matter of reaching optimal interpretations of Union law, but also a question of safeguarding the basic institutional infrastructure, including the judicial settings, of the Union and of its Member States.

In sum, the present-day Union is an organisation that has evolved substantially from the project it represented back in 1964 when the judgment in *Costa v ENEL* was delivered. The building blocks of the Union are made of constitutional principles and values with the force of law, giving rise to autonomous categories of citizenship, rights and democracy with a decisive impact on the everyday lives of citizens. An organisation of this nature promotes and implements political agendas with a significant transformative impact. Therefore, for this Union to achieve its aims, it needs to rely on a robust normative toolbox that ensures the effectiveness of the project. To see at the present time, when the Union has achieved an unprecedented degree of ambition and sophistication in its organisation, a crisis of its principle of primacy, is an outcome that seriously undermines the narrative described thus far.

The current crisis is not an isolated incident. The German Constitutional Court's judgment in the case of *Weiss*, declaring a judgment of the Court of Justice to be "objectively arbitrary" and an ECB decision *ultra vires*, is the tipping point of a trend that has only aggravated over time. It is true that the crisis in the *Weiss* case eventually found a pragmatic solution, but the reality is that the effect of the ruling was to send a clear message to all national jurisdictions inclined to depart from the common criteria set by the Court of Justice. If the only recognition of the principle of primacy comes from the case-law of the European Court of Justice and a Declaration annexed to the Treaties, the frailty of the Union's legal order is too obvious for all to see. In a Union that intends to play a transformative role in promoting societal change in times of existential challenges, this frailty is a price too high to pay.

---

[24] Case C-357/19 *Euro Box Promotion* EU:C:2021:1034).

[25] See Laurent Pech, Patryk Wachowiec and Dariusz Mazur, "Poland's Rule of Law Breakdown: A Five-Year Assessment of EU's (In)Action" (2021) 13 *Hague Journal on the Rule of Law* 1.

4 Living with a Fragile Principle of Primacy in an Invigorated Union

It is tempting to affirm that challenges to the principle of primacy are an inherent feature of the integration process, and that the Union should be ready to tackle them in a pragmatic way. To some extent, the entire history of European integration has witnessed various challenges of this kind, generally solved through political compromise or discrete manoeuvrings. In the same way that the Union has struggled through many crises by focusing on problem-solving rather than problem-raising, the challenges to primacy could be approached in a similar way, relying on the good will of all of the stakeholders to reach a reasonable compromise.

This approach is tempting, and it could be even considered to be the correct way forward. However, it is a strategy that gambles on the successful management of previous crises, whilst the current crisis of primacy is taking place in an entirely different context. This can be seen by depicting the different scenarios that could ensue in a Union with a fragilised primacy at the basis of its legal order.

A fractured primacy is not an acceptable normative premiss on which to build essential policy measures like Next Generation EU, joint purchases of vaccines or energy resources, or measures of support in the field of defence while a deathly war is taking place in a neighbouring country. The list of external shocks that are shaking the foundations of the Union is growing longer, now including climate change as an additional and long-term risk for the Member States and its citizens. These challenges are not internal shocks provoked by a Member State or group of Member States. On the contrary, they are external shocks that affect the Union and its Member States as a whole. The response of the Union to these shocks has an existential dimension, inasmuch as its failure can risk the collective failure of all the Member States, including the risk of their very existence. Whilst a fragilised primacy was traditionally concerned with the internal market, the new and invigorated Union hardly has any margin of error, and a broken primacy that entitles any national stakeholder to depart from the uniform implementation of Union law can be a lethal manoeuvre with far-reaching implications.

The same applies to the current federal-like institutional arrangements, which demand a high degree of cooperation among the Union and the national authorities. As entire policy fields turn towards mechanisms and forms of highly integrated administrative performance, this model can only operate on the basis of a robust principle of primacy accepted by all of the players, particularly national authorities. A supervisory mechanism for credit institutions cannot be effective if the decisions of the ECB do not have primacy over the decisions of national authorities, particularly when there is a discrepancy in the interpretation of Union law. The European Public Prosecutor must rely on the uniform interpretation provided by the Court of Justice, not on the diverse national interpretations that the national higher courts can provide of the same provision. As the Union navigates towards highly integrated methods of administrative action, the principle of primacy must act as a firm foundation accepted by all of the stakeholders. Otherwise, the structure becomes unstable, fragilised and destined to fail, together with its policy aims.

As the Union becomes more rights-centered and a statue of citizenship evolves, questions of values and principles will emerge, in which a variety of views will create divergences among the Member States. Values-based reasoning in the case-law of the Court or in the legislative process will trigger more complex conflicts in which the final word will leave unsatisfied stakeholders. Religion in the workplace, the protection of privacy and its conflicts with public security, the protection of animals and its balancing with entrenched cultural practices, etc.... The Union is called to have a say in many of the current socictal debates that were traditionally separate from the discussions over the internal market. However, these debates are directly or indirectly part of Union policy now, and the Union legislature and its courts cannot be driven to have a say in these matters while the principle of primacy is being questioned by the highest courts of the Member States. For the Union to have a robust fundamental rights policy and an authoritative criterion settling such matters in a complex and diverse Europe, once the decision is made, it is imperative that the principle of primacy deploy its full force.

Seen in this light, the current crisis of the principle of primacy is not just another bump in the road, like other previous crises seen in the past. The current challenges to primacy are a much more unsettling and significant threat which imperils the Union's efforts to provide robust responses to existential challenges. For that reason, pragmatism and low-key responses will not solve the problem that has now emerged. The crack is not in a Chinese flower vase, it is a crack that is slowly and constantly expanding in the concrete heart of a gigantic water dam.

5 A Future for the Principle of Primacy

The alternatives to taking a pragmatic approach to the crisis of primacy are not self-evident. They run from idealistic and politically naïve proposals to overcomplicated solutions with uncertain chances of success. In any event, a quick review is well deserved, whilst the use of idealistic but politically challenging solutions should not be overlooked. What seemed impossible in European integration a decade ago has become the rule today (Next Generation EU was hardly conceivable in the midst of the euro crisis in 2012)—a sign that it is important to keep an open mind when exploring options for overcoming the primacy crisis.

The first proposal is a classic: the introduction of a primacy clause in the Treaties with binding force of law in all the Member States. This option was explored in 2004 in the Constitutional Treaty, in its Article I-6, according to which "the Constitution and law adopted by the institutions of the Union in exercising competences conferred on it shall have primacy over the law of the Member States".[26] It can be argued that such a provision is currently in force today through the indirect means of Declaration

[26] Draft Treaty establishing a Constitution for Europe (OJ C 169, 18.7.2003, pp. 1–150).

17 on primacy, but that is not correct. Declaration 17 is a non-binding act annexed to the Final Act of the Intergovernmental Conference which agreeed the Treaty of Lisbon, and was adopted to confirm that the non-enactment of the Constitutional Treaty and its Article I-6 in no way affected the status of the principle in Union law. Furthermore, Declaration 17 is a restatement of the Court's case-law as explained by a legal opinion of the Council, not as a solemn statement of the Member States. Even as a multilateral Declaration, its construction shows the efforts of the Member States to avoid upsetting the balance kept between European Union law's unilateral and broad conception of primacy and the limits set to it by national superior courts.[27]

Would the introduction of a provision like Article I-6 resolve the primacy crisis? Probably not. To a certain extent, the current law, even as it now stands, has already incorporated a primacy clause through the authoritative interpretation of the Treaties developed by the Court of Justice. After almost sixty years since the judgment in *Costa v ENEL*, it can be argued that the Member States have had plenty of opportunities to amend the scope of this doctrine by way of a Treaty amendment, but nothing of the kind has occurred. On the contrary, in amendment after amendment, the Member States have seemed eager to expand the competences of the Union upon the understanding that Union law held primacy over national law, including constitutional law. This tacit acceptance of primacy by the masters of the Treaties, together with the clear and unconditional case-law of the Court of Justice, has not stopped the supreme and constitutional courts of the Member States from setting benchmarks limiting the scope of Union law's primacy. An explicit recognition of the principle in the articulated text of the Treaties would probably keep the *status quo* as it now stands, irrespective of the clarity of the message being conveyed in such a provision.

There is a variant to this option which would possibly change the fate of the proposal: an explicit recognition in the Treaties of the primacy clause, together with the incorporation of the very same provision in the Constitutions of all the Member States, would significantly improve the chances of success in settling the principle in a robust and stable way for the long term. By enshrining a principle of primacy in a dual fashion, in both the Treaties and national constitutions, a firm commitment from all legal orders ensues, setting a conflict rule that provides clear guidance on what legal order (and jurisdiction) prevails over the other. National courts could no longer assert that the final word on the interpretation of the Treaties, on matters such as the distribution of competence, can be assumed, even exceptionally, by a domestic jurisdiction. The mandate would be clear and the authority of Union law would prevail. The technique has already been used in the past, particularly in the Treaty on Stability, Coordination and Governance (also known as the Fiscal Compact), signed on 2 March 2012 by the then Member States (with the exception of the United Kingdom and the Czech Republic).[28] This Treaty provides in its Article 3(2) for

[27] See Ferdinand Weber, "The Identity of Union Law in Primacy: Piercing Through Euro Box Promotion and Others" (2022) 7 *European Papers*, No. 2.

[28] Treaty on Stability, Coordination and Governance in the Economic and Monetary Union (2012) (Document 42012A0302(01).

the duty of Member States to introduce rules on fiscal discipline and stability, but "preferably constitutional rules".

Despite the robustness of such a solution, and irrespective of its feasibility undergoing twenty-seven constitutional amendments, the truth is that this proposal would not dispel the risk of constitutional conflict and, eventually, another challenge to primacy. Whilst such a clause will contribute to end conflicts mostly in the field of competence (granting the Court of Justice the ultimate word in determining the scope of the Union's jurisdiction), it will not stop national constitutional courts from claiming their own constitutional identities, particularly as regards issues that touch on points close to values and principles, in which balancing acts are necessary. Also, in constitutions that have "eternity clauses" or provisions that are not subject to amendment, any interference by Union law would be subject to these red lines, irrespective of the scope and terms provided in the primacy clause. These matters will be for national constitutional courts to resolve, which will give them sufficient leeway to continue to claim the last word in the ongoing discussion over the authority of Union law in the Member States.

The limitations of the previous proposals explain why in part, discussions on the ways to overcome the crisis of primacy have a procedural angle, focusing not so much on the substance of the primacy clause itself, but on the procedures that allow the European Union to assert both its authority and that of its legal system. Procedural solutions do not solve the very crux of the matter, but they act as buffers to prevent constitutional conflict from materialising into a crisis. To this end, these proposals are a middle ground between the maximalist option of constitutional reform and the pragmatic approach.

A first procedural option is the creation of a mixed chamber in the Court of Justice, comprised of sitting judges of the Court of Justice and of national constitutional and supreme courts.[29] The mixed chamber would be a last-instance jurisdiction to hear actions against a decision of the Court of Justice on a point of Union competence. Its jurisdiction could also extend to hearing cases on fundamental rights. But above all, the role of the mixed chamber would be to settle a claim of primacy coming from the Union legal order and a national legal order. When such a conflict would arise and both jurisdictions would have had the chance of ruling on the matter, both the Union or the Member State concerned would have the right to bring the case to the mixed chamber. The mixed chamber's decision would settle the matter and rule through the voice of the joint legitimacy granted by its composition, thus providing a robust decision with sufficient authority to overrule either the Court of Justice's or the national superior court's claim. The result would not be a general confirmation of the primacy of one legal order over the other, but would rather be a composite answer solving a specific dispute and settling the matter until the next dispute would be raised.

There would be several procedural guarantees to ensure that the mixed chamber fulfilled its role in a balanced way. Its composition would be made up of thirteen

---

[29] Daniel Sarmiento and Joseph Weiler, "The EU Judiciary After Weiss", *Verfassungsblog*, 2 June 2020 and "The EU Judiciary After Weiss—A Reply to our Critics", *EU Law Live*, 6 July 2020.

judges, of which eight would be sitting judges of the Court of Justice on a rotating basis, and seven would come from national supreme and constitutional courts, also on a rotating basis. Although decisions could be made based on a consensus of all the sitting members of the mixed chamber, an *in dubio mitius* voting rule should apply: this would require that a decision validating a contested EU act be supported by at least eight judges. This rule would avoid having all of the judges of the Court of Justice siding with the Union, thus requiring at least the support of one judge of the national high courts to validate the contested act.

Another procedural proposal focuses on the US technique of "certification", a means by which federal courts can inquire of state courts about the correct interpretation of state law.[30] Extended to Union law, a "certification" procedure would empower the Court of Justice to refer questions of national law, on constitutional points of principle, to the Member States' highest courts. This tool could facilitate a dialogue between the Court of Justice and the highest courts of the Member States, but more specifically it would provide the Court with binding guidance about provisions concerning national identity, national competence or constitutional limits that risk colliding with Union law. This course of action, like the mixed chamber, would require specific rules, but probably not a reform of the Statute. At the present time, Article 24 of the Statute provides that the Court may "require the Member States and institutions, bodies, offices and agencies not being parties to the case to supply all information which the Court considers necessary for the proceedings." This provision could find further development in a future reform of the Rules of Procedure, entitling the Court of Justice to request a court of a Member State guidance on a point of interpretation of national law.

Like the mixed chamber, a European "certification" procedure would not solve the challenges raised by constitutional conflicts between the Union and its Member States. However, it would mitigate the chances of further conflict by providing a channel of communication between the Court of Justice and the Member States' highest courts, even in circumstances in which no prior preliminary reference had been made between the two jurisdictions. This would be a tool to facilitate mutual understanding, the outcome of which would be unknown in advance. The tool would also depend on the willingness of the Court of Justice to make use of it. The Statute and Rules of Procedures of the Court have a fair share of procedural options that have become obsolete or forgotten as a result of their lack of use by the Luxembourg judges. Procedural solutions would be buffers that would contribute either to preventing constitutional conflict or to helping fashion an acceptable final outcome, but they would not solve the inherent tension between two colliding and legitimate claims of authority emanating from the Union and one or more of its Member States.

---

[30] Alberto Nicòtina and Emil Martini, "From Monologues to Dialogue: The US "Certification" Procedure as a Source of Inspiration for EU Cooperative Judicial Federalism", (2022) *European Yearbook of Constitutional Law* 207.

6 Conclusion

The questioning of the principle of primacy of Union law has reached a tipping point. At the stage of European integration in which we currently stand, in which existential challenges have been delegated for their resolution to the Union's institutions, the risk of fragmenting the unity of the Union's legal order is too high. The Member States cannot confer such responsibilities on the Union while empowering their internal authorities to question the uniform implementation of Union law in their territory. The Union's institutional organisation provides sufficient guarantees of democratic accountability and legitimacy for Member States and their national jurisdictions to accept that the common rules enacted by the Union are uniform standards that supersede national law in its areas of competence. Control over the exercise of Union competence is a task that is well performed by the Court of Justice, a jurisdiction with seven decades of experience in adjudicating over the Union's jurisdiction. At the present stage of European integration, the undermining of primacy is a self-destructive practice that harms the overall project, but its individual members too. Considering the relevance of the existential challenges at stake, it is worrying to witness how the ongoing defence of an indeterminate "constitutional identity", solely defined by a court of law, can rally its defenders to the point of undermining policies addressed to deal with some of society's existential challenges.

Behind the curtain of the notion of constitutional identity lies nationalism and its many faces, a force that is difficult to handle or rationalise when it touches the core of identity politics in the Member States. The history of Europe, including its most recent history, provides sound proof of the ability of nationalism to elude the real problems of the people and to embrace discourses that turn out to be self-destructive in the long term. The challenges that have been recently faced or are currently faced by the Member States, ranging from a global pandemic, to energy crises, to climate change, have arrived along with significant numbers of vaccine sceptics, climate change deniers and conspiracy theory supporters questioning either the existence of the problem or its solutions. In such a context, it is unsurprising still to encounter primacy-deniers refusing to accept Union law's power to supersede national law. Primacy denialism can be as destructive as the force of nationalism, embracing core values in the name of ethereal goals, whilst sacrificing the edifice that keeps society together to address common challenges.

However, in the same way that nationalism will not disappear and must be interiorised and channelled through the democratic process, the same should apply to scepticism concerning the primacy of European Union law. For that reason, attempts to settle the matter by introducing a strict primacy clause in the Treaties or in the Constitutions of the Member States, are destined to fail. As long as primacy deniers continue to haunt the Union and its legal order, the presence of primacy clauses in writing will not repeal the underlying ideology supporting the attacks. Therefore, the way forward is to channel those claims and prove them wrong through appropriate procedures, in a way that reflects all the interests at stake and eventually tips the balance in favour of a European majority. The mixed chamber is an example of how to proceduralise a primacy clause, refusing to eradicate the concerns of primacy sceptics, but embracing them and giving them voice in a composite procedure in which a decision must finally emerge. Nothing will stop a national court or a Member State from refusing to comply with a decision of the mixed chamber, but at such point it will be obvious that the only way forward for that Member State will be to exit the European project. After a ruling of the Court of Justice followed by a decision of a body representing not only all the Member States, but also the voices of constitutional courts, the Member State which is the source of the dissenting opinion will face a choice: to carry on with its European journey or take a different path.

The Janus of European Sovereignty—A Franco-Estonian Perspective

Julia Laffranque

> *In the absence of justice – what is sovereignty but organised robbery?*
> *Saint Augustine*

1 Introduction: The Sovereign Meaning of Sovereignty

1.1 Talking About Sovereignty: The Importance of Perspectives

One complexity in the topic of sovereignty consists of the fact that sovereignty itself is a sovereign phenomenon and not easily definable even though during different periods of time those in power have frequently given a meaning corresponding to how they liked to see it, stretching the definition of sovereignty as they have liked.[1]

Sovereignty is abstract and practical at the same time, and an issue which is somehow constantly on the agenda. It is a topic that surfaces every now and then, forming the subject of heated debates and discussions. This can be in the context of European Union (EU) integration whenever sovereignty is on the table: e.g., in 1992 when closely contested referendums in France and in Denmark relating to the

[1] The quotation at the top of the page is taken from St. Augustine, *Book IV* of *The City of God*: "And so, if justice has been removed, what are kingdoms but great robber bands? For what are robber bands but little kingdoms?" (Available online at <https://www.sabidius.com/latin/latin-translation/augustine-de-civitae-dei-book-iv/> Accessed 11 October 2023).

Judge of the Supreme Court of Estonia and visiting professor, University of Tartu.

J. Laffranque (✉)
Tartu, Estonia
e-mail: julia.laffranque@riigikohus.ee

G. Barrett et al. (eds.), *European Sovereignty*,
https://doi.org/10.1007/978-3-031-71851-9_5

Maastricht Treaty occurred producing different results;[2] in 2005, when the "European Constitution" (the Treaty Establishing a Constitution for Europe) was voted down by the people in France and the Netherlands (while referendums took place in several other countries, with other electorates voting in favour[3]) and where again, sovereignty was an issue; or (in the framework of EU enlargement and the accession of new countries to the Union) e.g., in the discussions on sovereignty which occurred in Estonia and other Central and Eastern European countries when they joined the European Union almost twenty years ago.[4] Nowadays again, when we look at the question of the rule of law in Poland and Hungary, but also in Romania, or look at the Constitutional and Supreme Court rulings in some other countries, such as Denmark, the Czech Republic and Germany–we see the role that the national sovereignty of Member States *vis-à-vis* the European Union plays. But sovereignty arises as an issue as well in connection with the European Union itself–is the EU sovereign e.g., in relation to economic, energy or climate crises or in relation to the rise of artificial intelligence? Last, but not least, sovereignty is on our minds on a daily basis because of the ongoing war by Russia in Ukraine which makes us all, especially in Europe, particularly vulnerable. It would be a good thing to learn from history.

We lawyers have also been arguing about sovereignty for a long time. Sometimes these arguments seem abstract to us, especially when it comes to the relationship between the European Union and its Member States: as long as there is no real threat of losing sovereignty, these discussions remain theoretical. Of course, in a way, Member States (but also the EU itself) lose the sole exclusive power to exercise certain functions, but they share sovereignty voluntarily.

We know, however, from the past, and unfortunately, are seeing now in connection with Russia's war in Ukraine, that both independence and sovereignty can be very fragile notwithstanding how valuable they are to us. Compared, for example, to the delegation of parts of functions of Member States' sovereignty voluntarily to the European Union, the very real threat presented to sovereignty by military invasion is of course much more serious, The reason why e.g., Estonia joined the EU, and more

---

[2] A referendum on the Maastricht Treaty was held in France on 20 September 1992. It was approved by only 51% of voters. A referendum on the Maastricht Treaty was also held in Denmark on 2 June 1992. It was rejected by 50.7% of voters on a turnout of 83.1%. It is interesting to note however, how thirty years later, on 1 June 2022, a referendum on the abolition of the defence opt-out, one of the country's opt-outs from the EU, was held in Denmark which the vote going in favour of this abolition. Seemingly, the current situation with war in Ukraine had implications for the vote, as this was the third referendum to be held in relation to Denmark's opt-outs and the first time that the vote went in favour of abolition of the opt-out. (In 2000, the Danish electorate rejected the adoption of the euro as national currency, and in 2015 a proposal to modify the justice opt-out was also rejected).

[3] Spain was the first country to hold a referendum on the Treaty Establishing a Constitution for Europe: on 20 February 2005, Spanish voters backed the treaty with 76% voting in favour to 24% against, on a turnout of 43%.

On 29 May 2005, the French people rejected it by a margin of 55% to 45% on a turnout of 69%. On 1 June, the Dutch people rejected it as well by a margin of 61% to 39% on a turnout of 62%. Notwithstanding these rejections, Luxembourg subsequently held a referendum on 10 July 2005 approving the Constitution by 57% to 43%.

[4] See the Estonian example below under heading 3.1.

particularly, the reason why it acceded to NATO, was to guarantee its own safety, whereby delegating certain tasks to these organisations (the EU and NATO) is a kind of assurance of that security–just as deepening European integration is an assurance for the sovereignty of the European Union *vis-à-vis* outside threats.

It is popular to discuss sovereignty, even if this is unfortunately often done without really realising what the concept means or in deliberately being provocative regarding possible threats to sovereignty: in such discussions, polarisation should be avoided and constructive thinking and action welcome. Perhaps we should invent a completely new phenomenon to replace the traditional understanding of sovereignty?

In ancient Roman religion and myth, *Janus* is the god of beginnings, gates, transitions, time, duality, doorways, passages, frames, and endings. This is a good symbol for trying to understand, analyse and further develop or transform our understanding of sovereignty.

Starting at the beginning, let us take two examples in our quest for the grail of sovereignty–those of France and of Estonia–the latter a country, the Constitution of which, in its first paragraph (in its second sentence), proclaims that independence and sovereignty are timeless and inalienable; thus encompassing east and west, north and south, and old and new democracies. Let us further put this in the context of European Union law.[5]

Furthermore, in discussing sovereignty, we must not forget what is most important–the individual and his or her rights and sense of justice. Law and justice are there to guarantee that human rights will always be upheld.

1.2 A Holistic Definition: One Possible Attempt

Sovereignty can be looked at as the highest authority in the political-legal hierarchy; we note, e.g., that according to the French Constitution, national sovereignty belongs to the people, who exercise it through their representatives and by means of referendums[6]; and, similarly, that the Estonian Constitution says that supreme power is vested in the people.[7]

In attempting a holistic definition, we too can understand sovereignty to mean the ultimate right to decide on political-legal matters; to signify in jural form the nature and quality of political relationships with respect to governmental regimes.[8]

[5] There will be somewhat more emphasis on Estonia, as the discussions about Estonia's sovereignty and relevant case law are lesser known to the European legal public.

[6] Article 3 of the 1958 French Constitution; (available online at <https://efaidnbmnnnibpcajpcglclefindmkaj/ https://www.conseil-constitutionnel.fr/sites/default/files/as/root/bank_mm/anglais/constiution_anglais_oct2009.pdf> accessed 11 April 2023).

[7] Article 1 of the 1992 Estonian Constitution; available online at <https://www.riigiteataja.ee/en/eli/ee/521052015001/consolide/current> accessed 11 April 2023).

[8] See e.g., Martin Loughlin, "Why Sovereignty?" in: *Sovereignty and the Law: Domestic, European and International Perspectives*. Richard Rawlings, Peter Leyland and Alison Young, (eds.), (Oxford Academic 2013) 34.

In addition to the foregoing, in order to fully grasp sovereignty, it is also important to consider the influence of the sovereign: the universality of its acts, and the autonomy that characterises sovereignty, i.e., that the sovereign must be independent in its relations, both internally and externally. Thus, in order to define sovereignty, four components are essential: the seat (i.e., that it involve the highest power in the political-legal hierarchy); hierarchy (i.e., that it involve the final authority in the political-legal hierarchy); influence (i.e., that it involve universality in each stream of action) and autonomy (i.e., that the sovereign must be independent in its relations with other parties (both internal and external).

Sovereignty in international law means the ability of a state to exercise its power: *de jure* sovereignty refers to having the right to do this, *de facto* sovereignty refers to having the actual ability to exercise it.[9] A separate question is whether the law is sovereign, i.e., whether it is above politics; thus whether a sovereign right is a real right that can be exercised even against the will of political branches of government, insofar as the constitution is respected and that any violation of the constitutional order will constitute a *coup d'état* or a revolution, regardless of intent.

In relations with the European Union, for example, we must bear in mind that the European Union itself does not have this ultimate competence, that is to say, the competence to decide on its own competences (or *Kompetenz Kompetenz* as the matter is so well elaborated in German doctrine[10]). The competences of the European Union have been voluntarily granted and delegated to it by the Member States. The Member States have freely replaced some of the tasks involved in exercising their own competences through the grant and delegation of competences to the institutions of the EU, in particular to the European Parliament (which is directly elected by the people) but also to the European executive, the European Commission; as well as to the Council of the European Union (in which are represented the Member States themselves), which, together with the European Parliament, adopt so-called secondary European legislation. On the other hand, it has been argued that within the European Union as far as the European Union dimension is concerned, the States separately do not possess *Kompetenz Kompetenz*, but rather all the states together possess *Kompetenz–Kompetenz*, with the consequence of this being that the exercise of this function is necessarily a collective exercise.[11]

---

[9] Neil MacFarlane and Natalie Sabanadze, "Sovereignty and self-determination: Where are we?" (2013) 68(4) *International Journal* 609.

[10] Martin Große Hüttmann in Martin Große Hüttmann and Hans-Georg Wehling, (eds.) *Das Europalexikon*, (3rd edition, Dietz 2020) see <https://www.bpb.de/kurz-knapp/lexika/das-europalexikon/177087/kompetenz-kompetenz/> accessed 2 April 2023).

[11] Raffaele Bifulco and Alessandro Nato, "The concept of sovereignty in the EU—past, present and the future", (Reconnect/European Commission 2020) 85.

2 The Past: National Sovereignty as Understood Classically

2.1 The French Notion of the Supremacy of Sovereignty

The concept of sovereignty derives originally from the French word *la souveraineté*, which in turn is descended from Latin, *superanus*. One of the first conceptions of sovereignty, it was used in the sixteenth century by the Frenchman Jean Bodin, to strengthen the power of the French king against the rebellious feudal lords.[12] Bodin's concept of absolute sovereignty is often exaggerated,[13] but it must be seen in the context of the conflicts between Catholics and Huguenots, and in particular of the St. Bartholomew's Day massacre in 1572. Can we thus say that Bodin's notion was that the sovereign Prince was really accountable only to God?

Montesquieu developed a theory according to which the sovereign, although the highest power in the state, is not above the law.[14] Philosophers such as Thomas Hobbes, John Locke and Jean-Jacques Rousseau have also influenced the concept of sovereignty,[15] with the doctrine of popular sovereignty finding expression in the United States Declaration of Independence in 1776.[16]

Jurists prior to 1789 were primarily concerned with laying legal foundations for the omnipotence of the monarch and the rights of the king in the face of the resistance the king was encountering in the ordinary exercise of his power. In later times, lawyers have made use of the theory of the rule of law to place limits on the power of the state and, in particular, to limit the omnipotence of parliament that derives from the theory of national sovereignty.[17]

The Declaration of the Rights of Man and of the Citizen (*Déclaration des droits de l'Homme et du citoyen de 1789*), a civil rights document dating from the time of the French Revolution inspired by Enlightenment philosophers and adopted by

---

[12] Andrew, Edward, "Jean Bodin on Sovereignty", (2011) 2 *Republics of Letters: A Journal for the Study of Knowledge, Politics, and the Arts* 75.

[13] See interestingly about Bodin's concept, Dieter Grimm, "Bodin's Significance for the Concept of Sovereignty" Part B(1) of Dieter Grimm, *Sovereignty* (Columbia University Press 2015) 13.

[14] Charles Louis de Secondat, Baron Montesquieu, *De l'Esprit des Loix*, II, 1. (Available online at <https://efaidnbmnnnibpcajpcglclefindmkaj/ https://upload.wikimedia.org/wikipedia/commons/1/12/Montesquieu%2C_De_l%27Esprit_des_loix_%281st_ed%2C_1748%2C_vol_1%29.pdf> accessed 11 April 2023). See also M.J.C Vile, Chap. 4 in *Constitutionalism, and the Separation of Powers*, (2nd edition, Liberty Fund 1998) 22.

[15] See e.g., Manzoor Laskar, "Summary of Social Contract Theory by Hobbes, Locke and Rousseau" (unpublished paper, April 4, 2013). (Available online at <https://ssrn.com/abstract=2410525> or <http://dx.doi.org/10.2139/ssrn.2410525> accessed 11 April 2023).

[16] It was also an example for many other states. See regarding the importance of the Declaration of Independence for concepts of fundamental rights, Randy E. Barnett, "The Declaration of Independence and the American Theory of Government: 'First Come Rights, and Then Comes Government'" (2019) 42(1) *Harvard Journal of Law & Public Policy* 23.

[17] See also Alain Laquièze, "État de Droit and National Sovereignty in France" in Pietro Costo and Danielo Zolo, (eds.), *The Rule of Law—History, Theory and Criticism*, Springer: 2007, pp. 261–291, at p. 261.

France's National Constituent Assembly in 1789, proclaims in its Article III that the principle of all sovereignty resides essentially in the nation: no body or individual may exercise any authority which does not proceed directly from the nation.[18] This Declaration was later explicitly referred to in the preamble of French constitutions. Furthermore, the Preamble to the Constitution of 27 October 1946, which also has constitutional value, proclaimed that the French Republic "conforms to the rules of public international law" (see para 14 thereof) and that "subject to reciprocity, France consents to the limitations of sovereignty necessary for the organisation and defence of peace" (see para 15).[19]

Sovereignty (which, it has been decided "can only be national"[20]) appeared also in the first sentence of the Preamble to the Constitution of 4 October 1958 of France which declared that:

> The French people solemnly proclaim their attachment to human rights and to the principles of national sovereignty as defined by the Declaration of 1789, confirmed and completed by the Preamble to the Constitution of 1946, as well as to the rights and duties defined in the Charter of the Environment of 2004.[21]

2.2 *Sovereignty: the Pride of Estonian National Self-Determination*

The freedom and independence of Estonia have not come easily. Estonia has been populated since almost the end of the ice age, its national inhabitants being mainly Finno-Ugrians; it was violently Christianised by Bishop Albert of Riga and the Order of the Sword-Brothers, which was later transformed into the Livonian Order. It came temporarily and partially (only northern Estonia) under Denmark's rule, later coming under that of the Swedish Kingdom and Russian Czar's Empire, even if the upper hand nevertheless belonged nevertheless continuously to German landlords. The Estonian people fought for their freedom and existence down through the centuries.[22]

In 1918, the decisive year, alarming reports alerted Estonians of approaching German troops who might occupy the whole country, while the Russian Bolsheviks

[18] Text available e.g., at <https://www.conseil-constitutionnel.fr/le-bloc-de-constitutionnalite/declaration-des-droits-de-l-homme-et-du-citoyen-de-1789> accessed 11 April 2023). See also regarding sovereignty and for a comparison with the United States Declaration of Independence, *Discours sur la Déclaration des droits de l'homme et du Citoyen* (1 August 1789), available online at <https://www.assemblee-nationale.fr/histoire/sur%20la-declaration-des-droits-de-l-homme.asp> accessed 11 April 2023).

[19] Available online at: https://www.conseil-constitutionnel.fr/en/constitution-of-4-october-1958.

[20] Decision of the Conseil Constitutionnel, no. 76–71 DC of 30 December 1976.

[21] Available online at <https://www.conseil-constitutionnel.fr/en/constitution-of-4-october-1958> accessed 31 January 2024.

[22] See Seppo Zetterberg,, *Eesti ajalugu* (Tänapäev 2009) and Ilmar Talve, *Eesti Kultuurilugu* (Ilmamaa 2004).

(then in power) were fleeing. The Estonian Salvation Committee,[23] which composed of three men: first, the lawyer Konstantin Päts, the future head of state and president of Estonia; secondly, the lawyer and editor-in-chief of the daily newspaper Päevaleht, and later first minister of justice, Jüri Vilms, and thirdly (last, but not least) Konstantin Konik, a doctor, professor, and later member of the Estonian Parliament (*Riigikogu*) as well as minister of education and social affairs—took advantage of this moment and decided to declare Estonia an independent state. The Manifesto for all the peoples of Estonia (the Manifesto)[24] was drafted.[25] The question then arose of finding a suitable city in which to proclaim independence in the best and boldest way.

In fact, it was 23 February 1918, at eight o'clock in the evening, when the Manifesto, the wonderful founding document of Estonian statehood, was read out publicly and solemnly from the balcony of the Endla Seltsimaja, a theatre in the sea-side resort, city of Pärnu, by torchlight. These moments are described in detail in order to demonstrate the pride Estonians have historically taken in their belief in their right to national self-determination which is part of sovereignty.

The Manifesto quotes the national epic "Kalevipoeg" written by Friedrich Reinhold Kreutzwald[26] and perfectly summarises the basic principles and values of the Estonian state as being respect for, respectively, human rights, the rule of law, democracy, and minorities. For example, the Manifesto states that all citizens of the Republic of Estonia, irrespective of religion, nationality, or political outlook, find equal protection before the laws and courts and that national minorities living within the borders of Estonia–Russians, Germans, Swedes, Jews and others–will be guaranteed their rights to ethnic and cultural autonomy. The concluding chapter of the Mainfesto begins by expressing the daring hope:

> Estonia! You stand on the threshold of a promising future, where you can freely and independently determine and control your own destiny! Start building your own home, where order and justice will prevail, so that you can be a worthy member of the family of civilised nations! All sons and daughters of the homeland, let us unite as one man in the sacred work of building the homeland! The sweat and blood of our ancestors, shed for this land, demand it, our future generations oblige us to do so.[27]

It was in Pärnu, at the beginning of the birth of Estonia, that the Manifesto was read out in public for the first time by the courageous Hugo Kuusner, a brave man,

---

[23] *Wanematekogu otsus Päästekomitee loomisest—decision to create the Salvation Committee of Estonia of 19 February 1918*, published in State Gazette (Riigi Teataja), No 1, 27 November 1918; available online at <https://dea.digar.ee/cgi-bin/dea?a=d&d=AKriigiteataja19181127.2.4&e=-------et-25--1--txt-txIN%7ctxTI%7ctxAU%7ctxTA> accessed 11 April 2023.

[24] State Gazette (Riigi Teataja), No 1, 27 November 1918, 1, available online at <https://web.archive.org/web/20211118011933/; https://www.riigiteataja.ee/failid/manifest.html> accessed 11 April 2023).

[25] By Karl Ast, Jüri Jaakson, Juhan Kukk and Jüri Vilms, see *Encyclopedia Estonica*, available at <https://web.archive.org/web/20220701104517/; http://www.estonica.org/et/Iseseisvusmanifest/> accessed 11 April 2023.

[26] Friedrich Reinhold Kreutzwald, *Kalevipoeg*, (SE&JS, 2019 edition).

[27] *Manifest kõigile Eestimaa rahwastele,* State Gazette (Riigid Teataja), RT No 1, 27 November 1918, 1, point 7, available online at <https://web.archive.org/web/20211118011933/; https://www.riigiteataja.ee/failid/manifest.html> accessed 11 April 2023).

and a jurist by training. As a member of the Constituent Assembly of Estonia and its Constitutional Committee, Kuusner later participated in the creation of the first Estonian Constitution.

The first Estonian Constitution was adopted by Constituent Assembly on 15 June 1920 and entered into force in December of the same year.[28] Paragraph one of the Constitution stated that Estonia is an independent, *rippumatu*[29] republic where state power is in the hands of the people.[30] Writing in the legal monthly review "Õigus (Law)" in the same year, Professor Eduard Berendts of the University of Tartu said that justice is the basis of the Estonian Constitution and must be the guiding star for the legislature, the executive, and the courts.[31]

The second Estonian Constitution was adopted by referendum in 1933 and came into force in 1934.[32] Legally speaking it is actually the law amending the previous constitution, but it is widely considered as the constitution of 1933 (this being the year it was adopted by the people, not when it entered into force).[33] Here again, paragraph one proclaimed that Estonia shall be an independent, "*rippumatu*" republic, where sovereign power is in the hands of the people.

Four years later, on 1 January 1938, the new Constitution came into force. It remained the last constitution of pre-World War II Estonia.[34] In this constitution, sovereignty was for the first time mentioned as "sõltumatu" (there exists also a word "suveräänne")[35] in Estonian. The first paragraph—which remained the cornerstone of Estonia's independence and sovereignty in the Constitution of the Republic—was rephrased or modernised as follows: "Estonia shall be an independent and sovereign ("sõltumatu/non-dependent") republic, where the supreme authority is vested in the people."

According to the Estonian legal scientist Artur Tõeleid Kliimann, Estonia's independence is represented in its existence as a separate state.[36]

---

28 State Gazette (Riigi Teataja), RT, No. 113/114, 9. August 1920, 243.

29 An expression the literal meaning of which is "unhinged", and which can be seen as something equivalent to "sovereign".

30 State Gazette (Riigi Teataja), RT, No. 113/114, 9. August 1920, 243.

31 Eduard Berendts,. *Eesti Vabariigi Riigikohus ja 1920. a. põhiseaduse printsiibid. 1. osa, Õigus* 1920/2, p. 43; and *2. osa., Õigus* 1920/3, p. 56.

32 RT, No. 86, 628, 28. October 1933.

33 Eerik-Juhan Truuväli, *Põhiseaduse teel* (Ilo 2008) 148.

34 RT, No. 71, 590, 3. September 1937. As when speaking about the 1933 constitutional amendments, the special state of defence which was proclaimed in the context of the economic and political situation of 1930s must be taken into consideration, see e.g., Eerik-Juhan Truuväli, *Põhiseaduse teel* (Ilo 2008) 208.

35 The word "suveräänne" was nevertheless used on 16 November 1988, when the then Supreme Council of the Estonian Soviet Socialist Republic (SSR) adopted a declaration on the Sovereignty of the Estonian SSR, see ENSV *Ülemnõukogu ja Valitsuse Teataja* (1988) 48, 685.

36 Artur-Tõeleid Kliimann, *Eesti iseseisvuse areng (The evolution of Estonian independence),* in Õigus (Law) 1935, No 2, pp. 49–50.

The current Constitution, which is now more than thirty years old, was adopted by the Estonian people in a referendum on 28 September 1992.[37] It has been amended on a few occasions,[38] the most important of which, the only amendment by referendum, was on 14 September 2003, when the Constitution was supplemented by a law enabling Estonia to join the European Union on 1 May 2004.[39]

The Constitution of 1992 stipulates again in the first paragraph that supreme power in Estonia belongs to the people, that Estonia is an independent and *sovereign* (in Estonian the word "sõltumatu" is used again, thus not the exact word "suveräänne", but it has been translated as sovereign)[40] and in addition also a democratic republic.[41] It also sets out fundamental rights, freedoms and duties (based to a large extent on the model of the European Convention on Human Rights (ECHR)).

Although the wording of the Constitution does not use *expressis verbis* the exact concept of sovereignty, the principle of the sovereignty of the Estonian state can be read from the wording of the first paragraph.[42]

The Constitution lists the institutions of the state and their functioning: the legislature (the *Riigikogu*); the President; the Government as the executive; local government; the judiciary; the Chancellor of Justice; finance and the state budget; the Bank of Estonia and the National Audit Office; foreign relations; and national defence.

Paragraph 1 of the Constitution in force has a second sentence which concretises that Estonia's independence and sovereignty ("sõltumatus") are timeless and

---

[37] RT No. 26, 349, 6 July 1992; amended as: RT I 2003, 29, 174; RT I 2003, 64, 429; RT I 2007, 33, 210; RT I, 27 April 2011, 1; RT I, 15 May 2015, 1. (The numbers reflect those in the Estonian State Gazette).

[38] The first amendment was adopted in 2003 as a matter of urgency, increasing the number of local elections from three to four years, and entered into force in 2005.

The second amendment was adopted in 2003 and came into force in 2004. This was the amendment concerning accession to the EU commented upon in this paper.

The third amendment was adopted by two successive legislatures in 2007 and entered into force the same year. This amendment added the protection of the Estonian language to the preamble of the Constitution.

The Fourth Amendment was adopted again by two consecutive sessions of *Riigikogu* in 2011 and entered into force the same year. The purpose of the amendment was to streamline the governance of national defence and strengthen control over the Defence Forces.

The Fifth Amendment was adopted again by two successive sessions of the *Riigikogu* in 2015 and entered into force the same year. The amendment lowered the voting age for local government councils from 18 to 16.

[39] RT I No. 64, 429, 5 October 2003.

[40] See the Estonian Constitution in English, available online at <https://www.riigiteataja.ee/en/eli/521052015001/consolide> accessed 25 July 2023.

[41] Artur-Tõeleid Kliimann has noted that in the decision of 15 November 1917 of the Estonian Land Council it was stated that Estonia was a democratic republic. In the above-mentioned Manifesto of 1918, it was added that Estonia was an independent democratic republic, and in the document about provisional arrangements for the government of the Republic of Estonia of 4 July 1919, it was stressed that Estonia was independent and sovereign ("sõltumatu") democratic republic. See in *Taasvabanenud Eesti põhiseaduse eellugu* (Juura 1997) 22.

[42] See Hent Kalmo, *Commentary of the first paragraph of Estonian Constitution, Põhiseaduse kommenteeritud väljaanne* (Juura 2020) (Available online at <https://pohiseadus.ee/sisu/3470/paragrahv_1> accessed 19 July 2023.).

inalienable. This sentence was inserted into the Constitution in order to emphasise the importance of Estonia's independence and sovereignty among the constitutional values and the timelessness of national self-determination. According to the discussions of the Constitutional Assembly, the introduction of § 1(2) into the text of the Constitution is an attempt to provide an additional guarantee for Estonian statehood, namely that Estonian independence and sovereignty can only be surrendered by referendum through an amendment to the Constitution.[43]

Despite the fact that according to the Estonian constitutional order, in domestic relations, sovereignty means a monopoly on the exercise of public power, in international relations, the exercise of state power of Estonia is constrained by the sovereignty of other states, which every country must respect. Public power is bound by the Constitution and the Estonian State must adhere to international law.

Estonia has a strong constitutional tradition, now just over a hundred years old. Justice, the rule of law, democracy and human dignity are still the cornerstones of our constitutional order. The Constitution is like everyone's Bible: everybody in Estonia, irrespective of nationality, race, colour, sex, language, origin, religion, political or other convictions, wealth, or social status, can, if necessary, obtain justice under it.

The Constitution must not remain just beautiful words on paper. It is part of reality and part of citizens' lives. Nor can the Constitution be seen in isolation from the constitutional culture, from the extent to which people know and are aware of their fundamental rights, or from constitutional review, which is carried out by the courts and must function properly. Knowledge of the Constitution begins at home and at school and continues throughout life. Understanding sovereignty and its evolving definition is part of that culture and education.

3 The Present: the European Dimension of Sovereignty

The Roman god Janus is usually depicted as having two faces. Sovereignty also has at least two faces: the traditional, national one, classical concept from the past which we have just elaborated above, but also the international, more modern one, that we will analyse in the text below. The latter includes the relationship between national Member States and the supranational EU. Furthermore, the European Union itself has ambitions concerning its own sovereignty.[44]

We could expand on the "two faces" theory with an additional question: does the European Union have a double face? Does it have double standards: one set for its Member States—requirements concerning the rule of law, democracy, fundamental

---

[43] See Põhiseadus ja Põhiseaduse Assamblee (Constitution and Constitutional Assembly), Tallinn: Juura, 1997, pp. 526 and 564.

[44] This was acknowledged and built upon by the French President Macron in his speech in the Sorbonne on 26 September 2017 on a new initiative for Europe where he stated that "the only way to guarantee our future is to re-establish a sovereign, united and democratic Europe." (Available online at <https://www.elysee.fr/en/emmanuel-macron/2017/09/26/president-macron-gives-speech-on-new-initiative-for-europe> accessed 26. September 2023.).

values which prompt the Member States to give up some of their powers in exercising sovereignty, even to lose for the sake of "common values" some of their national identity despite the safeguarding clause in the Treaty on European Union (Article 4(2) TEU)—and another set for itself? The reality is that some of the criteria set for Member States would not be met by the European Union itself, e.g., by reason, *inter alia,* of the democratic deficit in the European Union, excessive bureaucracy[45] and the fact that the EU has not yet joined the European Convention on Human Rights.[46]

The European Union itself also needs to adhere to the rule of law,[47] in order to be an example to its Member States and to other international organisations. This is the only way it can put itself in a position to demand high standards of others.

To go even further: does the European Union have also a double face in treating different Member States differently or in expanding various demands depending on which candidate countries it is dealing with. One point is clear—the criteria, requirements and standards, e.g., concerning the rule of law, for European Union accession, etc. should be the same for all. Such respect for the equality of States is also key to gaining acceptance for living with a nuanced sovereignty which, in a way, is actually reduced to strategic autonomy.

3.1 Pragmatic Solutions to Win Acceptance of European Integration

Barack Obama, while he was US president, expressed the view that big nations should not bully smaller ones, that the sovereignty of nations must be respected, and that disputes must be resolved peacefully, including through mechanisms like international arbitration.[48]

But how to protect universal human rights in a world of sovereign states, if many of them still jealously guard themselves from interference by outside authorities,

---

[45] Former President of the European Commission (and President of the Governing Board of the Academy of European Law (ERA)), Jean-Claude Juncker, stated at the ERA 30th Anniversary Congress on 13 October 2022 in Trier that over-regulation by the EU has had an impact on EU citizens and that despite attempts to cut red tape (i.e., reduce bureaucracy), the EU is "famous" for being the bastion of bureaucracy.

[46] Hence e.g., the former Finnish Chancellor of Justice Paavo Nikula has said that if the EU itself wanted to join the EU, it would not qualify, because it has not signed the European Convention on Human Rights. See Paavo Nikula's speech, "The human rights within [the] EU—key issue in political integration", in Athens 11 February 2000, at the conference *Towards a Political Unification of Europe?* organised by the Andreas Papandreou Foundation and European Public Law Center.

[47] This was also noted by European Commission Vice-President Vera Jurova in her contribution to the ERA 30th Anniversary Congress in Trier on 14 October 2022.

[48] President Obama, speaking in Vietnam regarding territorial disputes in the South China Sea, 24 May 2016. Available at CNA (Channels News Asia): see <https://www.facebook.com/ChannelNewsAsia/posts/big-nations-should-not-bully-smaller-ones-president-obama-speaking-in-vietnam-on/10153650786237934/> accessed 21 July 2023.

remains one of the most pressing dilemmas in contemporary politics and law around the world.[49]

However, with time, there has been increased talk of shared sovereignty. No one state alone is as strong and powerful as when it acts jointly with others, while differentiated sovereignty also allows for better intervention in the affairs of other states, for example when there are serious human rights violations.

As a result of developments in Europe, many functions of state power have been transferred to the supranational European Union. This started with economic aspects and then spread into many other fields of life and law, such as social and fundamental rights.[50] To a certain extent this has been inevitable. It was argued for on a world scale (and in terms of a new world order) by Rockefeller who preferred the idea of the supranational sovereignty of an intellectual elite and world bankers to the national auto-determination practised in past centuries.[51]

These circumstances have led to an attempt to give new meaning to the concept of sovereignty as such. There have been efforts to find a balance in the content of the relationship between the European Union and its Member States, and a large number of concepts–such as the pooling of sovereign rights, multi-level sovereignty, the joint exercise of sovereignty by states, European sovereignty, strategic autonomy/sovereignty, open strategic autonomy, technological sovereignty and digital sovereignty[52]–have been used and written about in academic circles.[53]

The notion of European 'strategic sovereignty' is increasingly important to debates about the European Union, which—thanks to rapidly shifting global geopolitical and technology trends, and the seeming fragmentation of the multilateral order—is being forced to confront its own position in international affairs.[54] However defined, there is a need to focus on the practical nature of economic and technological interdependence, multilateralism and strategic partnerships.[55]

---

[49] See David Armitage, "The Declaration of Independence in Global Perspective" (Available online at <https://ap.gilderlehrman.org/history-by-era/road-revolution/essays/declaration-independence-global-perspective> accessed 11 April 2023)).

[50] See e.g., Joseph Weiler, "The Transformation of Europe" (1991) 100 *Yale Law Journal* 2403.

[51] William Caniano, *The Powers That Be: America's Dirtiest Secrets* (Publish America 2007) 120.

[52] Digital sovereignty was extensively debated during the ERA 30 years conference on 14 October in Trier, e.g., in the speech of Prof. Anu Bradford who compared the economic rule of law of EU with the state of affairs in a now-digitalised China which, in ignoring the rule of law, is nonetheless outpacing Europe in terms of its economy. This in turn seems to reduce the EU's economic and technological sovereignty.

[53] In Estonia, see e.g., Mario Rosentau, *Suveräänsus Euroopa Liidus* (Riigikogu Toimetised 2003), available online at <https://efaidnbmnnnibpcajpcglclefindmkaj https://rito.riigikogu.ee/wordpress/wp-content/uploads/2016/03/Suver%C3%A4%C3%A4nsus-Euroopa-Liidus.pdf> accessed 19 July 2023.

[54] *Achieving Strategic Sovereignty for the European Union,* online workshop, requested by the European Parliament's Committee on Foreign Affairs AFET Committee from April 2021. (Available online at chrome-extension://efaidnbmnnnibpcajpcglclefindmkaj/https://www.europarl.europa.eu/RegData/etudes/STUD/2021/653634/EXPO_STU(2021)653634_EN.pdf> accessed 21 July 2023).

[55] *Ibid.*

This inevitably raises the dilemma for Member States of balancing the tasks of defending national sovereignty and the obligations arising from the process of European integration. The need for national constitutions to reflect this was long ago recognised in both countries being focussed upon here, France and Estonia.

In 1992, new articles (Articles 88-1 to 88-4) were added to the French Constitution, the effect of which is that only the people, or their representatives, who are the bearers of sovereignty and to whom the higher power belongs, can decide and approve—following a special procedure—the limitation of French sovereignty, or, better said, the transfer of competence deriving from sovereignty to a supranational organisation.[56] Here, it is important not to confuse the international concept of sovereignty, as set out in paragraph 15 of the preamble to the French Constitution of 1946, with the national concept of sovereignty, found both in Article 3 of the Declaration of the Rights of Man and of the Citizen and in Article 3(1) of the French Constitution. The two concepts have different internal logics. At national level, sovereignty is solitary, single (involving one nation and one people) and knows neither superiors nor equals, whereas at international level it is multiple (e.g., involving all Member States of the European Union) and knows at least equals (because all Member States are sovereign).[57]

After Estonia regained its independence in 1991 and before the country delegated some competencies associated with sovereignty to the European Union, intensive discussions about the shift in the meaning of sovereignty in contemporary Europe took place. However, one should note that prior to Estonia's accession to the European Union, amending the Estonian Constitution in order to enable Estonia to join the European Union in accordance with the rule of law was for the most part a taboo subject among politicians, who feared that a perceived need to amend the Constitution in a referendum might negatively impact the prospects of accession to the European Union.[58]

Lawyers, however, tried to explain that, since the Constitution strongly emphasised the importance of sovereignty, and since accession to the European Union would inevitably have an impact on this, then if accession to the European Union was

---

56 See Rodolphe Laffranque, "EL/EÜ lepingute konstitutsionaliseerimise protsess ja liikmesriikide suveräänsus. Dilemma Prantsuse õiguse vaatepunktist nähtuna" (Constitutionalising of EU/EC treaties and sovereignty of Member States. Dilemma from French Perspective) (2000) 8 *Juridica* 537.

57 Alain Pellet, "Le Conseil constitutionnel, la souveraineté et les traités—A propos de la décision du Conseil constitutionnel du 31/12/1997 (Traité d'Amsterdam)" (1998) 4 *Cahiers du Conseil constitutionnel*.

58 Julia Laffranque, "Pilk Eesti õigusmaastikule põhiseaduse täiendamise seaduse valguses. Euroopa Liidu õigusega seotud võtmeküsimused põhiseaduslikkuse järelevalves" (A Glance at the Estonian Legal Landscape in the Light of the Constitution of the Republic of Estonia Amendment Act), (2007) 8 *Juridica* 523, also published in English in Julia Laffranque, "A Glance at the Estonian Legal Landscape in View of the Constitution Amendment Act", (2007) XII *Juridica International* 55.

desired, a shift in the constitutional concept of sovereignty had to be reflected in law.[59] Finally, this writer, together with three other colleagues, succeeded in presenting the Constitution of the Republic of Estonia Amendment Act (CREAA), as a compromise option. This provided for Estonian membership of the European Union and in it the so-called safeguard clause has also been interpreted to mean that Estonia can only belong to a European Union that respects the fundamental principles of the Estonian Constitution.[60]

It is gratifying to note that CREAA was approved in the referendum on Estonia's accession to the European Union on 14 September 2003 by a substantial majority of 66.83% of those voting, on a turnout of 64.06%,[61] one of the highest turnouts ever in Estonia and (as noted above) the only time the 1992 Constitution has been amended by referendum.

The Constitution of the Republic of Estonia Amendment Act comprises only four paragraphs, while the text of the Constitution itself remained unchanged, but must be read and interpreted in the light of CREAA i.e., in the light of the rights and obligations assumed by Estonia on its accession to the European Union.[62] It has been recognised widely in Estonian legal literature that the role of the CREAA in Estonian constitutional law is significant.[63]

---

[59] See also Julia Laffranque, "Constitution of the Republic of Estonia in the Light of Accession to the European Union", (2001) VI Juridica International 207 and Julia Laffranque, "Co-existence of the Estonian Constitution and European Law", (2002) VII *Juridica International* 17.

[60] Julia Laffranque, Ülle Madise, Kalle Merusk, Jüri Põld, Märt Rask, "Põhiseaduse täiendamise seaduse eelnõust" (Draft Act to amend the Constitution) (2000) 8 *Juridica* 563.

[61] *Rahvahääletuse tulemuste kinnitamine (Approval of the Referendum Results),* Riigi Teataja (State Gazette), 5 October 2003, RT I 2003, 63,426. According to official data there were 867 714 persons with the right to vote entered on the electoral rolls. A total of 556 915 received a ballot paper and 555 835 voters took part in the referendum. 369 657 voters answered in the affirmative and 183 454 in the negative to the question on the ballot paper. The number of invalid ballot papers was 2724.

[62] See further Julia Laffranque, Carri Ginter, Lauri Mälksoo, Jüri Põld, Andres Tupits and Merli Vahar, "Commentary of the Constitution of the Republic of Estonia Amendment Act" in *Eesti Vabariigi Põhiseaduse Kommenteeritud Väljaanne* (Juura 2020) (Available online at <https://pohiseadus.ee/sisu/3665> (21 July 2023); Julia Laffranque, "The Constitution of Estonia and Estonia's Accession to the European Union" in 2004 (4) Baltic Yearbook of International Law 1; Julia Laffranque, "Estlands Grundgesetz und der EU-Beitritt" in Sven I. Oksaar and Niels von Redecker (eds.), *Deutsch-Estnische Rechtsvergleichung und Europa* (Studien des Instituts für Ostrecht/Peter Lang Europäischer Verlag der Wissenschaften 2004) 35.

[63] Andra Laurand, *Põhiseaduse täiendamise seaduse kommentaar* (Eesti teaduste akadeemia riigiõiguse sihtkapitali väljaanne 2023). (Available online at <https://pohiseadus.riigioigus.ee/v1/eesti-vabariigi-pohiseaduse-taiendamise-seadus/pohiseaduse-taiendamise-seaduse-kommentaar> accessed 21 July 2023).

3.2 *The Judicial Approach to Sovereignty in Relation to a United Europe*

In giving life to nice words about perfect relationship between national sovereignty and European Union membership in constitutional texts, the role of the judiciary is irreplaceable. It is important not only in interpreting the constitution and laws, but also, if necessary, in filling in the gaps in regulation that the legislator either has forgotten about or intentionally avoided.

When political compromises cannot be reached, the courts–including the European Court of Justice–have often had to play a key role. Stone Sweet observed already some years ago that "in today's multi-level European polity, the sovereignty of the legislature and the supremacy of the national executive are dead. In a match or contest, the European legislature, together with the judiciary, reigns supreme."[64]

Yet French President Macron recalled the most fundamental aspect underpinning the relationship between States and the (international) judiciary while visiting the European Court of Human Rights (ECtHR). "We have not handed over our legal sovereignty to the Court," he said, but rather "[w]e have provided the citizens of Europe with an additional guarantee that human rights will be upheld".[65] He compared the Court of Human Rights to "an essential bulkhead in protecting the nationals of the forty-seven member States[66] from abuses, totalitarian trends and the dangers that tomorrow's world will bring with it"–thus emphasising the weight of responsibility on judges' shoulders.[67]

The guardian of national sovereignty in France, the Constitutional Council (*Conseil constitutionnel*), has tried to define the point at which the transfer of the power to exercise national sovereignty to the European Union requires a constitutional amendment.

In the 1970s, the *Conseil constitutionnel* used to distinguish between the limitation of sovereignty and the transfer of sovereignty. Only in the latter case was a change to the Constitution mandatory.

The view of the Constitutional Council since the Maastricht judgment in 1992 has been however, that a transfer is not necessarily itself a limitation of sovereignty: respect for national sovereignty does not preclude France from concluding external agreements in order to take part in "the creation and development of an international

---

[64] Alec Stone-Sweet, *Governing with Judges: Constitutional Politics in Europe* (Oxford University Press 2000) 127.

[65] *Discours du Président de la République, Emmanuel Macron devant le conseil de l'Europe à Strasbourg* (at the European Court of Human Rights), 31 October 2017. (Available online at <https://www.elysee.fr/emmanuel-macron/2017/10/31/discours-du-president-de-la-republique-emmanuel-macron-devant-le-conseil-de-leurope-a-strasbourg> accessed 22 July 2023).

[66] As of today, there are 46 Member States in Council of Europe since Russia's exclusion in March 2022.

[67] See also Raimondi, Guido, *Opening Speech at the Solemn Hearing of the European Court of Human Rights on 26 January 2018*, available online at <https://efaidnbmnnnibpcajpcglclefindmkaj/https://www.echr.coe.int/documents/d/echr/speech_20180126_raimondi_jy_eng> accessed 21 July 2023.

organisation which is permanent, has legal personality and is endowed with the power to take decisions on the basis of a transfer of competences agreed by the Member States".[68] This decision gives a logical meaning to the concept of limitation of sovereignty in paragraph 15 of the Preamble to the 1946 Constitution and this so-called judicial amendment of the Constitution, or at least in a re-reading (*relecture*) of paragraph 15 of the Preamble to the 1946 Constitution with reference to the notion of devolution/transfer of powers has subsequently been confirmed in the text of the Constitution, in the context of its above-described 1992 amendment (Article 88-2: 'France accepts the transfer of powers…').

The Constitutional Council has defined the essential conditions for the exercise of national sovereignty (*les conditions essentielles d'exercice de la souveraineté nationale*) on the basis of three elements: (1) respect for the institutions of the French Republic; (2) the timelessness of the nation; and (3) the guarantee of citizens' rights and freedoms. It has checked whether the area of transfer of powers concerns the exclusive rights of the state (*droits régaliens* or 'regal rights'), i.e., the right of the state to establish an army, to exercise customs control, to mint its own currency, etc. and whether there will be a total abolition of competences (which would require an amendment of the Constitution) or only the creation of shared competences. The decision-making power of France is a fundamental criterion for the exercise of national sovereignty: if it were abolished, this would mean the end of sovereignty. The method of supervision described above has also been confirmed by the *Amsterdam* Decision of the French Constitutional Council.[69]

The French Supreme Courts hesitated a long time before recognising the process of constitutionalisation of the European Union treaties and the primacy of European Union law, despite the clear case law of the European Court of Justice in this regard. Hence, in the beginning, the French judiciary showed itself hesitant to recognise the supremacy of European Union law and thought initially that in case of a subsequently adopted national law which was contrary to a previously adopted European Community act, the rule *lex posteriori derogat leges priori* applied, and this despite the fact that this issue had been resolved by Article 55 of the French Constitution, which provides that foreign treaties, once ratified, take precedence over national laws.[70] Even when the ordinary courts–which the Constitutional Council had given the power to apply Article 55 of the Constitution[71]–modified this position,[72]

[68] Decision of the Constitutional Council in Traité de Maastricht 9 April 1992, nr 92–308 DC, *Recueil* 55.

[69] Decision of the Constitutional Council in Traité d'Amsterdam, 31 December 1997 DC, nr 92–308 *Recueil* 344.

[70] Karen Alter, *Establishing the Supremacy of European Law: The Making of an International Rule of Law in Europe* (Oxford Academic 2003) at124-181. See also, Juscelino Colares, "The Reality of EU-Conformity Review in France" (2012) 18 Columbia Journal of European Law 369, available at <https://surface.syr.edu/lawpub/66> accessed 11 October 2023.

[71] Decision of the Constitutional Council, No 74–54 DC, *Recueil* 19.

[72] Chambre mixte de la Cour de Cassation, 24 May 1975, A.J.D.A. 1975, 567.

the Supreme Administrative Court/Council of State (the *Conseil d'État*) remained conservative on the point up until the so-called *Nicolo* judgment in 1989.[73]

Since 2004 (the issue having been clarified in 2006), the Constitutional Council has developed a body of case-law specific to laws the purpose of which is to transpose into domestic law a European Union directive.[74] According to this case law, while Article 88–1 of the French Constitution imposes a constitutional requirement to transpose European Union directives, the transposition may not normally run counter to a rule or a principle inherent in the constitutional identity of France. Unless such a rule or principle is challenged, however, the Constitutional Council does not have jurisdiction to review the conformity with the Constitution of legislative provisions that merely draw the necessary consequences from unconditional and precise provisions of a European Union directive. This jurisdiction is reserved to French administrative courts, if necessary, making a preliminary reference to the European Court of Justice. The same applies where an infringement of the rights and freedoms protected by the Constitution originates in an act of the European Union when those rights and freedoms *are also protected* by the European legal order (e.g., freedom of expression,[75] the right to respect for one's private life,[76] the right to equality before the law[77] and the freedom to conduct business[78]). In other words, here again the Constitutional Court does not have jurisdiction to review for conformity with the Constitution.

However, if, on the other hand, the rules, and principles are inherent in France's constitutional identity, it is up to the Constitutional Council itself to ensure compliance. In fact, this safeguard clause (*clause de sauvegarde*) reflects Article 4 para 2 TEU.

Without going into further details of the extensive jurisprudence of the French courts (such as e.g., in particular the so called *French Data Network* judgment of the Council of State,[79] which also included a preliminary ruling from the European

---

[73] Decision of the Council of State, 20.10.1989 *(Nicolo), Recueil Lebon*190.

[74] Decision of the Constitutional Council, 10.06.2004, No 2004–496, Loi pour la confiance dans l'économie numérique; decision of the Constitutional Council, 27 July 2006, No 2006–540, Loi relative au droit d'auteur et aux droits voisins dans la société de l'information.

[75] Decision of the Constitutional Council, 29 July 2004, No 2004–498; Decision of the Constitutional Council, 26 July 2018, No 2018–768.

[76] Decision of the Constitutional Council, 29 July 2004, No 2004–499.

[77] Decision of the Constitutional Council, 26 July 2018, No 2018–768.

[78] Decision of the Constitutional Council, 26 July 2018, No 2018–768.

[79] See e.g., the so called French Data Network judgment of the French Council of State (French Council of State (Conseil d'État), French Data Network and others> accessed 21 April 2021), Nos. 393099, 394,922, 397,844, 397,851, 424,717, 424,718), which concerned the conflict between the right to privacy and the protection of personal data, and the need to ensure the effectiveness of the fight against crime, on the one hand, and the issue of primacy of EU law on the other. The Council of State decided to break with previous case law which seemed to accept, as a general rule, the primacy of fundamental rights standards set by the European Court of Justice, in order to reject the standards set by the latter for the protection of personal data, in favour of an approach facilitating the justifications presented by police and intelligence services. See Turmo, Araceli, "National security as an exception to EU data protection standards: the judgment of the Conseil d'État in French Data Network and others", (2022) 59(1) Common Market Law Review 203.

Court of Justice;[80] as well as the views of the Constitutional Council regarding European Union law and European integration), it is appropriate to examine briefly a recent decision of the Constitutional Council–that of 15 October 2021,[81] which states in essence that the application of a provision of a European Union law can only be rejected if it contradicts a principle that is inherent to French constitutional identity.[82]

In this case, the French Council of State had requested a preliminary ruling (*question prioritaire de constitutionnalité*) from the Constitutional Council on the conformity with the French Constitution of a provision of French law implementing the Convention Implementing the Schengen Agreement and Directive 2001/51 supplementing Article 26 of the Convention implementing the Schengen Agreement, as regards the obligation on air carriers to return third-country nationals when their entry into France is refused. The applicant in the main proceedings, Air France, had alleged that those provisions had the effect of delegating to a private person the general administrative police powers inherent in the exercise of public force, in violation of Articles 9 and 12 of the Declaration of the Rights of Man and of the Citizen of 1789, in addition to Article 66 of the French Constitution. In order to determine the scope of the review to be carried out, the Constitutional Council had to assess whether contested national provisions resulted from the transposition of a European directive and, if so, whether those provisions merely drew the necessary consequences of the unconditional and precise provisions of that directive. Finding that this was the case at hand, the Constitutional Council reserved the exercise of its competence in such cases only to circumstances where the national provisions transposing the directive put in danger the applicability of a rule or a principle which was inherent in the constitutional identity of France and which did not find equal protection in the EU law.

This was the first time that the Constitutional Council spelled out precisely the criterion "rules or principles that do not find equivalent protection in European Union law."[83] The Constitutional Council specifically held that the right to security, the principle of personal responsibility (*principe de responsabilité personnel*) and the principle of equality before public burdens (*égalité devant les charges publiques*)

---

[80] Joined Cases C-511/18, C-512/18 and C-520/18 *La Quadrature du Net and Others v Premier ministre and Others* European Court of Justice (Grand Chamber), 6 October 2020 (on requests for a preliminary ruling from the Conseil d'État (France) and the Cour constitutionnelle (Belgium).

See e.g., Xavier Tracol, "The two judgments of the European Court of Justice in the four cases of Privacy International, La Quadrature du Net and Others, French Data Network and Others and Ordre des Barreaux francophones et germanophone and Others: The Grand Chamber is trying hard to square the circle of data retention" (2021) 41 *Computer Law and Security Review* 105,540.

[81] Decision of the Constitutional Council, 15.10.2021, No 2021–940 QPC, *Société Air France (Obligation pour les transporteurs aériens de réacheminer les étrangers dont l´entrée en France est refusée).*

[82] The judgment relates to compliance with the rights and freedoms that the French Constitution guarantees of Article L. 213–4 and 1° of Article L. 625–7 of the Code for Entry and Residence of Foreigners and Right of Asylum (CESEDA).

[83] Decision of the Constitutional Council, 15.10.2021, No 2021–940 QPC, *Société Air France*, para 13.

do not constitute rules or principles inherent in the constitutional identity of France insofar as they enjoy equivalent protection under European Union law.

However, the prohibition on delegating to private persons general administrative police powers inherent in the exercise of public force, based on Article 12 of the Declaration of the Rights of Man and of the Citizen of 1789, "constitutes according to Constitutional Council a principle inherent in the constitutional identity of France" which is specific to the French constitutional order.[84] It reflects a specific requirement regarding the conditions for the use of a public police force and the exercise of police powers, which had no equivalent in European Union law. The result was that the Constitutional Council was indeed competent to examine whether the contested rules were in conformity with constitutional rules and principles but found in the case at hand that the contested provisions did not transfer to carriers any decision-making power or render carriers accountable for any obligation to supervise a person or to exert any constraint on that person in order to fulfil their obligation to reroute. The Council declared that the contested provisions were in conformity with the Constitution.[85]

The Estonian Supreme Court which acts both as the supreme administrative, and the constitutional court of Estonia, seems to have also struggled with the concepts of supremacy, later described as 'primacy' of European Union law and in interpreting the above-mentioned safeguard clause of the Constitution of the Republic of Estonia Amendment Act.

It has however, after an initial, and one could even say, extremely EU law-friendly approach,[86] expanded its competence to review the constitutionality of EU-related national law perhaps even to a greater extent than the French Constitutional Council has dared to do.

Already long before Estonia's accession to the European Union, i.e., as early as in the 1990s, directly after the regaining of Estonian independence and the re-establishment of the Supreme Court[87] in Tartu (the second largest city of Estonia,

---

[84] Provisions that allegedly delegate police powers in breach of Article 12 of the Declaration of 1789 could not therefore be challenged on the basis of EU law, since there is currently no European standard preventing such delegation.

[85] See in detail, Commentaire, Conseil Constitutionnel. (Available online at <https://mail.google.com/mail/u/0/#inbox?projector=1> accessed 21 July 2023).

[86] See also Julia Laffranque and Rodolphe Laffranque, "Les modifications apportées à la Constitution estonienne du fait de l'adhésion à l'Union Européenne et leur mise en ouvre par la Cour d'Etat" (2008) 1 *Revue d'études politiques et constitutionnelles est-européennes* 91.

[87] The Supreme Court of Estonia comprises nineteen judges and is composed of four chambers: the Administrative Law Chamber, the Criminal Law Chamber, the Civil Law Chamber and the Constitutional Review Chamber. The last is composed of nine justices who are at the same time members of either administrative, criminal, or civil law chambers and the president of the Court. The Grand Chamber of the Supreme Court, the so-called Supreme Court *en banc*, comprising all justices of the Supreme Court, is the highest body of the Court, which decides on the most important constitutional matters. Constitutional review can be in the form of abstract constitutional review (initiated by the Chancellor of Justice who also has the functions of an Ombudsman) or the President of the Republic, or a local government council; or in the shape of concrete constitutional review (which is initiated by the courts, and comprising most of the cases) or as opinions (which are

where the oldest University and law faculty also have their seat), the Supreme Court recognised the importance of the European Convention on Human Rights, the precedents of the so-called Strasbourg Court (the European Court of Human Rights), European Union law (including the case-law of the European Court of Justice) and European principles as part of the general principles of Estonian law.[88]

European law also featured in dissenting opinions of judges and the Supreme Court referred to the Charter of Fundamental Rights of the European Union (the Charter) well before Estonia's accession to the EU, and indeed before the Charter even became legally binding under EU law.[89]

The first of the four chambers of the Supreme Court to apply, implement and interpret European Union law, was the Administrative Law Chamber which also made the first Estonian preliminary reference to the European Court of Justice and even drafted a possible solution for the preliminary ruling.[90] This proposal of a solution was however not followed by the European Court of Justice, because, according to the Luxembourg Court, the principle of legal certainty was not considered violated in the case at hand in changing the rules for agricultural subsidies due to budgetary constraints.[91]

---

initiated by Parliament, and have been used only once in connection with euro in 2006). There is no classical individual constitutional claim in Estonian law, but this is possible if no other avenues exist to protect the fundamental rights, and it has exceptionally been granted. The Supreme Court as constitutional court is competent to review the constitutionality and legality of laws and resolutions adopted by the *Riigikogu* (Parliament of Estonia), which have entered into force; the constitutionality and legality of laws, which have not been promulgated by the President of the Republic and have not entered into force; the constitutionality of decrees issued by the President as well as resolutions by *Riigikogu*; the constitutionality of international treaties which have not entered into force; and the constitutionality and legality of legislation of general application. All courts can find that a law is contrary to the Constitution, but they must then initiate the constitutionality review at the Supreme Court because only the highest court of the country can invalidate a law: the Supreme Court shall declare wholly or partly invalid any law or other legislation if it conflicts with the spirit or provisions of the Constitution.

[88] Supreme Court of Estonia, judgment of 30.09.1994, in case III-4/A-5/94—RT (Riigi Teataja, State Gazette) I 1994, 80, 1159. See also, Laffranque, Julia, Euroopa Inimõiguste Kohus ja Eesti õigus (The European Court of Human Rights and Estonian law) (2017) *Juura* 22.

[89] See e.g., the dissenting opinions of Judge Rait Maruste (then president of the Surpeme Court of Estonia) in the mid-1990s. The earliest reference to the Charter can be found in 2003, when the Constitutional Review Chamber expressed its view that the right to a good administration as embodied in the Charter, can be found in para 14 of the Constitution, Constitutional Review Chamber of the Supreme Court, judgment of 17 February 2003, in case 3-4-1-1-03, para 15. See more on the case law in the speech given by Julia Laffranque, "Euroopa Liidu Põhiõiguste harta Eesti õiguses" (The Charter in Estonian law), available online at <https://era-comm.eu/stream/interview_JL_EE.mp4?fbclid=IwAR0MO5w32hq0PU0sokpbPijBZpV96c4Ees-ZTQX5uIPVa4WLhdbT1FRrqm0> accessed 22 July 2023).

[90] *Otsa Talu JK*, Order of the Administrative Chamber of the Supreme Court for a preliminary reference, 14 May 2007, in case 3–3-1–95-06.

[91] European Court of Justice, 4.06.2009, *Otsa Talu*, C-241/07.

The Administrative Law Chamber also tried to develop a running order for examining Estonian law which transposed European Union law:[92] first, one should look at the compatibility of the national law with EU law and if there was space and necessity for further examination, one should also review the constitutionality of the contested national law. The Supreme Court, as the constitutional court, initially followed this quite logical rule,[93] but denied, for example, the competence of the legal chancellor (the Chancellor of Justice) (who also has the functions of the ombudsman) to initiate abstract review of laws due to their incompatibility with European Union law (see the judgment of 19 April 2005, examined below).

Among the most famous Supreme Court decisions concerning the relationship between the Estonian Constitution and the European Union law, the following are worth mentioning:

(a) the decision of the Grand Chamber of the Supreme Court (the Supreme Court *en banc*) of 19 April 2005, which dismissed the application of the Chancellor of Justice to have the first sentence of § 5(1) of the Political Parties Act declared unconstitutional and invalid insofar as it did not allow citizens of other Member States of the European Union to belong to a political party. There was an accompanying dissenting opinion contesting the majority finding that it was impossible for the Chancellor of Justice to contest the compatibility of a national law with European Union law if this law was connected to the Estonian Constitution;[94]
(b) the Opinion of the Constitutional Review Chamber of the Supreme Court of 11 May 2006 on the interpretation of paragraph 111 of the Constitution and the relevant dissenting opinions;[95]
(c) the decision of the Grand Chamber of the Supreme Court of 1 July 2010 rejecting the application of the Chancellor of Justice concerning the unconstitutionality

[92] Decision of Administrative Law Chamber of 5.10.2006 in the so-called sugar surplus stock case 3–3-1–33-06; decision of the Administrative Law Chamber of the Supreme Court of 7 May 2008, *OÜ Aiva Baltic*, in case 3–3-1–85-07.

[93] According to the Supreme Court, the order of operations was as follows: "in a situation where, within one and the same case, the conformity of a provision to both, the Constitution and EU law is questioned, the court adjudicating the matter has first to check the conformity of the Estonian law with EU law."(see judgment of 26.06.2008, in case 3–4-1–5-08 at para 31).

[94] Judgment of the Grand Chamber of the Supreme Court, 19 April 2005, in case 3–4-1-1-05. The Supreme Court said that different possibilities exist for bringing national law into conformity with the EU law, and that neither the Constitution nor EU law provide for the existence of constitutional review proceedings for this purpose. The supremacy of application of EU law does not mean that an abstract review procedure over national law should exist on the national level. The legislator is competent to decide whether it wants to regulate the procedure for declaring invalid Estonian legislation which is in conflict with EU law. See also dissenting opinion of Justice Julia Laffranque, on the judgment of the Grand Chamber of the Supreme Court in case No 3–4-1–1-05, joined by Justices Tõnu Anton, Peeter Jerofejev, Hannes Kiris, Indrek Koolmeister and Harri Salmann. (Available online at <https://www.riigikohus.ee/et/lahendid?asjaNr=3-4-1-1-05>. The judgment and dissent are available online in English at <https://www.riigikohus.ee/en/constitutional-judgment-3-4-1-1-05> accessed 25 July 2023).

[95] Opinion of the Constitutional Review Chamber of the Supreme Court, 10 May 2006, in case 3–4-1–3-06, available in English at <https://www.riigikohus.ee/en/constitutional-judgment-3-4-1-3-06> accessed 25 July 2023).

of the provisions of the European Parliament Election Act, the Local Government Council Election Act and the *Riigikogu* Election Act prohibiting outdoor political advertising, and the dissenting opinions attached to the decision;[96]

(d) the decision of the Grand Chamber of 12 July 2012, which once again rejected the application of the Chancellor of Justice, this time for a declaration that Article 4(4) of the Treaty establishing the European Stability Mechanism (ESM) was unconstitutional and (as usual) the dissenting opinions of the minority judges;[97]

(e) the judgment of the Grand Chamber of the Supreme Court of 15 December 2015 on the constitutionality of renewable energy, and the dissenting opinions;[98] and most recently

(f) the judgment of the Grand Chamber of the Supreme Court of 15 March 2022 on the constitutionality of a national law transposing an equality directive, as well as dissenting opinions.[99]

It is worth focussing on aspects of some of the above-listed decisions which concern sovereignty, in particular the most recent decision, the judgment of 2022.

In 2006, an opinion of the Supreme Court was requested by the Estonian Parliament on joining the euro area and, in particular, on how to interpret the Constitution in the light of introduction of the euro in Estonia. (This concerned paragraph 111 of the Estonian Constitution, concerning the role of the Bank of Estonia). This is the only Supreme Court opinion under this procedure to date. The Supreme Court had been vested with this new competence just before the request by the parliament. The Supreme Court's Constitutional Review Chamber ruled by majority that the supremacy of European Union law in the event of any conflict with national law applied also *vis-à-vis* the Estonian Constitution (see para 16 of the Opinion). Apart from this bold statement, however, the Chamber did not address the so-called safety clause of the CREAA and possible situations where this safeguard would come into play at all. The Opinion was accompanied by two dissents[100] and caused quite a degree of controversy in academic literature.[101]

Several years later, in 2022 the Supreme Court in its composition as the Grand Chamber further nuanced its position by confirming that

---

[96] Judgment of the Grand Chamber of the Supreme Court, 1 July 2010, in case 3–4-1-33-09, available online in English at <https://www.riigikohus.ee/en/constitutional-judgment-3-4-1-33-09> accessed 25 July 2023.

[97] Judgment of the Grand Chamber of the Supreme Court, 12 July 2012, in case 3–4-1–6-12.

[98] Judgment of the Grand Chamber of the Supreme Court, 15 December 2015, in case 3–2-1–71-14.

[99] Judgment of the Grand Chamber of the Supreme Court, 15 March 2022, in case 5–19-29/38.

[100] That of Justices Villu Kõve and Erik Kergandberg, in case 3–4-1–3-06.

[101] Laffranque, Julia, "Sõltumatu ja demokraatlik õigusriik Riigikohtu praktikas Eesti Euroopa Liidu liikmesuse kontekstis" (An Independent and Democratic State Based on the Rule of Law in the Practice of the Supreme Court. Estonia in the Context of European Union Membership) (2009) 7 *Juridica* 486; Madis Ernits, Carri Ginter, Saale Laos, Marje Allikmets, Paloma Krõõt Tupay, René Värk and Andra Laurand, "Eesti põhiseadus: Euroopa Liidu õiguse piiramatu esimusega seotud ootamatud küsimused" (The Estonian Constitution: unexpected issues related to the unrestricted supremacy of European Union law) —*Riigiõiguse aastaraamat* (*Constitutional law Yearbook, Estonia*) 3/2022, pp. 132–191, p 139.

> Under paragraph 1 of the CREAA, Estonia may belong to the European Union, proceeding from the fundamental principles of the Constitution. Paragraph 2 adds that, with regard to Estonia's membership in the European Union, the Constitution shall be applied taking into account the rights and obligations arising from the treaty of accession. Thus, the principle of primacy of European Union law applies to the entirety of Estonian national law, including the Constitution (e.g., C-399/11: *Melloni*, para. 59; C-378/17: *An Garda Síochána*, para. 49; C-564/19: IS, para. 79; C-497/20: *Randstad Italia*, paras 52–53), but **only insofar as this is not contrary to fundamental constitutional principles.**[102]

It is important to note that the Supreme Court itself had, in essence, stated (in 2008) that it was not to be ruled out that the treaties amending the founding treaties of the European Union and such stipulations of European Union law as delegated to the EU new competencies would be scrutinised (reviewed) by the Supreme Court to assess their concordance with fundamental Constitutional principles inherent to Estonia.[103]

In a significant judgment of 12 July 2012 concerning the constitutionality of the Treaty establishing the European Stability Mechanism, the Supreme Court noted *obiter dictum* that "the Supreme Court *en banc* is of the opinion that the CREAA does not authorise the integration process of the European Union to be legitimised or the competence of Estonia to be delegated to the European Union to an unlimited extent."[104]

However, in concrete terms the Supreme Court did not see that the limits had been reached by the European Stability Mechanism Treaty. Notably, the Supreme Court majority stated that an international treaty is an instrument by which each contracting state undertakes to behave in a certain way in specified cases. This means that a State thereby waives the possibility of choosing a different course of conduct in such cases. A State thus gives up a part of its sovereignty, however small that part may be in a particular case.[105]

The Grand Chamber of the Supreme Court held that since the Constitution allows the conclusion of foreign agreements, "the Constitution, despite the strict wording of the sovereignty clause, does not require adherence to absolute sovereignty".

It is a kind of paradox that thanks to Estonia's membership of the European Union, we are now perhaps talking more about our Constitution's inclusion of the term 'sovereignty' than would otherwise be the case. Discussing what the basic principles of our Constitution are is of course extremely useful for the development of democratic statehood based on respect for human rights and the rule of law.

In 2015, the Supreme Court found that the fact that any provisions are compatible with European Union law cannot lead to the conclusion that the same provisions

---

[102] Judgment of the Grand Chamber of the Supreme Court, 15 March 2022, in case 5–19-29/38, para 41. Emphasis added by the author to emphasise the change as this caveat was not added back in 2006.

[103] Administrative Law Chamber ruling of 7 May 2008, in case 3–3-1–85-07, *OÜ Aiva Baltic*, para 39.

[104] Judgment of the Grand Chamber of the Supreme Court, 12 July 2012, in case 3–4-1–6-12, para 223.

[105] *Ibid*, para 129.

are also compatible with the Estonian Constitution or that declaring a provision unconstitutional and repealing it would constitute a breach of European Union law, paving its way to modify the order of operations agreed upon previously which had ordered the courts first to check a provision's conformity with European Union law and only then, if need be, the constitutionality.[106]

In 2021, the Supreme Court added that the fact that a contested norm belonged to the scope of European Union law did not mean that constitutional review was automatically precluded. Insofar as the activity of a Member State was not regulated by European Union law, the Member State could implement its own fundamental rights standards as far as this did not endanger the level of protection offered by the Charter or the supremacy, uniformity or effectiveness of European Union law.[107]

More recently, in a decision of 15 March 2022, where the Supreme Court found that the dismissal of a deaf and dumb prison guard and the acts on which this dismissal was based were contrary to the Estonian Constitution, the Supreme Court clarified the relationship between the Constitution and European Union law.[108] The Supreme Court developed a new methodological rule, establishing that there is a freedom of choice between constitutional review and European Union compliance control, as follows:

> Neither EU law, nor the Constitution nor procedural law give rise to the requirement that courts can check the constitutionality of national law connected with EU law only after they are convinced of its compatibility with EU law. Where a court has misgivings about the constitutionality of an Estonian law provision connected with EU law and falling within the scope of application of EU law, as well as about the compatibility of that provision with EU law, as a rule the court can weigh which of the two compatibility checks it will follow to resolve the case. In this regard, it is not ruled out that in resolving the case the court will

[106] Judgment of the Supreme Court of 15 December 2015, in case 3–2-1–71-14, para 81.

[107] Judgment of the Supreme Court of 20 April 2021, in case 5–20-10–13, paras 40–42.

[108] This decision of the Grand Chamber of the Supreme Court of Estonia has played an important role in clarifying the relationship between the Estonian Constitution and EU law and in ensuring equal treatment of persons with disabilities. The Supreme Court declared unconstitutional and invalid the provisions of a government decree that obliged a prison officer with impaired hearing to be dismissed from service and did not allow the hearing loss to be corrected, for example, with hearing aids or, if necessary, the officer's duties to be changed.

Beyond the specific case, this ruling has wider implications for the rights of people with disabilities. The Supreme Court pointed out that the Estonian Constitution, as well as EU and international law, emphasise the need to take reasonable measures to ensure equal treatment of persons with disabilities. Therefore, before dismissing a person on the grounds of disability, the State has an obligation to seek solutions that would allow him or her to continue working, provided that this does not impose a disproportionate burden on the employer.

According to the Supreme Court, the contested provisions of the government regulation were at the same time contrary to both the Estonian Constitution and EU law. Therefore, the Court had to decide whether to simply disapply the provisions in the specific case because of their conflict with EU law or to declare them unconstitutional and invalid as well. The Supreme Court chose to do the latter. See also the commentary, by Villu Kõve and Mait Laaring, "Põhiseadust ja Euroopa Liidu õigust tuleks vaadata partnerite, mitte rivaalidena" (the Constitution and EU law should be seen as partners, not rivals). *Postimees*, 16 March 2022. (Available online at <https://arvamus.postimees.ee/7478312/villu-kove-ja-mait-laaring-pohiseadust-ja-euroopa-liidu-oigust-tuleks-vaadata-partnerite-mitte-rivaalidena ≥ (accessed 23 July 2023).

disapply the Estonian provision on account of its conflict with directly applicable EU law, while simultaneously initiating constitutional review to check the constitutionality of the disapplied Estonian provision. However, "when initiating constitutional review in respect of a provision connected with EU law, the prohibition arising from direct effect of EU law on compromising the primacy, uniformity and effectiveness of EU law must be taken into account. However, when making choices the court must take into account that it may not disapply an Estonian law provision on account of its substantive unconstitutionality if the duty to establish the provision arises unavoidably from EU law. The court has a duty to give reasons.[109]

The Supreme Court justified the shift in its case law by referring to the significant developments in the European legal space that had occurred in interpreting and applying the European Convention on Human Rights and European Union law, including the Charter. With that in mind, the Supreme Court *en banc* deemed it necessary to develop further its previous positions regarding the issue of constitutional review of Estonian law provisions connected with European Union law.[110] Understandably, this shift caused quite an amount of confusion and resulted in dissenting and concurring opinions by several judges.[111] It remains to be seen how this judgment will be implemented and respected in the future case-law of Estonian courts.

It is noteworthy that while processing the case, the Supreme Court, for the first time as a constitutional court (*ex officio*) requested a preliminary ruling from the European Court of Justice–which also interpreted European Union law as precluding national legislation which imposed an absolute bar to the continued employment of a prison officer whose auditory acuity did not meet the minimum standards of sound perception prescribed by that legislation, without allowing it to be ascertained whether that officer was capable of fulfilling those duties (where appropriate, after the adoption of reasonable accommodation measures as foreseen in the respective EU directive).[112]

It can be seen on the basis of these examples, that, over time, both French and Estonian courts have considered the right to self-determination, the rule of law and constitutional identity with regard to European Union law, as well as constitutionality review over national laws transposing and implementing European Union law. The priority for both jurisdictions seems to be determining how to ensure the most effective protection of the rights of individuals, both in terms of substance and procedural economy, i.e., in terms of quality and speed.

It is desirable that in general in the European Union, competence disputes between national and supranational courts should be less significant, and the protection of fundamental rights should prevail. In this light, the constitutional/supreme courts of

---

[109] Judgment of the Grand Chamber of the Supreme Court of 15 March 2022, in case 5–19-29/38 para 47.

[110] Ibid, para 40.

[111] Dissenting opinion of Justices Hannes Kiris and Viive Ligi, 5–19-29/40; dissenting opinion of Justice Tambet Tampuu, 5–19-29/41, concurring opinion of Justice Julia Laffranque, joined by Justice Saale Laos, 5–19-29/41.

[112] EU Directive 2000/78/EC of 27 November 2000 establishing a general framework for equal treatment in employment and occupation forbids discrimination on the bases of disability. See judgment of the European Court of Justice of 15 July 2021, in Case C-795/19, *Tartu Vangla* EU:C:2021:606.

the two Member States examined, have a very important role to play alongside the European Court of Justice, the European Court of Human Rights and the highest jurisdictions of other European countries. In this context, awareness on the part of national courts of their country's constitutional identity is necessary for entering into a positive dialogue with others.

4 Conclusion: The Future of Sovereignty–Outlawed Like Banned Books in Fahrenheit 451?

The Roman god *Janus* presided over the beginning and ending of conflict, and hence war and peace. Europe–in fact, the whole world–is unfortunately still witnessing war at the time of the writing of this paper. What will the impact of all this be on the present and future of the EU legal structure and of the sovereignty of European Union and its Member States? What will its impact be on European Union defence and security, migration and fiscal policies?

The present writer is sceptical insofar as the future of European sovereignty is concerned: the European Union will likely not be the master of its own future, controlling its own destiny. But neither will the Member States separately and therefore the future of national sovereignty is also not particularly bright.

We have seen, based on the above-analysed examples of France and Estonia that sovereignty has developed from having a strong, inalienable value in terms of the constitution and statehood to a more pragmatic concept which is open to internationalisation and European integration. We have also seen that the concept according to which nowadays sovereignty is open to flexibility and internationalisation, is subject to certain reservations in that the judiciary often step in as a compromise between politicians and concretise the notion of sovereignty.

No matter how much we theorise about sovereignty, we can never really predict what the practical impact of e.g., ambitious powers attempting to exercise and also impose their national sovereignty outside the State's own territory, both on the national and the European level, will be in the future. Also, there will remain a certain distinction between the two levels of sovereignty: national and European, despite attempts to unify them.

Sovereignty, even if we invent a new term for it, or a special theory for European sovereignty, will remain both a right and a duty.[113]

It has been noted that sovereignty and the right to rule cannot be conferred on anyone as the result of an academic discussion. Sovereignty is acquired by force and power and violence.[114] Or to put matters in a manner more favourable to science,

---

[113] See Jacob Weinrib, "Sovereignty as a Right and as a Duty: Kant's Theory of the State" in Claire Finkelstein and Michael Skerker (eds.), *Sovereignty and the New Executive Authority* (Oxford Academic 2018).

[114] Mustafa Kemal Ataturk quotes, available online at <https://www.azquotes.com/quote/952282> (23 July 2023).

which is less violent, but just as radical, "science has made unrestricted national sovereignty incompatible with human survival. The only possibilities are now world government or death."[115]

Will the future of the sovereignty be like that of books in the excellent dystopian novel by Ray Bradbury, *Fahrenheit 451*?[116] This remains to be seen. The survival of sovereignty, its transformation and future in its positive aspects depend to our mind on two important factors: institutions and people.

4.1 Sovereignty and Institutions

The more democratic, transparent and respectful towards fundamental rights and the rule of law the institutions of Member States and the European Union are, the more chance there is that sovereignty will be understood and exercised harmoniously, usefully and without abuse.

Sovereignty cannot be taken out of context, but must be seen in conjunction with democratic legitimacy, the rule of law and the protection of human rights. Unfortunately, taking it out of context is one of the biggest mistakes made so far in the discourse about sovereignty. In general, there is too little of looking at the global picture in both law and politics regarding the European Union. Contrary to the common understanding, strong institutions at EU level arguably also reinforce national institutions and make them stronger.

There is nothing as such wrong, should France wish to defend the competences of its parliament (the National Assembly and Senate) and have the national parliament play a greater role in the adoption of European legislation, so that democracy in Europe and sovereignty in France are guaranteed.[117]

Yet sovereignty, as we have seen, cannot be created in a vacuum. That is why there is increasing talk in the European Union e.g., of establishing supranational lists for European Parliament elections, so that a candidate who is on the French list can

[115] Akṣapāda, *Philosophical consultations of Bertrand Russell* (independently published 2019) 73.

[116] Ray Bradbury, *Farenheit 451* (Ballantine Books 1953). It is admirable, and at the same time terrifying, how well the American writer predicted in 1953 what we are witnessing more than half a century later: superficiality, mediocrity, advances in technology that not only help but make us dependent, hinder our imagination and frighten us, fake news and misinformation, disregard for human feelings, disrespect for the environment, and no books, just to name some few items in common between the novel and contemporary reality. One of the most tragic points about it is that it has not only been the system and institutions that have made such changes for the worse possible. It has also been the people themselves, who have stopped reading. "Remember, the firemen are rarely necessary. The public itself stopped reading of its own accord". (*Op. cit.*, p 83.).

[117] Rodolophe Laffranque, "EL/EÜ lepingute konstitutsionaliseerimise protsess ja liikmesriikide suveräänsus. Dilemma Prantsuse õiguse vaatepunktist nähtuna" (Constitutionalising of EU/EC treaties and sovereignty of Member States. Dilemma from French Perspective), in (2000) 8 *Juridica* 537 at 542.

be elected in Estonia, etc.[118] It is also being argued that the post of President of the European Commission should not be filled on the basis of political backroom deals, but rather should be a '*Spitzenkandidat*', i.e., that the candidate of the party that won the direct election to the European Parliament, who was known to everyone during the campaign, should become President of the Commission.[119] This is something that can be done in future European Parliament elections if the political will and popular support for doing so exist.

These ideas of democratisation are also supported by the 'ordinary citizens' who participated in the debate on the future of the European Union with their own proposals.[120]

On the question of sanctions, it has already been said that the right of one state to intervene in the affairs of another state when human rights are being violated is incorporated in the new definition of sovereignty, and that such rights are also given to international organisations and courts. We have also examined in depth the role of judiciaries in preserving and at the same time modernising sovereignty. It is important that the judiciary's role survive crises, not only related to security and populism, but also concerning the environment (involving the Green Deal, and energy policy) and digitalisation (involving cyber threats, etc.) and that the sources of law, both national and European Union, and both procedural and substantial, be sufficient to face these challenges and at the same time respect the principle of proportionality and fundamental rights.

Would a new competence court composed among others of judges of national supreme courts (similarly to the Panel established by Article 255 TFEU) add value to the way in which the highest courts or constitutional courts of Member States cope with allegedly *ultra vires* activities of the European Court of Justice?[121]

---

[118] Committee on Constitutional Affairs, European Parliament (Rapporteur: Domènec Ruiz Devesa), *Report on the proposal for a Council Regulation on the election of the members of the European Parliament by direct universal suffrage, repealing Council Decision (76/787/ECSC, EEC, Euratom) and the Act concerning the election of the members of the European Parliament by direct universal suffrage annexed to that decision* (4.4.2022–(2020/2220(INL)). (Available online at <https://oeil.secure.europarl.europa.eu/oeil/popups/ficheprocedure.do?lang=en&reference=2020/2220(INL) ≥ accessed 23 July 2023.

[119] *Election of the President of the European Commission Understanding the Spitzenkandidaten process*, European Parliament Briefing Document from 2019, available online at <https://efaidnbmnnnibpcajpcglclefindmkaj/ https://www.europarl.europa.eu/RegData/etudes/BRIE/2018/630264/EPRS_BRI(2018)630264_EN.pdf> accessed 23 July 2023.

[120] See the ideas about strengthening European Democracy of the Conference on the Future of Europe. See in this regard e.g., Proposal on transnational EU-wide election lists, available online at <https://wayback.archive-it.org/12090/20230216205448/ https://futureu.europa.eu/en/processes/Democracy/f/6/proposals/55> accessed 23 July 2023). As Prof. Christine Landfried observed during her talk, *A Federal Future for the European Union?* at the 30 Years of ERA Congress on 13 October 2022 in Trier, when the people are asked for their opinion on the future of the European Union, the answer must be taken seriously.

[121] Joseph Weiler and Daniel Sarmiento, "The EU Judiciary After Weiss—Proposing A New Mixed Chamber of the Court of Justice", *EU Law Live*, 1.06.2020. (Available online at <https://eulawlive.com/op-ed-the-eu-judiciary-after-weiss-proposing-a-new-mixed-chamber-of-the-court-of-justice-by-daniel-sarmiento-and-j-h-h-weiler/> accessed 23 July 2023.

One of the dangers we see (in addition to over-regulation and bureaucracy), is also the tendency for the European Union and its institutions to duplicate tasks, e.g., on fundamental rights (on the part of the Commission and the Fundamental Rights Agency of the EU). As has been rightly pointed out, a genuine concerted European Union effort to better balance economic, security and normative interests must avoid institutional and personality-driven jealousies.[122]

4.2 Sovereignty and People

One of the essential elements in talking about sovereignty comprises people and their human rights, including European Union citizens and their fundamental rights and freedoms. In the context of EU sovereignty, European Union citizenship is crucial—as is solidarity. If it is true to say that when poverty comes in at the door, love flies out the window,[123] what about solidarity and the social dimension in difficult times—how can they survive? When times are tough, unity should be particularly necessary, but it is also particularly difficult to achieve.

The lack of a European people has been seen as one important shortcoming in the legitimation of the European Union, because the treaties cannot be connected to a European people, but rather to individual Member States. We have underlined above the importance of equality of states, yet, in fact, if citizens understand that it is not only the Member States that need to be treated equally, but they themselves—as Jean Monnet, one of the founding and spiritual fathers of the European Union, said, it is the people that need to be united, not the states[124]— then they will certainly be more interested in the European dimension, because at the moment e.g., people in France, as well as in Estonia tend to forget that we are all Europe rather than there being a France and Europe, an Estonia and Europe and so on.

As has been rightly argued, while this might not be covered under a conventional reading of Article 18 TFEU, the prohibition of discrimination based on nationality could be understood as also including a comparison between the situation of a person subject to European Union law in one Member State with the situation of a person

---

122 Daniel Fiott (with Riccardo Alvaro, Niclas Poitiers, Jana Puglierin, Pauline Weil and Guntram Wolff) *European Sovereignty: Strategy and Interdependence* (Chaillot Paper No. 169, European Union Institute for Security Studies 2021) at 42.

123 Ulla Neergard, "When Poverty Comes in at the Door, Love Flies Out the Window': The Influence of Eurozone Reforms upon the Social Dimension of the EU—And Vice Versa?" (2016) 7(2) *European Labour Law Journal* 168.

124 Speech by Jean Monnet, President of the High Authority, at the opening session of the Common Assembly (Strasbourg, 11 September 1952), available online at <https://efaidnbmnnnibpcajpcglclefindmkaj/ https://ec.europa.eu/historical_archives/archisplus/files/MONNET_1952_09_11_EN.pdf> accessed 23 July 2023.

subject to European Union law in another Member State or States, and expressing the objective or principle that equality must also be upheld in this constellation.[125]

When we look at popular movements related to questions of sovereignty, they are quite similar in the two countries commented upon in this article, despite the differences in democratic experience and history. Of course, Estonians rarely come onto streets to manifest and demonstrate, unlike the French (and would disapprove of doing harm, and destroying property and streets as was seen with the *gilets jaunes*). Nonetheless, Estonians, for reasons explained above, feel very strongly about sovereignty as do the French.

France has been said to have "welfare nationalism":[126] it has been humorously suggested that the French symbol was a rooster, but is now a rooster in wine sauce.[127] (De Gaulle famously also asked how one could govern a country where there are 246 varieties of cheese.[128]) However, the French also have a very highly developed political culture: newspapers are read widely and even in public transportation. Moreover, already at school, children are interested in politics, social issues, and debates on current affairs matter (even if according to Stendhal, France is a country where it's more important to have an opinion on Homer than to have read Homer.[129])

A culture of demonstrations is also well established, especially in the public sector: reasons, for taking all issues on to the streets include, among others, the fact that to demonstrate (rather to engage in a peaceful assembly) is regarded as a fundamental right and it is a right which is readily exercised, as e.g., it was during the famous 1968 student uprisings, as well as in more recent demonstrations concerning pension reform and against police violence. All pretexts for protesting against government are used.[130] This has forced the government e.g., to push legislation through parliament using votes of confidence on numerous occasions in France. Interestingly, the Estonian Parliament has also recently utilised an extraordinary session to pass many controversial laws (concerning e.g., taxes, as well as same-sex marriage) using such

---

[125] Marcus Klamert, "Rationalizing Supremacy. Supremacy, effectiveness, and two standards of equality in EU law", *Verfassungsblog*, 18 October 2021. (Available online at <https://verfassungsblog.de/rationalizing-supremacy/> accessed 23 July 2023).

[126] A description attributed to Vincent Martigny, a professor for political science at Nice University and the École Polytechnique. See Lisa Louis, "France: Pension reform spells crisis for Macron", *Deutsche Welle*, 17 March 2023. (Available online at <https://www.dw.com/en/france-pension-reform-spells-crisis-for-macron/a-65031192> accessed 11 October 2023).

[127] Cesborn, Gilbert: "L'emblème de la France, c'était le coq. C'est aujourd'hui le coq au vin", *Le Figaro*, undated (available online at <http://evene.lefigaro.fr/citation/embleme-france-etait-coq-aujourd-hui-coq-vin-12410.php> accessed 24 July 2023).

[128] "Comment voulez-vous gouverner un pays où il existe 246 variétés de fromage?", citation attributed to Général de Gaulle in Ernest Mignon, *Les Mots du Général* (Paris 1962).

[129] "La France est un pays où il est plus important d'avoir une opinion sur Homère que d'avoir lu Homère", attributed to Stendhal and available online at <https://www.dicocitations.com/citations/citation-32893.php> accessed 24 July 2023.

[130] France is a country that loves to change their government if it is always the same, as was said by Honore de Balzac ("La France est un pays qui adore changer de gouvernement à condition que ce soit toujours le même"). (Available online at <https://citations.ouest-france.fr/citation-honore-de-balzac/france-pays-adore-changer-gouvernement-78692.html> accessed 24 July 2023).

votes for laws relating to the issue of trust in the government, thus avoiding a second reading in the parliament.[131]

Estonia, with its still-idealistic patriotism, with somewhat less welfare, but with instead some degree of a small-country complex, and living in constant fear of its big neighbour in the east (a fear which has unfortunately turned out to be justified) has–even if for different reasons–much in common with France, as far as sovereignty is concerned.

For Estonians, there is only one Estonia and that is unique, whether it is the land of our birth, our homeland, motherland, fatherland, or all of them at once. Just as no one can replace mother or father, sister or brother, grandmother, or grandfather, no one can replace Estonia, not even the European Union. Estonians know that independence and freedom are very fragile. Some of us have had the fortune to be present at historical moments of the restoration of Estonia's sovereignty and to sing Estonia free again during the 'singing revolution' of the 1990s, and finally to be able to study enjoying academic freedom and free speech. The writer, Jaan Kross, also a lawyer by training, has aptly asked how many cases there are in the world, as there have been in Estonia's case, of two grants of independence in one human generation.[132]

Estonians realise how terrifying it is to have fallen asleep in a free country, only to wake up the next morning in an occupied country or in the middle of a war–that is why they cannot take lightly the issue of belonging to NATO and the European Union. Some of us have also had the opportunity to participate in those historic moments when Estonia was preparing to join these international organisations. As explained above, finding the best solution to the issue of how to join the European Union while respecting the rule of law and amending the constitution did not come easily. This is why, it is important, in order to understand sovereignty, for ordinary people (French and Estonians in our example) to understand the Charter.[133] The Charter is a document similar to Chapter 2 of the Estonian Constitution, but exists in a pan-European context, is published in all official languages of the European Union, including the Estonian language, goes hand in hand with constitutions of the Member States and the European Convention on Human Rights, and includes not only fundamental rights and freedoms, but also social and economic rights, rights that come with European citizenship and modern rights concerning e.g., bioethics. Both

---

131 See e.g., Loora-Elisabet Lomp, "Üle 24 tunni istungit, Riigikogu võttis vastu kaheksa seadust", *Postimees*, 20.06.2023, available online at<https://www.postimees.ee/7799245/video-ule-24-tunni-istungit-riigikogu-vottis-vastu-kaheksa-seadust> accessed 24 July 2023); "Ajalooline otsus: Eesti seadustas samasooliste abielu" (historical decision, Estonia has legalised same-sex marriage), *ERR*, 20 June 2023. (Available online at <https://www.err.ee/1609012283/ajalooline-otsus-eesti-seadus tas-samasooliste-abielu> accessed 24 July 2023).

132 Jaan Kross, in the newspaper *Rahva Hääl*, 29 April 1995.

133 The author of this paper has been the only member of the Scientific Committee of the European Union Agency for Fundamental Rights (FRA) of Estonian origin, and to have been selected in a close Europe-wide competition for five years, in a non-renewable capacity, thus serving the Committee from 2018–2023, and has on many occasions disseminated the Charter in Estonian at Estonian schools, universities and court houses.

the Estonian Constitution and the Charter attach the utmost importance to peace, freedom of expression and education.

The European Union would be making a mistake, if it did not take into consideration the feelings of people, as described above using the example of France and Estonia. The cultural heritage of sovereignty is not something one can just overrule with a myth of European sovereignty, unless real security is offered. Austrian-American economist, historian, logician, and sociologist, Ludwig von Mises has rightly pointed out that "sovereignty must not be used for inflicting harm on anyone, whether citizen or foreigner."[134]

[134] Ludwig von Mises, *Omnipotent Government: The Rise of the Total State and Total War* (Libertarian Press 1985). (Available online at <https://www.azquotes.com/author/10190-Ludwig_von_Mises/tag/sovereignty> accessed 24 July 2023).

Judicial Sovereignty

The Broadening of EU Competences Through the Case Law of the Court of Justice: Myth or Reality?

Koen Lenaerts

Abstract This keynote speech responds to criticism that is expressed from time to time to the effect that the Court of Justice would favour an extensive interpretation of EU competences and of the material scope of EU law, in violation of national sovereignty. It demonstrates that portraying the Court of Justice as a biased promotor of a 'centralist' vision of the EU is not correct. Member States regularly succeed in disputes with the EU over competence or the scope of application of EU law, irrespective of the legal area concerned. Moreover, the Court deals with those issues on the basis of settled, non-contentious principles such as effectiveness and institutional balance, and in accordance with stable methods of interpretation.

The Academy of European Law (ERA) was created in 1992 following a recommendation of the European Parliament. That creation, which immediately followed the signature of the Maastricht treaty, was justified by the unprecedented development of EU legislation under the *Delors* Commission, and the ensuing need to develop EU law training among legal practitioners. The expansion of EU law has significantly accelerated ever since, in areas such as environmental protection, non-discrimination, judicial cooperation in criminal matters, public health and the banking union, which makes the ERA even more necessary today than 30 years ago. Marc Van der Woude is right when he declares in the last annual report of the Academy[1] that any legal professional's knowledge is incomplete these days if missing the Union dimension

[1] The Academy of European Law (2021) Annual Report. https://www.era.int/upload/dokumente/24634.pdf, p. 7. (Accessed 24.10.2022).

President of the Court of Justice of the European Union and Professor of European Union Law, Leuven University.

Keynote speech delivered at the ERA Jubilee Conference—30 years of the Academy of European law (13.10.2022). All opinions expressed herein are personal to the author. This speech was previously published in ERA Forum Volume 24, Number 4, December 2023, p. 589.

K. Lenaerts (✉)
Luxembourg, Luxembourg
e-mail: Secretariat_President-Cour@curia.europa.eu

G. Barrett et al. (eds.), *European Sovereignty*,
https://doi.org/10.1007/978-3-031-71851-9_6

of a legal discipline. I want to pay special tribute to the Academy for its role as a 'transmission belt' of knowledge on EU law towards a wide variety of legal professionals. As they are increasingly exposed to EU law in their practice, the Academy's qualitative training programmes contribute to the effectiveness of that law, besides training provided by other key actors such as the European Judicial Training Network (EJTN) and the Council of Bars and Law Societies of Europe (CCBE). Moreover, the role of the Academy is not limited to training. As this congress itself demonstrates, it is also a useful forum of discussion among practitioners and policymakers on the development of EU law.[2]

The ERA's success story that we celebrate today, however, should not make us lose sight of the confidence crisis that the EU is currently undergoing, as part of a broader rejection of political institutions by a growing fraction of European citizens. That crisis can be seen in the progress made by extremist, often anti-EU political movements in many Member States. Confidence in the EU depends on a vast number of factors: the stability of its institutions; its capacity to address challenges raised by digitalisation, cybercrime, climate change, threats for biodiversity, innovation by and competitiveness of European businesses in the global economy, price stability and security of access to food, energy and pharma-products in times of crisis; the Union's capacity to show unity when the continent faces major geopolitical threats for its stability and security, such as the war in Ukraine; or simply the Member States' capacity to communicate positively about the EU and its protective role for citizens in ever-more aspects of their daily lives. All that is necessary to consolidate 'European sovereignty' in the 21st Century. However, such sovereignty is only conceivable *within the limits set out in the Treaties*. In particular, the Union can be legitimate and thus inspire confidence only if it acts within the competences conferred upon it by its 'basic constitutional charter'.[3] In this keynote speech, I shall comment on criticism that is expressed from time to time, to the effect that the Court would almost systematically favour EU competence in violation of the Member States' sovereignty.[4] I cannot share that view and will explain why.

---

[2] In the aforementioned annual report, Jean-Philippe Rageade mentions for example the role of the ERA in the context of the Conference on the Future of Europe. Ibid, p. 11.

[3] Judgment of 23.4.1986, Les Verts v Parliament, 294/83, EU:C:1986:166, para 23.

[4] See, for example, Weiler JHH and Sarmiento D (2020) The EU Judiciary After Weiss—Proposing a New Mixed Chamber of the Court of Justice, EU Law Live. https://eulawlive.com/the-eu-judiciary-after-weiss-proposing-a-new-mixed-chamber-of-the-court-of-justice-a-reply-to-our-critics-by-j-h-h-weiler-and-daniel-sarmiento/. (accessed 24.10.2022). These authors explain: "despite its fundamental and indispensable contribution to European integration, the European Court of Justice has shown itself over the years to have one blind spot. It has not proved to be a strict guarantor in policing the limits to EU competences and jurisdiction. The very limited number of cases where it has flagged a breach of competence have been the exception that proves a very general rule of broad EU competence. This is probably due to a misconceived vision of federalism, in which the federal vision is (wrongly) associated with a centralist understanding of the EU".

1 Methodology

Two preliminary observations must be made on methodology. First, besides issues of EU competence in the narrow sense, issues concerning the material scope of EU law have to be taken into account. That scope, for example of the prohibition of State aid, indeed determines the extent to which EU law circumscribes the action of the Member States when they exercise their own competences.[5]

Second, the critical comments to which I referred in the introduction put much emphasis on unsuccessful actions for annulment introduced by Member States against EU legislative acts. Yet, even within that category of proceedings, there are cases where the Court annulled or invalidated the challenged acts, either on grounds of a lack of competence as in the famous *Tobacco Advertisement* case[6] or of a violation of fundamental rights as in the *Test-Achats*[7] or *Digital Rights Ireland*[8] cases. More fundamentally, a realistic picture of the Court's case law requires considering other categories of proceedings, such as preliminary rulings or appeals, in which the Court also frequently addresses issues of competence in the broad sense.

2 Three Horizontal Principles Governing the Court's Jurisdiction on Competence

I now turn to three horizontal principles that I consider essential when assessing the Court's role on issues of competence.

First, the Court of Justice has exclusive jurisdiction to give the definitive interpretation of EU law, including Treaty provisions attributing competences to the Union or governing their exercise. It has moreover exclusive jurisdiction to declare an EU measure invalid. As the Court explained in its judgment in *RS* delivered in February 2022, accepting an *ultra vires* doctrine allowing national courts to second-guess and depart from the interpretation of EU law contained in a judgment of the Court of Justice, would breach the equality of the Member States before the Treaties.[9] It would

---

[5] According to settled case law, Member States are required to exercise competences that they retain in accordance with EU law. See e.g., on extradition, the judgment of 13.11.2018, Raugevicius, C-247/17, EU:C:2018:898, para 45.

[6] Judgment of 5.10.2000, *Germany v Parliament and Council*, C-376/98, EU:C:2000:544.

[7] Judgment of 1.3.2011, *Association belge des Consommateurs Test-Achats and Others*, C-236/09, EU:C:2011:100.

[8] Judgment of 8.4.2014, *Digital Rights Ireland and Others*, C-293/12 and C-594/12, EU:C:2014:238.

[9] Judgment of 22.2.2022, *RS (Effect of the decisions of a constitutional court)*, C-430/21, EU:C:2022:99, para 22.

show disrespect towards the other Member States and their peoples that continue to honour EU law on a reciprocal basis.[10]

However, that exclusive competence does not mean that the Court 'imposes' its views without any consideration for national courts. Only a cooperative dialogue with them enables the Court of Justice to stay perfectly connected to the realities on the ground when saying what the law of the EU is, including on issues of competence.[11] I am, therefore, particularly satisfied when I read in national judgments that the Court's 'message', including on issues of competence in the broad sense, has been well received and understood. For example, according to the landmark judgments in *Melloni*,[12] *Akerberg Fransson*[13] and *Taricco 2*,[14] the Member States can enforce their own standards of protection of fundamental rights going beyond the minimum protection offered by the Charter, provided that the 'primacy, unity and effectiveness' of EU law are respected. This means in practice that it is only in the absence of fully determined legislative choices at EU level that a Member State may apply its own standards of protection, insofar it does not render ineffective the EU legislation that it implements. That possibility does not exist if the EU legislation at issue reflects such fully determined choices. The *Bundesverfassungsgericht* correctly applied that distinction in its decisions *Recht auf Vergessen I*[15] and *Recht auf Vergessen II*.[16] Another example is a judgment of the *Corte Costituzionale* delivered in 2022. That court refers to the judgment in *RS* to conclude that the Italian Supreme Court of Cassation should directly set aside a provision of national law that is incompatible with EU law, as interpreted in a preliminary ruling, without first having to ask the Constitutional Court to strike down that provision as unconstitutional.[17]

The second principle is effectiveness of EU law. That principle underpins the Court's avoidance of interpretations of EU secondary law undermining its *effet utile*.[18] However, it can also serve as a guiding principle when assessing the scope of EU legislative competences. For example, in the case *Czech Republic v Parliament and*

[10] See Lenaerts K (2020) No Member State is More Equal than Others, Verfassungsblog. https://verfassungsblog.de/no-member-state-is-more-equal-than-others/ (accessed 24.10.2022).

[11] See, on constructive dialogue between the Court of Justice and constitutional courts of the Member States, Sciarra S (2022) Can Constitutional Courts and the Court of Justice of the EU Speak Common Words?, Eurojus. http://rivista.eurojus.it/wp-content/uploads/pdf/here-3.pdf (pp. 67–78, especially pp. 76–78). Accessed 24.10.2022.

[12] Judgment of 26.2.2013, *Melloni*, C-399/11, EU:C:2013:107.

[13] Judgment of 26.2.2013, *Åkerberg Fransson*, C-617/10, EU:C:2013:105.

[14] Judgment of 5.12.2017, *M.A.S. and M.B.*, C-42/17, EU:C:2017:936.

[15] BVerfG, *Recht auf Vergessen I*, orders of 6.11.2019, 1 BvR 16/13. See also Lenaerts K (2019) The Role of the Court of Justice in the Interpretation and Application of the Charter. Speech delivered at the European Committee of the Regions 134th plenary session on 11.4.2019, p. 8.

[16] BVerfG, *Recht auf Vergessen II*, 1 BvR 276/17.

[17] Corte Costituzionale, judgment of 8.2.2022, 67/2022.

[18] See, for example, judgment of 16.6.2015, *Rina Services and Others*, C-593/13, EU:C:2015:399, para 37, where the Court has decided that "an interpretation of Article 3(3) of Directive 2006/123 to the effect that Member States may justify, on the basis of primary law, a requirement prohibited by Article 14 of that directive would deprive that provision of any practical effect by ultimately undermining the ad hoc harmonisation intended by that directive".

Council,[19] that Member State called into question the adequacy of Article 114 TFEU as a legal basis of the EU Directive amending the Directive on firearms.[20] It argued that the amending Directive primarily served public security purposes, rather than improving the functioning of the internal market. The original Directive established a harmonized minimum framework for the possession and acquisition of firearms and for their transfer between Member States. The amending Directive drew the lessons of terrorist attacks in Europe in 2015 and 2016, in particular by establishing a new system for marking firearms and specifying the data to be filed in the Member States' databases. The Czech Republic argued that the correct methodology for assessing the legal basis was to appraise whether those measures *as such* primarily concerned the functioning of the internal market. The Court applied a different methodology. The EU legislature should be able to 'adjust' the balance that it has previously reached between improvement of the internal market and other general interests such as public safety, in order to take into account changed circumstances. The amended directive forms part of the relevant normative 'context' of the amending directive, which means that the latter *considered in isolation* cannot be decisive. What matters in terms of legal basis is the overall normative result of the amendment. That approach was necessary to preserve the *effet utile* of the legislative competence at issue.

The third and last principle is institutional balance, which has an impact on the intensity of judicial review. That principle means that, in areas entailing choices of a political or complex nature, the legality of a measure adopted by the EU political institutions can be affected only if the measure is *manifestly inappropriate* having regard to the objective pursued. Thus, the judgment in *Slovakia and Hungary v. Council*[21] concerned a challenge against a Council decision requiring the relocation of 120,000 migrants from Italy and Greece to other Member States. The decision took into account the exceptional burden that such a huge influx of migrants had on those Member States of the Mediterranean area. The applicant Member States argued in particular that the small number of relocations since the entry into force of the mechanism demonstrated its obviously inappropriate character. The Court rejected that argument. It noted that judicial review of the decision could not amount to a retrospective assessment of its effectiveness. It must be limited to examining whether the prospective analysis carried out by the Council was manifestly incorrect in the light of the information available when the contested decision was adopted. The relocation mechanism was not manifestly inappropriate for helping Greece and Italy to cope with a massive influx of migrants, in the light of the available statistical data. That cannot be regarded as undue deference *vis-à-vis* the political institutions of the Union. It is, on the contrary, standard restraint by a court in a democratic society to avoid crossing the line between law and politics. In other words, the Court of Justice

[19] Judgment of 3.12.2019, *Czech Republic v Parliament and Council*, C-482/17, EU:C:2019:1035.

[20] Directive (EU) 2017/853 of the European Parliament and of the Council of 17.5.2017 amending Council Directive 91/477/EEC on control of the acquisition and possession of weapons (*OJ* L 137, 24.5.2017, p. 22).

[21] Judgment of 6.9.2017, *Slovakia and Hungary v Council*, C-643/15 and C-647/15, EU:C:2017:631.

cannot be expected to encroach upon the core prerogative of the EU legislature to decide politically which measures are the most appropriate response to a given issue.

3 Illustrations of Member States' "Victories" in Disputes with the EU Over Competence or Scope of Application of EU Law

Against that background, I shall now provide illustrations of decisions of the Court of Justice demonstrating that it has no bias in favour of the EU when dealing with issues of competence. As we will see, those examples are neither isolated, nor limited to a given area of EU law. On the contrary, they cover a wide range of areas, thus clearly showing that the Court's reasoning is guided by neutral, exclusively legal considerations rather than political preconceptions.

The EU's external relations offer a first series of examples on 'pure' issues of competence, i.e. concerning the existence and nature of an EU normative competence. A recent illustration of an unsuccessful attempt by the Commission to 'push' for EU exclusive external competence is the judgment *AMP Antartica* of 2018.[22] The case concerned in particular the scope of the EU's exclusive competence for the conservation of marine biological resources under the common fisheries policy,[23] and its relationship with the Union's shared competences in agriculture and fisheries and in environmental matters.[24] The Commission challenged decisions of the Council approving the submission of documents on behalf of the Union and its Member States at the annual meeting of an international commission on the Antarctica, aiming to create so-called 'Marine Protected Areas'. It argued in essence that the Union's exclusive competence for 'conservation of marine biological resources' covers the adoption of any measure directed at such conservation, whatever the objective pursued. The Court decided on the contrary that such exclusive competence only exists insofar as the conservation is pursued *under the Common fisheries policy*, which was clearly not the case with the planned Marine Protected Areas.[25] The challenged decisions, therefore, were correctly based on the Union's environmental competence, which is shared with the Member States. The Court also rejected the Commission's subsidiary argument based on an alleged 'affectation' of common EU rules by the challenged decisions.[26] Interestingly, it did not rule out any possible affectation but rather observed that the Commission had not provided sufficient evidence

[22] Judgment of 20.11.2018, *Commission v Council (Antarctic MPAs)*, C-626/15 and C-659/16, EU:C:2018:925.

[23] Article 3(1)(d) TFEU.

[24] Article 4(2)(d) and (e) TFEU.

[25] Ibid, Judgment of 20.11.2018, *Commission v. Council (Antarctic MPAs)*, para. 84.

[26] Article 3(2) TFEU. In the Commission's view, that affectation concerned, on the one hand, a multiannual position adopted by the Union in the CCAMLR and, on the other hand, two EU regulations on fisheries.

to that effect.[27] In other words, an exclusive competence of the EU resulting from affectation of common rules *cannot be presumed.*

It is moreover settled case law that the mere fact that provisions of an international agreement may have repercussions on trade does not suffice to attract it within the Common commercial policy, which is an area of exclusive competence.[28] Other bases of EU competence in the Treaties, shared with the Member States, would otherwise become nugatory.[29] There are even situations where the Court held that the EU lacks *any* external competence, be it exclusive or shared. Thus, in *Opinion 2/15 on the draft trade and investment agreement with Singapore*,[30] it concluded that only the Member States are competent to enter into an Investor-State Dispute Settlement (ISDS) mechanism. Contrary to the position defended by the Commission, the Court decided that the ISDS mechanism, 'which removes disputes from the jurisdiction of the courts of the Member States', cannot be of a purely ancillary nature to the 'substantive' provisions of the agreement and therefore cannot be entered into without the Member States' consent.[31]

I also cannot accept the view that the Court systematically promotes a "tentacular" conception of the scope of application of EU law. Thus, despite suggestions made in academic literature[32] and by some Advocates General,[33] the Court has maintained its case law on purely internal situations falling outside the reach of Treaty provisions on free movement. In the famous *Flemish care insurance* case,[34] two regional governments in Belgium challenged before the Constitutional Court of Belgium a Flemish decree establishing a 'care insurance scheme' covering certain costs related to dependence caused by serious or prolonged disability. That scheme applied to persons either residing in Flanders or the region of Brussels-Capital, or to persons working there and residing in a Member State other than Belgium. The applicant governments argued that the exclusion of persons working in those two regions but residing in Wallonia amounted to a restriction of free movement prohibited by EU law. The Court disagreed. Belgian nationals living in Wallonia and having never exercised their EU free movement rights are in a 'purely internal situation' and thus

---

[27] Ibid Judgment of 20.12.2018, *Commission v. Council (Antarctic MPAs)*, paras 121–124.

[28] See, for example, Opinion 3/15 (*Marrakesh Treaty on access to published works*) of 14.2.2017, EU:C:2017:114. The Marrakesh treaty promotes accessibility of published works for blind or visually impaired persons. The Court concluded that this treaty had only indirect effects on trade, thus rejecting the Commission's argument that the copyright limitations and exceptions for the benefit of those persons specifically concerned 'commercial aspects of intellectual property' that now form part of the CCP.

[29] Opinion 2/00 (*Cartagena Protocol on Biosafety*) of 6.12.2001, EU:C:2001:664, para 40.

[30] Opinion 2/15 (*EU-Singapore Free Trade Agreement*) of 16.5.2017, EU:C:2017:376.

[31] Ibid, para 292.

[32] See, for example, Tryfonidou A (2008) 'Reverse Discrimination in Purely Internal Situations: An Incongruity in a Citizens' Europe. Legal Issues of Economic Integration 35(1):43–67.

[33] See in particular Opinion of Advocate General Sharpston in *Government of the French Community and Walloon Government*, C-212/06, EU:C:2007:398, paras 153–155.

[34] Judgment of 1.4.2008, *Government of the French Community and Walloon Government*, C-212/06, EU:C:2008:178.

fall outside the scope of freedom of movement of persons.[35] EU citizenship does not call that into question, because '[it] is not intended to extend the material scope of the Treaty to internal situations which have no link with [EU] law'.[36] Only a Court *without* any bias in favour of extending the scope of EU law could make such a clear statement.

The Citizenship Directive[37] offers other examples where Member States successfully defended prerogatives which, they argued, that directive left to them. In *Dano*,[38] German authorities had refused to grant social allowances to an economically inactive Romanian national and her son legally residing in Germany. As German nationals in the same situation would be entitled to the benefits at issue, the referring Court had doubts whether that refusal was compatible with Article 24 of the Citizenship Directive. That provision states that migrant citizens should in principle benefit from equal treatment in the host Member State with nationals of that Member State, except for the granting of social assistance during the first three months of residence or, where appropriate, the period of seeking employment. That exception did not apply in this case because Mrs Dano had been a resident in Germany for more than three months and was not seeking employment there. Moreover, she did not benefit from permanent residence in Germany because she had not been legally resident in that Member State for at least five years. The Court accepted Germany's argument that granting social benefits to a person in the situation of Mrs Dano on equal footing with German nationals would run counter to the objective of the Citizenship Directive to protect financially the social assistance systems of the Member States. It means that Member States should be entitled to deny social benefits to economically inactive citizens who exercise their right to freedom of movement solely in order to obtain social assistance although they do not have sufficient resources to claim a right of residence in the host Member State.[39] That reasoning was confirmed in *Alimanovic*.[40]

Another important area where the Court has recently opposed encroachments on Member States' competences is State aid. A usually complex question, in that

---

[35] Ibid, paras 37 and 38.

[36] Ibid, para 39. That was confirmed on numerous occasions. See for example the judgment of 15.11.2016, Ullens de Schooten, C-268/15, EU:C:2016:874, paras 54 and 55.

[37] Directive 2004/38/EC of the European Parliament and of the Council of 29.4.2004 on the right of citizens of the Union and their family members to move and reside freely within the territory of the Member States amending Regulation (EEC) No 1612/68 and repealing Directives 64/221/EEC, 68/360/EEC, 72/194/EEC, 73/148/EEC, 75/34/EEC, 75/35/EEC, 90/364/EEC, 90/365/EEC and 93/96/EEC (*OJ* L 158, 30.4.2004, p. 77).

[38] Judgment of 11.11.2014, Dano, C-333/13, EU:C:2014:2358.

[39] Ibid, para 78.

[40] Judgment of 15.9.2015, Alimanovic, C-67/14, EU:C:2015:597. That said, an important nuance came in 2021 with the judgment of 15.7.2021, The Department for Communities in Northern Ireland, C-709/20, EU:C:2021:602. In essence, the Court decided in that judgment that a Member State "implements" a Union citizen's free movement rights under Article 21(1) TFEU when it grants that citizen a right of residence, *even if* that right does not satisfy the conditions laid down by the Citizenship Directive. That triggers the application of certain rights under the Charter and thus requires from the host Member State that it grants means of subsistence to the migrant citizen necessary to lead a life in keeping with human dignity.

regard, is whether a given tax regime confers on certain undertakings or categories of undertakings a 'selective advantage'. For example, the judgments *Commission v. Poland*[41] and *Commission v. Hungary*[42] concerned, respectively, a Polish tax on the retail sector and a Hungarian tax on turnover linked to advertisements. Both tax regimes have two common characteristics: (a) they are based on turnover rather than profit and (b) they apply progressive rates. In its examination of selectivity, the Commission considered that the progressive structure of those taxes did not form part of the 'reference system'. It argued that progressive rates would favour undertakings with a low turnover by unjustifiably alleviating the average tax rate applied to them compared with that borne by other undertakings subject to the higher levels of the scale of progressive rates. That advantage would derogate from a reference system consisting of a fictitious flat-rate turnover tax. Both the General Court and the Court on appeal disagreed with that argument. Determination of the characteristics constituting each tax falls within the discretion of the Member States. Therefore, they should be able to apply progressive rates to a turnover tax. The progressive structure of the tax regimes at issue thus formed part of the reference system and could not lead to a selective advantage.

Lastly, it is not exceptional for the Court to interpret EU asylum and migration law in a sense that leaves to the Member States the margin for which they pleaded. A good example is the judgment in *X and X*,[43] which concerned a provision of the Community Code on Visas allowing delivery of a visa with limited territorial validity on humanitarian grounds. Syrian nationals had requested visas on such grounds at the Belgian embassy in Beirut, declaring that they intended to apply for asylum when they would reach Belgium. Belgian authorities rejected those requests. They considered that the applicants' real intention was to stay in Belgium for more than 90 days and that allowing such requests would mean in practice that asylum can be applied for at a diplomatic post of a Member State, which was certainly not intended by the Community Code on Visas. The Court observed that this Code exclusively governs the issuance of visas for periods not exceeding 90 days. Considering the context in which the requests in the main proceedings were made, they clearly fell outside the scope of that Code. Moreover, in the absence of EU rules on the issuance of long-term visas and residence permits to third-country nationals on humanitarian grounds, their applications fell solely within the scope of national law and the Charter did not apply.[44] The Court emphasised that allowing requests for visas such as those at issue would undermine the system established by the Dublin III Regulation,[45]

---

41 Judgment of 16.3.2021, *Commission v Poland*, C-562/19 P, EU:C:2021:201.

42 Judgment of 16.3.2021, *Commission v Hungary*, C-596/19 P, EU:C:2021:202.

43 Judgment of 7.3.2017, *X and X*, C-638/16 PPU, EU:C:2017:173.

44 Ibid, paras 43 and 44.

45 Regulation (EU) No 604/2013 of the European Parliament and of the Council of 26.6.2013 establishing the criteria and mechanisms for determining the Member State responsible for examining an application for international protection lodged in one of the Member States by a third-country national or a stateless person (*OJ* L 180, 29.6.2013, p. 31).

because third country nationals could lodge applications for visas from abroad with the sole aim of obtaining international protection in the Member State of their choice.

4 Concluding Remarks

Those examples demonstrate that it is not correct to portray the Court of Justice as a biased promotor of EU competences or a 'centralist' vision of the EU. The reality is much more complex. I do not deny that the Court regularly contributes to the consolidation of the EU when it rules on issues of allocation of competences and material scope of EU law. However, it does not do so with a political objective in mind. On the contrary, such case law is guided by settled, non-contentious principles such as effectiveness and institutional balance, and applies stable methods of interpretation. Moreover, the Court refrains from a 'top-down', authoritarian approach on issues of competences in the broad sense. It rather enters into constructive and open dialogue with national courts, in particular courts of last instance. As Jean Monnet declared, "[b]eyond differences and geographical boundaries there lies a common interest". The common interest of the Court of Justice and of national courts if they want to reinforce their 'judicial sovereignty' in the EU is in my view to endeavour to further develop that dialogue, nurtured by frequent meetings of judges at the Court of Justice and in other fora. That ongoing dialogue, based on mutual respect as well as acceptance of the EU constitutional fabric, is a key condition to the EU's legitimacy and thus to the 'European sovereignty' in the future.

The Romanian Constitutional Court and the European Court of Justice—Parallel Monologues

Elena Simina Tănăsescu

1 From National to European Sovereignty

The old concept of sovereignty has survived number of challenges, from integration and globalisation to the transnational defence of human rights and environmental protection. Originating in the peace treaties signed at Westphalia in 1648, the political and legal construct of sovereignty has never ceased to evolve, moving from a state-centred approach towards a multi-level and pluralist paradigm. The European Union (EU) is the living expression of this post-modern conception regarding sovereignty,[1] proving that, far from undermining national sovereignty, integration has merely reinforced state sovereignty, expressed through parliament and people, by topping it with the supra-national level, expressed through supranational norms that address European citizens and the union of European peoples equally.[2] The EU and national constitutional orders inherently overlap. Thus, a pragmatic approach towards European sovereignty has come to light, whereby national and European sovereignty reinforce each other mutually.[3]

[1] Neil MacCormick, "Beyond the Sovereign State" (1993) 56 (1) *Modern Law Review* 1.

[2] Christopher Bickerton, *European Integration: from Nation States to Member States* (2012, Oxford University Press); Kaarlo Tuori, *European Constitutionalism* (2015, Cambridge University Press).

[3] Emmanuel Macron, (2017) "Discours du Président à la Sorbonne", 27 September, available online at <http://international.blogs.ouest-france.fr/archive/2017/09/27/macron-sorbonne-europe-verbatim-18567.html> accessed 10 December 2023.

Judge of the Constitutional Court of Romania and Professor, University of Bucharest. ORCID ID: 0000-0002-5547-7995.

E. S. Tănăsescu (✉)
Bucharest, Romania
e-mail: simina-elena.tanasescu@drept.unibuc.ro

G. Barrett et al. (eds.), *European Sovereignty*,
https://doi.org/10.1007/978-3-031-71851-9_7

However, national and European sovereignty have also been construed as being in opposition to each other.[4] The "ever closer union" initiated after the second world war has meant a constant sharing of powers between Member States and the European Union, a permanent shifting of decision-making competences from the national level to the supranational, an enduring struggle of national states against the expanding European super-state. This relentless movement has been accomplished through the founding treaties of the European Union, as agreed upon by (sometimes unsuspecting) Member States—but it has also been done through the case law of the European Court of Justice (ECJ).[5] Mere economic integration was perceived as less threatening to national sovereignty, but the creation in 1992 of the all-encompassing European Union, with its conferred but nevertheless expandable powers,[6] brought a reaction on the part of–among others–constitutional courts mindful of the danger represented by an increasingly stronger European sovereignty for the sovereignty of their respective states.[7]

Ever since the creation of the European Union, various theories have been put forward in order to reconcile national and European sovereignties, such as constitutional pluralism[8] and multilevel constitutionalism[9] or constitutional identity.[10] In an attempt to settle normative tensions, the Treaty of Lisbon has detailed the sharing of powers within the European Union, although it has not managed to limit the further expansion of the decision-making power of the European Union. Indeed, the principle of conferral, provided by Article 5 TEU, easily accommodates implicit powers for the European sovereign, thus raising inherent concerns for Member States. Every

[4] Nathalie Brack, Ramona Coman, Amandine Crespy (eds.) *Understanding Conflicts of Sovereignty in the EU* (2021, Routledge).

[5] Thomas Horsley, "Reflections on the Role of the Court of Justice as the 'Motor of European Integration': Legal Limits to Judicial Law-making" (2013) 50(4) *Common Market Law Review* 931.

[6] See in particular, Article 3, para.6 of the Treaty on the European Union (TEU), which provides that "the Union shall pursue its objectives by appropriate means commensurate with the competences which are conferred upon it in the Treaties".

[7] Jo Eric Khushal Murkens, "Bundesverfassungsgericht (2 BvE 2/08): 'We want our identity back': The revival of national sovereignty in the German Federal Constitutional Court's decision on the Lisbon Treaty" (2010) 25 *Public Law* 530; Vincent Power, "National sovereignty is alive and well in the European Union: The Wightman ruling of the Court of Justice of the European Union" (2019) 61(1) *Irish Jurist* 65.

[8] Constitutional pluralism contends that EU Member States together with the new supranational institutions now form a new locus of constitutional authority, where hierarchy no longer defines the various possible interactions. See Neil MacCormick, "The Maastricht-Urteil: Sovereignty Now" (1995) 1(3) *European Law Journal* 259 or Neil Walker, "Late Sovereignty in the European Union" in Neil Walker (ed.), *Sovereignty in Transition* (2003, Hart) 3–32.

[9] Multilevel constitutionalism envisages the European Union as a composed constitutional system, which includes both national and supranational levels of legitimate public power that influence each other and that involve both individual citizens and the peoples of Europe. (See Ingolf Pernice, *Fondements du droit constitutionnel européen.* (2002, Editions Panthéon Assas)).

[10] Luke Dimitrios Spieker, "Framing and managing constitutional identity conflicts: How to stabilize the modus vivendi between the Court of Justice and national constitutional courts" (2020) 57(2) *Common Market Law Review* 361.

now and then, some constitutional courts have been more eager than others to notice this overt European empowerment.[11] Occasionally, mutual judicial self-restraint on the part of the European Court of Justice and constitutional courts respectively has been helpful in avoiding clashes between sovereignty prerogatives and parallel claims of ultimate authority while, at the same time, safeguarding the fundamental rights of European citizens.[12]

Recently, iterative crises (the financial crisis, the migration crisis, the pandemic, war at the EU's borders etc.) have shaken the European Union and challenged again its sovereignty. Among these, the recent crisis of the rule of law within the European Union[13] stands out as one that has involved not only political institutions, both at national and supranational level, but also–or rather more so–courts: the European Court of Justice and the Member States' constitutional courts above all.

2 The Interplay Between National Courts and the European Court of Justice

It is a fact that European integration has been accomplished through law and relies heavily on courts, in particular on the system of judicial cooperation established by the preliminary-ruling mechanism provided by Article 267 TFEU.[14] Ordinary

[11] The classical example of this being the German Constitutional Court with its *Maastricht Treaty* judgment (Case 2 BvR 2134/92 and 2 BvR 2159/92, judgment of 12 October 1993) and with its *Lisbon Treaty* judgment (Case 2 BverfG 2/08, judgment of 30 June 2009).

[12] A good example may be the pan-European saga of the transposition of the European Arrest Warrant (2002/584/JHA): instead of framing the debate in terms of the protection of fundamental rights of national citizens versus the advancement of European judicial integration, constitutional courts preferred to review the constitutionality of the national legislation implementing the European Arrest Warrant and then proceeded to make only marginal corrections. Another illustrative example may be the pan-European saga of the constitutional review of the national transpositions of the Data Retention Directive 2006/24, which ended up with the invalidation of the European legal act by the ECJ in its judgment in Case C-293/12 *Digital Rights Ireland* (judgment of 8 April 2014, EU:C:2014:238).

[13] The rule of law crisis has drawn the attention of European and even international scholarship. Among many others, see Laurent Pech and Kim Lane Scheppele "Illiberalism Within: Rule of Law Backsliding in the EU" (2017) 19 *CYELS* 3; Melanie Smith, "Staring into the Abyss: A crisis of the rule of law in the EU" (2019) 25 *European Law Journal* 561; Tímea Drinóczi and Agnieszka Bień-Kacała (eds.), *Rule of Law, Common Values, and Illiberal Constitutionalism: Poland and Hungary within the European Union* (2020, Routledge & CRC Press); Elena Simina Tănăsescu, "The independence of justice as proxy for the rule of law in the EU. Case study—Romania" (2021) 3(1) *Nuovi Autoritarismi e Democrazie: Diritto, Istituzioni, Società (NAD)* 103; Anna Gora and Pieter de Wilde, "The essence of democratic backsliding in the European Union: deliberation and rule of law" (2022) 29(3) *Journal of European Public Policy* 342.

[14] See notably the judgments of the ECJ in Cases C-188/10 and C-189/10 *Melki and Abdeli* (judgment of 22 June 2010, EU:C:2010:363); Case C-614/14 *Ognyanov* (judgment of 5 July 2016, EU:C:2016:514); Case C-564/19 *IS (Illegality of the order for reference)* (judgment of 23 November 2021, EU:C:2021:949), Case C-430/21 *RS* (judgment of 22 February 2022, EU:C:2022:99).

courts of Member States are at the same time ordinary courts of the European Union, and the first ones to be confronted with claims of European citizens in search of efficient protection for the rights bestowed upon them by the legal order of the EU.[15] Every now and then, constitutional courts have also been invited to participate in this process: sometimes they have protected the fundamental rights of European Union citizens in competition with the ECJ.

But the relationship between the ECJ and the constitutional courts of Member States has been a complex one, scattered with ups and downs.[16] Although most often at European level, it is those decisions of constitutional courts in which they seem to oppose EU sovereignty that are spoken of,[17] the daily business of constitutional courts is relatively far removed from issues relating to interactions between European Union and national legal systems and closer to the fulfilment of the rule of law at grassroots level. The mutual influence of the European Court of Justice and of constitutional courts is generally fruitful for the protection of fundamental rights of European Union citizens,[18] while remaining beneficial also for European integration.[19]

Nevertheless, there are also instances of constitutional conflicts between the Court of Justice and constitutional courts, some constructive and some disruptive. The failure to engage in dialogue between the Romanian Constitutional Court (RCC) and the European Court of Justice, illustrated by the now (in)famous decision 390/2021 of the Romanian Constitutional Court and the equally renowned European Court of Justice judgment in *RS* of 22 February 2022[20] may be reckoned as one instance among many other examples of disruptive constitutional conflict. Mention must be made here that there are good hopes that, in the case of the Romanian Constitutional Court, this disruption has been only temporary and will remain short-lived.

---

[15] The codification of the principle of effectiveness, first, in the Charter of Fundamental Rights, and later in the Treaty on the European Union has not resulted in harmonised EU judicial protection of substantive rights derived from EU law. Rather, it has referred the issue again to national courts. For the difference between the principle enshrined in Art. 19 TEU and the subjective right guaranteed in Art. 47 of the Charter and the linguistic variation in Art. 19 TEU between French and English, see Sacha Prechal, "Effective Judicial Protection: some recent developments—moving to the essence" (2020) 13(2) *Review of European Administrative Law* 178.

[16] Ana Bobić, *The Jurisprudence of Constitutional Conflict in the European Union* (2022, Oxford University Press).

[17] See in particular the Czech Constitutional Court Decision Pl. ÚS 5/12, following the judgment of the European Court of Justice in Case C-399/09 *Landtova* (judgment of 22 June 2011, EU:C:2011:415); the Danish Supreme Court Decision in Case 15/2014, *Dansk Industri*, following the judgment of the Court of Justice in Case C-441/14 *Dansk Industri v Rasmussen* (judgment of 19 April 2016, EU:C:2016:278); and the German Bundesverfassungsgericht, Order of the Second Senate of 29 April 2021—2 BvR 1651/15 (the so-called *'PSPP'* case), following the judgment of the European Court of Justice in Case C-493/17 *Weiss and Others* (judgment of 11 December 2018, EU:C:2018:1000). More recently, see also the Polish Constitutional Tribunal Judgment of 7 October 2021 in *Case No. K 3/21.*

[18] See, for instance, judgment of the Court of Justice in Case C-36/02 *Omega* (judgment of 14 October 2004, EU:C:2004:614).

[19] See, for instance, judgment of the Court of Justice in Case C-62/14 *Gauweiler* (judgment of 16 June 2015, EU:C:2015:400).

[20] Case C-430/21 *RS* (judgment of 22 February 2022, EU:C:2022:99).

3 A Missed Opportunity to Engage in Dialogue Between the Romanian Constitutional Court and the ECJ

In a nutshell–and leaving many other aspects aside–Decision 390/2021 of the Romanian Constitutional Court stated that (i) the primacy of European Union law only applies to ordinary national legislation and not to the Romanian Constitution because it cannot be conceived as "removing or disregarding the national constitutional identity, enshrined in Article 11(3) in conjunction with Article 152 of the Basic Law"[21] and (ii) national courts do not have the power to examine the conformity with European law of national provisions found constitutional by the Romanian Constitutional Court in the light of Article 148 of the Romanian Constitution.[22]

Two judges signed a separate opinion declaring that both above-mentioned conclusions contradict not only binding European Union law and established case law of the ECJ, but also Article 148 of the Romanian Constitution,[23] which provides for the systematic and compulsory primacy of European Union law over national law.

In short–and passing over a lot of the substance of this landmark ruling too–in its judgment in *RS*,[24] the European Court of Justice reiterated that ordinary courts cannot be prevented from assessing the compatibility with European Union law of national legislation which the constitutional court has found to be consistent with a national constitutional provision providing for the primacy of EU law, all the more so under the threat of disciplinary liability on the part of the incumbent judge(s).

From the above summaries, it looks like each of the two courts remained confined in its own paradigm, proffering its own monologue.

4 Specific Background

Let us also briefly remind ourselves of the context of this dispute. Together with Bulgaria, Romania joined the European Union on 1 January 2007 subject to an original post-accession conditionality. A Cooperation and Verification Mechanism (CVM) established by Decision 2006/928/EC of 13 December 2006 with regard

---

[21] See para 81 of the ruling.

[22] See para 83 of the ruling.

[23] Article 148 of the Romanian Constitution explicitly provides that

> [...] "(2) As a result of the accession, the provisions of the constituent treaties of the European Union, as well as the other mandatory community regulations shall take precedence over the opposite provisions of national laws, in compliance with the provisions of the accession act." and [...] "(4) The Parliament, the President of Romania, the Government, and the judicial authority shall guarantee that the obligations resulting from the accession act and the provisions of para (2) are implemented".

[24] Case C-430/21 *RS* (judgment of 22 February 2022, EU:C:2022:99).

to Romania was intended to assess the progress made by the new Member State in the areas of judicial reform and the fight against corruption, based on a set of specific benchmarks. Until 2022,[25] the European Commission issued a report each year assessing the situation and presenting recommendations meant to correct the course of the Member State in its endeavours to comply with the EU *acquis* in the relevant areas. In 2023 the European Commission decided to formally put an end to the Cooperation and Verification Mechanism.[26]

However, as of 2016 and until 2020, regular reports issued by the European Commission mentioned "possible systemic threats to the rule of law". In fact, rule of law backsliding started to manifest in Romania after the general elections of December 2016,[27] while a short but intense attack on independent justice took place between 2018 and 2019, with the adoption of laws concerning the judicial system which, among other things, entailed the creation of a special prosecutorial section meant to investigate crimes carried out by magistrates, and introduced sub-optimal changes concerning the personal liability of magistrates.

Democratic decay and rule of law backsliding are phenomena which are not specific to Romania, or indeed only to countries which have recently joined the European Union, although they do raise certain concerns regarding the enlargement process.[28] But in order to counteract these developments, the European Union resorted to its customary creativity and managed actually to deepen integration. Thus, the EU devised new instruments, such as the Cooperation and Verification Mechanism, which were tailor-made for Bulgaria and Romania; the set of transversal instruments related to the rule of law,[29] which were meant for all Member States; and the general conditionalities attached to loans or funds.[30] Initially based on the

---

[25] In November 2022, the European Commission announced that the benchmarks under the Cooperation and Verification Mechanism had been satisfactorily met by Romania and that therefore monitoring under this instrument would stop, while the Member State would remain subject to the annual reports issued by the European Commission within the Rule of Law Mechanism (see <https://ec.europa.eu/commission/presscorner/detail/en/ip_22_7029> (last accessed on 23 December 2022).

[26] See Commission Decision (EU) 2023/1786 of 15 September 2023 repealing Decision 2006/928/EC establishing a mechanism for cooperation and verification of progress in Romania to address specific benchmarks in the areas of judicial reform and the fight against corruption.

[27] Elena Simina Tănăsescu (2019) "From Constitutional Democracy to Constitutional Decay?" in Violeta Beširević. (ed.) *New Politics of Decisionism* (2019, Eleven International Publishing) at pp. 177–191.

[28] It has been noted that some Member States have been happy to receive the benefits of EU membership—specifically the financial ones—while their commitment to European values, including the rule of law (see Article 2 TEU), has been lacking. (See Justyna Łacny, "The Rule of Law Conditionality Under Regulation No 2092/2020—Is it all About the Money?" (2021) 13 *Hague Journal on the Rule of Law* 79).

[29] See *A new EU Framework to strengthen the Rule of Law* (COM/2014/0158 final) and the related reports issued yearly by the European Commission within the Rule of Law Mechanism (see <https://commission.europa.eu/strategy-and-policy/policies/justice-and-fundamental-rights/upholding-rule-law/rule-law/rule-law-mechanism_en> accessed 10 December 2023); and *Strengthening the rule of law within the Union. A blueprint for action* (COM/2019/343 final).

[30] Regulation 2020/2092 of the European Parliament and of the Council of 16 December 2020 on a general regime of conditionality for the protection of the Union budget.

voluntary character of the compliance expected from targeted Member States, some of these new instruments have evolved and been transformed into compulsory tools, such as the Cooperation and Verification Mechanism. Others have been criticised by doctrine as being in excess of European Union competencies, such as the general conditionalities attached to EU funds.[31] But the general outcome of all these new instruments has been more efficient European integration and a constant expansion in European Union powers.[32] The European Court of Justice has closely followed these normative evolutions, at times even colliding with some Member States.[33] The missed opportunity to engage in dialogue between the Romanian Constitutional Court and the European Court of Justice has to be placed—and analysed—against this general background. Its disruptive characteristics may well remain confined to this context since, on other occasions, the Romanian Constitutional Court has used the opportunity to develop a constructive dialogue[34] with the Court of Justice, although it has not reached the "apotheosis of a supportive attitude".[35]

5 Brief Analysis

Specifically concerning the parallel monologues developed by the Romanian Constitutional Court and the European Court of Justice in the above-mentioned rulings, two conclusions can be drawn. On the one hand, judicial autarchy of the type illustrated by the Romanian Constitutional Court in its Decision 390/2021, where it resolved to ignore the primacy of European Union law and attempted to attract all national courts into the same type of absolutist attitude, cannot provide insulation from European integration–but it can induce legal consequences that may entail state responsibility and hamper its proper functioning.

---

[31] Michael Ioannidis, "Europe's new transformations. How the EU economic constitution changed during the eurozone crisis" (2016) 53 *Common Market Law Review* 1237.

[32] This has been the case notably with the creation of the European common currency (the 'euro') in the absence of economic integration among Member States; with European fiscal federalism introduced via the requirement of national balanced budgets after the financial crisis of 2008–2009 in the absence of political governance; and with the continuous transfer of fiscal powers from national to the supranational level through the Recovery and Resilience Plan after the COVID-19 pandemic. (See Elena Simina Tănăsescu, Eric Oliva (eds.) *Constitutional Law and the EU Balanced Budget* (2022, Routledge)).

[33] See, for instance, the judgment of the Court of Justice in Case C-156/21 *Hungary v Parliament and Council* (judgment of 16 February 2022, EU:C:2022:97) and Case C-157/21 *Poland v Parliament and Council* (judgment of 16 February 2022, EU:C:2022:98).

[34] See the judgment of the Court of Justice in Case C-673/16 *Coman* (judgment of 5 June 2018, EU:C:2018:385).

[35] According to Claes, the apotheosis of a supportive attitude that a constitutional court may display with regard to the ECJ involves not only compliance with the duty to refer a preliminary question to the Court of Justice but also implementation of the Court's ruling on the respective matter. (See Monica Claes, "Luxembourg, Here We Come? Constitutional Courts and the Preliminary Reference Procedure" (2015) 16 *German Law Journal* 1331).

On the other hand, upon accession to the European Union, ordinary courts of Member States are not only endowed with additional powers as ordinary judges of EU law, which require cooperation with the ECJ in order to ensure the effective protection of rights bestowed upon European citizens by both the national and the European legal orders, but they also become a sort of buffer between the European Court of Justice and their respective constitutional courts, permanent 'collateral victims' of the battle between those two giants. However, their role in the European judicial dialogue is too important for them to be sacrificed on the altar of a destructive interaction between the ECJ and constitutional courts. Rather their essential function within the European judicial paradigm should induce an open attitude towards a harmonious implementation of European Union law right across the spectrum of stakeholders, including the ECJ and constitutional courts, and various other actors, such as European citizens.

6 Primacy of European Union Law

Thus, on the one hand, the primacy of European Union law over the national legal systems of Member States no longer needs to any presentation to us. It is the established case law of the European Court of Justice,[36] with the status of a general principle of European Union law, and it is provided for in a declaration[37] annexed to the Final Act of the Intergovernmental Conference which adopted the Treaty of Lisbon. The European Court of Justice has form in declaring that EU law takes precedence over any provision of national law, including national constitutions.[38] Some constitutional courts, notably the German Federal Constitutional Court, have contested this all-encompassing approach based on the assumption that the European Union is a creation of Member States and, by extension, of their Constitutions and not vice versa. On the other hand, it is also fair to say that Member States have never attempted to correct the case law of the Court of Justice on primacy despite the many opportunities offered, in particular upon iterative revisions of the founding treaties of

---

[36] It is the settled case-law of the ECJ that, unlike standard international treaties, the Community and European Union Treaties established a new legal order, integrated into the legal systems of the Member States and which is binding on their courts. As Member States transferred certain powers to the EU, they limited their sovereign rights, and, in order for EU norms to be effective, these norms must take precedence over any provision of national law, including national constitutions. (See notably the judgments of the Court of Justice in Case 26/62 *van Gend en Loos* (judgment of 5 February 1963, EU:C:1963:1); Case 6/64 *Costa* (judgment of 15 July 1964, EU:C:1964:66); Case 11/70 *Internationale Handelsgesellschaft* (judgment of 17 December 1970, EU:C:1970:114).

[37] See Declaration 17 concerning primacy annexed to the Final Act of the Intergovernmental Conference which adopted the Treaty of Lisbon.

[38] See notably the judgments of the Court of Justice in Case 11/70 *Internationale Handelsgesellschaft* (judgment of 17 December 1970, EU:C:1970:114); Case 106/77 *Simmenthal* (judgment of 9 March 1978, EU:C:1978:49); and Cases C-357/19, C-379/19, C-547/19, C-811/19 and C-840/19) *Euro Box Promotion and Others* (judgment of 21 December 2021, EU:C:2021:1034).

the European Union.[39] On the contrary, Member States agreed on the Treaty establishing a Constitution for Europe, which failed to enter into force only due to the special situation at the time in two Member States (France and the Netherlands). Furthermore, the Member States subsequently agreed on Declaration 17 annexed to the Final Act of the Intergovernmental Conference which adopted the Treaty of Lisbon. It all boils down to a perceived competition between sovereignty prerogatives and parallel claims of ultimate authority among the European Union and the Member States.[40] Euclidian geometry could not solve the problem of squaring this particular circle and I will not attempt to find a solution to the competing European and Member States' sovereignties. It is sufficient here to acknowledge that the European Union cannot exist in the absence of the primacy of EU law, as the European Court of Justice has amply explained in its case law.

It is therefore even more interesting to note that, in the specific case of Romania, this acknowledgement has not only been the object of constant pre-accession evaluations, but also of a revision of the national constitution meant to pave the way for the country's accession to the European Union. The very fact that the amendment of the Romanian Constitution in 2003 introduced Article 148 into the text of the fundamental law is a proof that, in Romania, primacy of EU law has both supranational and constitutional value. As mentioned in the separate opinion to Decision 390/2021,

> it is the will of the Romanian constituent power to impose on all Romanian public authorities the systematic priority of application of EU law over conflicting provisions of national law, as a legal obligation at national level which duplicates the one established by the settled case-law of the CJEU at supranational level.[41]

Therefore, both Decision 2006/928/EC of 13 December 2006 and the Cooperation and Verification Mechanism it established enjoy primacy over contrary national provisions based on Article 148 of the Romanian Constitution and on the general principle of European Union law. The common perception that, although it had been meant as a cooperation tool between the European Commission and Romanian authorities, the Cooperation and Verification Mechanism grew into a fully-fledged and binding post-accession conditionality, does not alter its legal nature and consequences. Decision 2006/928/EC is and remains a normative act within the EU

---

[39] Karen J. Alter, "Who Are the 'Masters of the Treaty'? European Governments and the European Court of Justice" in Karen J. Alter, *The European Court´s Political Power* (2009, Oxford University Press) at p.109.

[40] Michael Dougan, "When Worlds Collide! Competing Visions of the Relationship between Direct Effect and Supremacy" (2007) 44 *Common Market Law Review* 931.

[41] Separate opinion to the Romanian Constitutional Court's decision 390/2021, signed by Livia Doina Stanciu and Elena Simina Tănăsescu and published in the Official Monitor no. 612 of 22 June 2021.

legal order.[42] The same applies to the benchmarks appended to the Cooperation and Verification Mechanism, as the European Court of Justice has clearly underlined.[43]

Nevertheless, the *yearly reports* issued by the European Commission are nothing more than a continuation of the pre-accession monitoring of this Member State–just as the reports issued yearly by the European Commission under the Rule of Law Mechanism are a monitoring tool of the significant developments relating to the rule of law in all Member States. They are not devoid of legal consequences, but they are not enforceable.[44] Their constraining value remains debatable, as the recent case law of the ECJ shows.[45] The fact that these reports are issued on the basis of directly applicable and enforceable normative acts of the European Union, which also benefit from primacy and are under the jurisdiction of the ECJ, cannot alter their legal nature as soft law.[46] Ordinary courts cannot be expected to disapply national provisions based on their contradicting findings in monitoring reports. In this tiny but formal and legal respect, Decision 390/2021 of the Romanian Constitutional Court is correct: the primacy of EU law cannot include such yearly reports of the Commission due to their non-normative value, i.e., because they are "recommendations, issued for political

---

[42] In this context it is worth mentioning that the Cooperation and Verification Mechanism has been criticised as inefficient, discriminatory and even illegitimate. See Dimitry Kochenov, *EU Enlargement and the Failure of Conditionality* (2008, Kluwer Law International); Linka Toneva-Metodieva, "Beyond the carrots and sticks paradigm: Rethinking the Cooperation and Verification Mechanism experience of Bulgaria and Romania" (2014) 15 *Perspectives on European Politics and Society* 534; Georgi Dimitrov, Anna Plachkova, "Bulgaria and Romania, twin Cinderellas in the European Union: How they contributed in a peculiar way to the change in EU policy for the promotion of democracy and rule of law" (2021) 22 *European Politics and Society* 167.

[43] See in particular paras 174 to 177 of the judgment of the Court of Justice in Cases C-83/19, C-127/19, C-195/19, C-291/19, C-355/19 and C-397/19 *AFRJ* (judgment of 18 May 2021, EU:C:2021:393).

[44] As also noted in the Opinion of Advocate General Bobek (EU:C:2020:746) in the judgment of the Court of Justice in Cases C-83/19, C 127/19, C 195/19, C 291/19, C 355/19 and C 397/19 *AFRJ* (judgment of 18 May 2021, EU:C:2021:393). For a critical appraisal of that Opinion see Ondrej Kadlec and David Kosar, "Romanian version of the rule of law crisis comes to the ECJ: The AFRJ case is not just about the Cooperation and Verification Mechanism" (2022) 59 *Common Market Law Review* 1.

[45] See in particular para 174 of the judgment of the Court of Justice in Cases C-83/19, C 127/19, C 195/19, C 291/19, C 355/19 and C 397/19 *AFRJ* (judgment of 18 May 2021, EU:C:2021:393):

> [...] it is true that the reports drawn up on the basis of Decision 2006/928 are [...] not addressed to Romania but to the Parliament and the Council. Furthermore, although those reports include an analysis of the situation in Romania and formulate requirements with regard to that Member State, the conclusions set out therein address 'recommendations' to Romania on the basis of those requirements.

[46] Oana Ştefan, "Apărarea statului de drept între noua guvernanţă şi guvernare, între autonomia dreptului European şi suveranitatea naţională (The defense of the rule of law between the new governance and government, between the autonomy of EU law and national sovereignty)" in Valeriu Stoica (ed.) *CJUE si CCR—Identităţi în dialog (Identities in Dialogue)* (2022, Universul Juridic) 430.

purposes, for the attention of the European Council and European Parliament" (para 45), not addressed to Romanian authorities.

For the sake of clarity, it is worth mentioning that the teleological explanations provided by the European Court of Justice with regard to the general constraining value of these reports are also correct.[47] It is true that the principle of sincere cooperation stipulated by Article 4 (3) TEU obliges any Member State to take all the measures necessary to guarantee the application and effectiveness of European Union law and to eliminate the unlawful consequences of a breach of that law, in particular of breaches of the values enshrined in Article 2 of the TEU, on the protection of which the European Court of Justice requires non-regression.[48] The ECJ asserted expressly that "in particular, Romania cannot adopt or maintain measures in the areas covered by the benchmarks which could jeopardise the result prescribed by those requirements and recommendations".[49] In other words, diminishing the independence of the administration of justice, despite contrary benchmarks and clear recommendations in European Commission reports, is equivalent to a breach of European Union law that may even entail state responsibility.[50] But this type of negative obligation (non-regression) belongs with the legislator, which should not have adopted or should have repealed the relevant laws, and not with the judicial system, which cannot either ignore or replace them. The empowerment of ordinary courts implied by this type of reasoning is far-reaching and may hurt the separation of powers and other domestic institutional arrangements that constitutional courts have to protect. The Romanian Constitutional Court was right to signal this aspect, although it did so in an awkward manner, purposefully ignoring the constraining force of benchmarks, the normative value of Decision 2006/928/EC and their blatant inconsistency with the laws pertaining to the reform of the Romanian judiciary that the Constitutional Court had reviewed and declared constitutional.

---

[47] See in particular paras 175 and 176 of the judgment of the Court of Justice in Cases C-83/19, C 127/19, C 195/19, C 291/19, C 355/19 and C 397/19 *AFRJ* (judgment of 18 May 2021, EU:C:2021:393):

> [...] the reports are intended to analyse and evaluate Romania's progress in the light of the benchmarks which Romania must address and [...] in order to comply with the benchmarks set out in the Annex to Decision 2006/928, Romania must take due account of the requirements and recommendations formulated in the reports drawn up by the Commission under that decision.

[48] See paras 63 and 64 in the judgment of the Court of Justice in Case C-896/19 *Republikka* (judgment of 20 April 2021, EU:C:2021:311).

[49] Paragraph 177 in the judgment of the Court of Justice in Cases C-83/19, C 127/19, C 195/19, C 291/19, C 355/19 and C 397/19 *AFRJ* (judgment of 18 May 2021, EU:C:2021:393).

[50] The ECJ has already ruled that, if a Member State fails to fulfil its obligations under EU law, the responsibility of that state may be established irrespective of the state agency whose action or inaction has been at stake, either according to Article 258 TFEU (see ECJ, *Commission v France (Advance payment)* Case C-416/17 (judgment of 4 October 2018, EU:C:2018:811) or according to the principle of state liability (see ECJ, *Köbler* Case C-224/01 (judgment of 30 September 2003, EU:C:2003:513).

7 Ordinary Courts as Buffers Between Constitutional Courts and the European Court of Justice

On the other hand, ordinary courts are not only the centrepiece of the judicial paradigm of European integration. However, more often than not, they fall between the cracks of judicial integration, which ideally should be perfected through judicial dialogue, but which is sometimes accomplished through judicial conflict. That ordinary courts can set aside national legislation found contrary to European Union law, particularly when this has also been confirmed in a ruling of the European Court of Justice, is well-known in EU law.[51]

In Decision 390/2021, the Romanian Constitutional Court declared that

> point 7 of the operative part of ECJ judgment in AFRJ is not based on the provisions of the Romanian Constitution [...] and the Romanian judge cannot be put in the position of deciding to give priority to the application of recommendations over national law [...] the more so when the relevant national law has been declared compliant with the national constitutional provision providing for the primacy of EU law by the national constitutional court.[52]

Point 7 of the operative part of ECJ judgment in *AFRJ* states that

> the principle of the primacy of EU law must be interpreted as precluding legislation of a Member State having constitutional status, as interpreted by the constitutional court of that Member State, according to which a lower court is not permitted to disapply of its own motion a national provision falling within the scope of Decision 2006/928, which it considers, in the light of a judgment of the Court, to be contrary to that decision or to the second subparagraph of Article 19(1) TEU.

The autarchy of the Romanian Constitutional Court in Decision 390/2021 is obvious when it requires the ECJ to use as a standard for the review it performs the Romanian Constitution and not European Union law. Its naughtiness becomes palpable when it accuses the European Court of Justice of applying European Union law to a specific case,[53] thus implying that the Court of Justice (in its *AFRJ* judgment) has acted *ultra vires*. Furthermore, any possibility for ordinary courts to review

---

[51] See point 7 of the operative part of the judgment of the Court of Justice in Cases C-83/19, C 127/19, C 195/19, C 291/19, C 355/19 and C 397/19 *AFRJ* (judgment of 18 May 2021, EU:C:2021:393):

> national courts — as courts applying EU law — are required, as far as possible, to interpret national law in conformity with the requirements of EU law in order to ensure the full effectiveness of EU law and are authorised to disapply on their own motion national provisions falling within the scope of Decision 2006/928 and which they consider, in the light of a judgment of the Court, to be contrary to that decision or to the second subparagraph of Article 19(1) TEU.

[52] Paragraph 85 of the Court's judgment.

[53] Paragraph 78 of Romanian Constitutional Court decision 390/2021:

> Although Article 267 TFEU does not empower the ECJ to apply the rules of Union law to a particular case, but only to rule on the interpretation of the Treaties and of acts adopted by the Union institutions, the referring court being responsible for ruling on those matters after making the necessary assessments, the ECJ does not confine itself to 'providing the national

the conformity with European Union law of national legislation found in conformity with Article 148 of the Romanian Constitution is ruled out because the Romanian Constitutional Court declares that a law which passes this constitutionality test is necessarily irreproachable, including from the perspective of European Union law. Consequently, an ordinary court is allowed neither to assess and set aside national legislation which has been deemed compatible with Article 148 of the Romanian Constitution by the Romanian Constitutional Court, nor to send preliminary questions to the European Court of Justice with regard to those national legal provisions. In Decision 390/2021 the Romanian Constitutional Court not only voluntarily eliminates any analysis or legal arguments that could contradict its dicta, but also flatly refuses the mere possibility that any types of review of laws other than the one that it performs are possible, a head-in-the-sand approach that fails any reality check.

The separate opinion to Decision 390/2021 observed that

> from the perspective of the RCC the present case does not involve a contradiction between the Romanian Constitution and the normative content of Decision 2006/928/EC, but the analysis of the compliance of some provisions of the national law on judicial organisation with the constitutional norms pertaining to the rule of law, equality and legality. At the same time, from the perspective of Romanian ordinary courts and of the European Court of Justice, the cases they had to rule upon referred to the compliance of some provisions of the national law on judicial organisation with clear, unconditional and effective legal provisions relating to the rule of law and the independence of the judiciary from EU law.

The norms reviewed are the same, but the standards used and the courts performing the review are different. Therefore, it is possible that the results produced by two different types of review are also different.

In its *RS* judgment,[54] the European Court of Justice felt compelled to state that "deterring a national court hearing a case governed by European Union law from exercising the discretion or satisfying the obligation, under Article 267 TFEU, to refer to the Court of Justice questions concerning the interpretation or validity of acts of EU law"–because the national court is bound by a decision of the national constitutional court that has found the national legislation consistent with a national constitutional provision providing for the primacy of European Union law–is contrary to EU law: and the more so when the above is all done under the threat of disciplinary liability for the respective national judge(s).

Ordinary courts in Romania seemed trapped whichever direction they decided to take. If they complied with the decision of the Romanian Constitutional Court, they were bound not to comply with the judgment of the European Court of Justice and, thus, incurred liability for infringing EU law; if they complied with the judgment of the ECJ, they were not obeying the decision of the Romanian Constitutional Court

> court with the elements of interpretation of European Union law which may be useful to it in assessing the effects of one or other of its provisions', as it has held in its own case-law.

For a similar critique of some judgments of the ECJ see Monica Claes and Maartje de Visser, "Are you networked yet? On dialogues in European Judicial networks" (2012) 8(2) *Utrecht Law Review* 104.

54 Case C-430/21 *RS* (judgment of 22 February 2022, EU:C:2022:99).

and, thus, could have seen their disciplinary liability engaged. In addition, where the Romanian Constitutional Court, had declared legal provisions compliant with Article 148 of the Constitution, ordinary courts could no longer address preliminary questions to the European Court of Justice.

This was an untenable situation for several reasons. First, because such an institutional arrangement infringes the independence of the administration of justice, a paramount prerequisite of any state governed by the rule of law,[55] and it is important to underline here once more that the rule of law is a standard for the constitutionality review performed by the Romanian Constitutional Court as well as for the review performed by the European Court of Justice.[56] Secondly, because in Romania the Romanian Constitutional Court has only conferred powers, whereas ordinary courts enjoy a general jurisdiction; therefore, limiting their all-encompassing jurisdiction through decisions of the RCC contradicts the tenets of the national judicial architecture. Thirdly, because forbidding the interaction of ordinary courts with the European Court of Justice equates to denying the effectiveness of Romania's integration in the European Union and contradicts the very purpose of the constitutional amendment[57] adopted in 2003, as well as the Accession Treaty signed and ratified by Romania in 2005. Last but not the least, because such an approach is in contradiction with established case law of the European Court of Justice.[58] It is therefore logical that Romanian ordinary courts resorted to strategic litigation, addressing the European Court of Justice in "waves",[59] while the Court of Justice obliged them by confirming its constant case law in favour of the independence of justice.[60]

In the institutional triangle created by constitutional courts, ordinary courts and the European Court of Justice, ordinary courts enjoy the most delicate position: a buffer between two giants, with which they nevertheless have to cooperate loyally. The interaction between the European Court of Justice and constitutional courts does not necessarily have to pass through the mediation of ordinary courts. Recent case law of the ECJ has shown instances where this type of interaction has been mediated

[55] Elena Simina Tănăsescu, "The independence of justice as proxy for the rule of law in the EU. Case study—Romania" (2021) 3(1) *Nuovi Autoritarismi e Democrazie: Diritto, Istituzioni, Società (NAD)* 103.

[56] Paul Craig "The Rule of Law and the EU: Responsibility, Independence and Rights" in Allan Rosas, Juha Raitio and Pekka Pohjankoski (eds.), *The Rule of Law's Anatomy in the EU: Foundations and Protections* (2023, Hart Publishing/Bloomsbury Publishing) 29.

[57] Over time, a number of Member States have revised their Constitutions in order to allow more efficient European integration. See François-Xavier Millet, "How Much Lenience for How Much Cooperation ? On the first Preliminary Reference of the French Conseil Constitutionnel to the Court of Justice" (2014) 51(1) *Common Market Law Review* 195.

[58] See notably the judgment of the ECJ in Case C-188/10 *Melki and Abdeli* (judgment of 22 June 2010, EU:C:2010:363).

[59] Mădălina Moraru and Raluca Bercea, "The First Episode in the Romanian Rule of Law Saga: Joined Cases C-83/19, C-127/19, C-195/19, C-291/19, C-355/19 and C-397/19, Asociatia Forumul Judecatorilor din România, and their follow-up at the national level" (2022) 18(1) *European Constitutional Law Review* 85.

[60] Starting with the seminal judgment of the Court of Justice in Case C-64/16 *Associação Sindical dos Juízes Portugueses* (judgment of 27 February 2018, EU:C:2018:117).

by the European Commission through infringement procedures.[61] Issues regarding 'the final arbiter'[62] on disputes pertaining to European Union powers and their limits may arise in absence of preliminary references from ordinary courts of Member States. However, the European Court of Justice and constitutional courts should be able to develop their own direct dialogue. Nevertheless, irrespective of their open and straightforward interaction or implicit and indirect interplay, both the European Court of Justice and constitutional courts may wish to be careful not to crush ordinary courts, who remain the foot soldiers of European Union law.

8 Conclusion

The conclusions set out here may be well known but deserve nonetheless to be remembered. The dialogue between the European Court of Justice and constitutional courts is and remains necessary. In some cases, the judicial dialogue between the ECJ and constitutional courts has evolved from sharp conflict to careful confrontation and, even further, to a genuine exchange of ideas.[63] When mediated by ordinary courts, the ordinary courts have either thrived or, on the contrary, they have endured harsh consequences, but they have remained an essential link in the European judicial dialogue. However, for this European judicial dialogue to be complete, it has to encompass direct interaction between the European Court of Justice and constitutional courts and not only their interplay mediated by other actors.[64] The European Union legal order provides for an efficient tool for this dialogue to take place, namely the judicial cooperation induced by the preliminary reference regulated by Article 267 TFEU. Several constitutional courts have used it, some with more success than others.[65]

---

[61] See, for instance, the judgment of the Court of Justice in Case C-192/18 *Commission v. Poland* (judgment of 5 November 2019, EU:C:2019:924) or Case C-619/18 *Commission v. Poland* (judgment of 11 July 2019, EU:C:2019:615) or Case C-791/19 *Commission v. Poland* (judgment of 15 July 2021, EU:C:2021:596) as well as the ruling of the Polish Constitutional Tribunal in *Case No. K 3/21* (judgment of 7 October 2021).

[62] Mattias Kumm, "Who is the final arbiter of constitutionality in Europe: Three conceptions of the relationship between the German Federal Constitutional Court and the European Court of Justice" (1999) 36(2) *Common Market Law Review* 351.

[63] Marta Cartabia, "Europe as a Space of Constitutional Interdependence: New Questions about the Preliminary Ruling" (2015) 16 (6) *German Law Journal—Special issue: 'Preliminary References to the Court of Justice of The European Union by Constitutional Courts'* 1791.

[64] The indirect dialogue mediated by the European Commission through the infringement procedures should rather be avoided.

[65] For instance, the Belgian Constitutional Court has been noted for its openness towards European law, a point demonstrated by the large number of references for preliminary rulings it has made to the ECJ. See Willem Verrijdt, "Belgium" in Stefan Griller, Lina Papadopoulou and Roman Puff (eds.), *National Constitutions and EU Integration*, (2022, Hart Publishing) at p. 29. On the fruitful dialogue between the Italian Constitutional Court and the ECJ, see Silvana Sciarra "First and Last Word: Can Constitutional Courts and the Court of Justice of the EU Speak Common Words?" (2022 (3) *Eurojus*) available online at <https://rivista.eurojus.it/wp-content/uploads/pdf/here-3.pdf> (last accessed on 23 December 2022).

As far as direct dialogue between the European Court of Justice and constitutional courts is concerned, the ECJ has consistently claimed exclusive jurisdiction on matters relating to the validity of European Union law, thus implying that it has the last word on the conferral of powers within the European Union, with the risk of alienating constitutional courts and despite the fact that European sovereignty and national sovereignty are intertwined. On the other hand, constitutional courts are used to having the last word in matters relating to the fundamental laws of their lands and to perform the role of the last guardians of the fundamental rights of their citizens, sometimes forgetting that these are also European citizens endowed with fundamental rights at European level as well. For its part, the Romanian Constitutional Court has already been advised "to accept that it cannot have the last word on the primacy of European Union law"[66] and to use more often the mechanism of preliminary references,[67] a mechanism already used by it — although only once — in the past.

Against this general background, it is interesting to note that, in the particular case at hand, at the end of the day and despite the contrary will of the Romanian Constitutional Court, an indirect and implicit dialogue of sorts did start between the European Court of Justice and the Constitutional Court of Romania, but this was mediated by ordinary courts, which had to fight for the acknowledgment of their jurisdiction. Let us hope that future iterations of interactions between the Romanian Constitutional Court and the European Court of Justice will be direct, open, fruitful and will go beyond the current stage of parallel monologues.

[66] Fabian Gyula, "Principiul primordialității dreptului Uniunii Europene și ideea identității constituționale promovată de Curtea Constituțională a României (The principle of primacy of EU law and the ideea of constitutional identity promoted by the Constitutional Court of Romania)" (2022) XXI (7) *Curierul Judiciar* 389.

[67] The Romanian Constitutional Court had explicitly refused to send a preliminary question to the ECJ on the laws pertaining to the judicial reform in Decision no.137/2019. This has been considered by Romanian scholarship to have been a missed opportunity. (See Constantin Pintilie, "Curtea Constituțională a României la o răscruce de drumuri (The Constitutional Court at a Crossroads)" (2021, *Juridice*) available online at <https://www.juridice.ro/732329/curtea-constitutionala-a-romaniei-la-o-rascruce-de-drumuri.html> accessed on 10 December 2023).

National and European Sovereignty in the European Union: An Irresoluble Conflict? The Position of the Czech Constitutional Court

Jiří Zemánek

Abstract This article seeks to argue that sovereignty is no longer attributable only to a State. It is also attributable to the European Union in areas of high politics. Its role is a functional, instrumental one: to legitimise and authorise the conferring of elements of the power of national authorities on supranational institutions as well as to safeguard *ultima ratio* their appropriate use.

This article seeks to argue that sovereignty is no longer attributable only to a State. It is attributable to the European Union in areas of high politics, as well. Its role is a functional, instrumental one: to legitimise and authorise the conferring of elements of the power of national authorities on supranational institutions as well as to safeguard *ultima ratio* their appropriate use. The multilevel nature of European Union law justifies functionally equal criteria being used in considering constitutionality, of both the national and European kind.

1 The Sovereignty Doctrine

The Czech Constitutional Court has offered from the outset of its case-law raised by the joining of the European Union a rather restrained doctrine of state sovereignty. To the extent that the criteria of justice do not stop at the border of a nation State, the autonomy of its constitutional order, the exclusivity of public power as a *pouvoir constitué* and the *Kompetenz-Kompetenz* of its *pouvoir constituant* do not form a sufficient definition of sovereign statehood. Sovereignty is no longer attributable only to the entity of a State. It is attributable to the European Union in the areas of high politics, as well.

Judge of the Constitutional Court of the Czech Republic (2014–2024).

J. Zemánek (✉)
Brno, Czechia
e-mail: jiri.zemanek@usoud.cz

G. Barrett et al. (eds.), *European Sovereignty*,
https://doi.org/10.1007/978-3-031-71851-9_8

Sovereignty has a functional role in legitimising and authorising the conferring of the public power of national authorities on supranational institutions, 'bottom-up' through a decision of the people on distribution of its parts (and not as a mere *summa potestas* or an assembly of the competencies of the State). This distribution can take place either via an elected parliament or directly, through a referendum on the ratification of a Treaty on Accession to the European Union.

The Czech Constitutional Court built on the statement that President Václav Havel had made in the European Parliament on 8 March 1994 when he said that "we are ready to give up a piece of our State sovereignty in exchange for jointly administered sovereignty of the European Union, since we know–like other Europeans–that it is worthwhile (it will pay many times over)."

The Court rejected in this context the fear of a draining away or erosion of sovereignty through a mere delegation of competencies.

2 The Multilevel Nature of European Union Law

The legal order of the European Union is multilevel,[1] a notion which evokes the whole, and is based on a consistency in the values of the various parts of the Union. But do judicial authorities make this cross-European Union effective enough to neutralise potential conflicts between national constituencies and the centre of the European integration project–each claiming autonomy within their respective domains–so as to bring these 'competing autonomies' into a scheme of mutual complementarity rather than rivalry?

The co-existence of two–national and supranational–judicial levels requires openness to cooperation, the ability to engage in self-reflection, a readiness to preview the externalities of their own behaviour and willingness to adopt (or internalise") impulses from the case-law of the other, i.e., a capacity for what has been termed by Anne Peters "*lernende Anpassung*". It means understanding oneself as a part of de facto union of European judiciaries with a comparative perspective.

This kind of international communication or dialogue is served by already existing procedural instruments, such as the preliminary ruling procedure under Article 267 TFEU, the EU Pilot mechanism[2] and the Consultative Council of European Judges of

[1] See, among others, Ingolf Pernice, Multilevel constitutionalism in the European Union, (2002) 27 EL Rev. 509 and J. H. H. Weiler, A Constitution for Europe? Hard Choices, (2002) 40 JMCS 4.

[2] EU Pilot is a mechanism facilitating informal dialogue between the Commission and a Member State concerning potential non-compliance with EU law. Although not compulsory, it can be used before launching a formal infringement procedure under Art. 258 TFEU, when an issue seems likely to be resolved through informal dialogue. The Commission and Member States share information on particular cases using the EU Pilot online database and communication tool. The Commission sends a query to the Member State concerned, which will normally have ten weeks to reply, with the Commission then normally itself having ten weeks to assess this response.

the Council of Europe,[3] the use of which–intended to be more supportive than defensive–would be desirable. This is a matter of finding a sustainable balance between the individual roles in the double mandate of judges as national and European interpreters of applicable laws, looking for a common *modus operandi*, and being aware of (1) a dimension reflecting the explicit and implicit limits of the redefinition of the position of national Constitutions in the wake of EU accession, and (2) a dimension legitimising due execution of transferred European Union competencies, which is a pre-condition for the functionality of the '*Rest-Kompetenz*' at national level. This would be a contribution of the *de facto* judicial union to understanding sovereignty in a multilevel system not as a matter of conflict, but as a pooled phenomenon, reflecting the respective identities–both national and European ones.

3 Europeanisation of the Czech Constitution

The integration clause of the Constitution offers a rather broad space for the development of a profile of Czech membership of the EU by the case-law of the Czech Constitutional Court. In its first post-EU-accession decisions,[4] the Czech Constitutional Court stipulated two conditions for a transfer of competencies to the European Union to occur: keeping the essential requirements for a democratic state governed by the rule of law[5] and the execution of entrusted substantive competencies by the European Union institutions in a way compatible with maintaining the basics of State sovereignty, thus not endangering the fundamentals of a State governed by the material rule of law. As long as the exceptional situation of a breaching of these conditions does not occur, the Czech Constitutional Court will not review the compliance of the European Union acts with the Czech constitutional order.

In two *Treaty of Lisbon* cases,[6] the Czech Constitutional Court dealt with the topic of sovereignty, refering to Jellinek's thesis that a self-limitation of one's own powers is not a recognition of a sovereign's insufficiency, but a manifestation of its full sovereignty. Instead, the Czech Constitutional Court, claiming a certain *de facto* decline of the 'classical' understanding of this notion in contemporary world, pointed out that sovereignty is not a purpose in itself, but a means of achieving the fundamental values of a democratic State governed by the rule of law.

This open-minded declaration met with criticism by some introverted-minded constitutionalists, who asserted that sovereignty is indivisible and claimed that the

---

[3] The Consultative Council of European Judges is an advisory body of the Council of Europe on questions concerning the competence, impartiality and independence of judges. Its membership is composed exclusively of judges.

[4] Pl. ÚS 37/04 *Directive on anti-discrimination*; Pl. ÚS 50/04 *Sugar quotas III;* Pl. ÚS 66/04 *European Arrest Warrant;* Pl. ÚS 36/05 *Medicaments regulation*; Pl. 56/05 *Squeeze out*; Pl. 12/08T-*Mobile*; III. ÚS 31/97 *Škoda Auto*; available online at <www.usoud.cz/en/decisions> accessed 31 January 2024.

[5] Article 9 para 2 of the Constitution.

[6] Pl. ÚS 19/08 *Treaty of Lisbon I*; Pl. ÚS 29/09 *Treaty of Lisbon II*.

Czech judiciary would lose control over respect for the democratic values of the rule of law (incorporated in the Treaties as equivalent to the national constitutional values), as a result of the European authorities taking decisions directly affecting individuals at national level, on the basis of powers attributed to the European Union by its Member States.

However, the Czech Constitutional Court tried to demonstrate, by reference to the case-law of the European Court of Justice, that effective protection of values, equivalent to "the material core of constitutionality", as codified in Article 9 para 2 of the Czech Constitution, is evidently guaranteed at European Union level, too. The Czech Constitutional Court called this protection "a common task" of both judiciaries. A double *ex ante* control by national constitutional courts, as required by the German Federal Constitutional Court, the *Bundesverfassungsgericht* (with its references to an *ausbrechende Rechtsakte*[7] and *Identitätskontrolle*[8]) was superfluous.[9]

In spite of the lack of any statement in the Czech Constitution on a unified Europe to be constructed with protection of the same principles of democracy, the rule of law and fundamental rights at a level equal to that at national level,[10] the Czech Constitutional Court seems to be open to understanding its own role within a conception, whereby national and European sovereignty are not in an irresolvable conflict, but rather in a system of complementarity, with national constitutions as *Teilverfassungen.*[11] The case-law of the Czech Constitutional Court will be consolidated in this respect, accepting the autonomy of European Union law.[12]

4 A Failure to Communicate, Rather then Heresy, on the Part of the Czech Constitutional Court

The one and only case of the Czech Constitutional Court, in which its dynamic (or "pragmatic") European Union law doctrine ran out, ensued from the conflict between the Supreme Administrative Court and the Czech Constitutional Court on the applicability of the EC Regulation on social security schemes of persons moving within the European Community. This was a specific case involving Czech citizens–now pensioners–who had been employed before the dissolution of Czechoslovakia

---

[7] An *ausbrechende Rechtsakte*, in the case-law of the *Bundesverfassungsgericht*, refers to a legal instrument of the European institutions or bodies which transgresses the limits of the sovereign rights conferred on those institutions or bodies.

[8] *Identitätskontrolle*, in the case-law of the *Bundesverfassungsgericht*, is a control to ensure that the constitutional identity of the State is not trespassed upon.

[9] See also *European Constitutionalism in the Context of Judicial Dialog* (2017, Constitutional Court, Brno).

[10] Conditionality of constitutional development of this kind is a *Staatsziel* (or State objective) prescribed in Article 23 para 1 of the German Constitution, the *Grundgesetz*.

[11] This translates as 'partial constitutions', a concept of long standing in German legal thought.

[12] Luboš Tichý, Rainer Arnold, Jiří Zemánek, Richard Král and Tomáš Dumbrovský, T. *Evropské právo* (European Law) (5th edition, 2014, Beck), para. 46.2.2.

(on 1 January 1993) in the territory of Slovakia, as a part of the Czechoslovak Federation at that time.

The Court adjudicated that such an application of the EC Regulation would be retroactive and unconstitutional as contrary to the principles of constitutionalism, since the division of the Czechoslovak Federation had happened long before both separate successor States joined the European Union (on 1 May 1 2004). Therefore, the territory of Slovakia could not be understood–from the Czech perspective–as a territory of a foreign State, justifying the applicability of the EC Regulation. Entitlements to supplementary payments based exclusively on the Czech citizenship of their beneficiaries and the respective international treaty agreed by Czech and Slovak Republics, could not be discriminatory towards the citizens of other (now) European Union Member States, including Slovak citizens, and break European Union law, as the European Court of Justice had concluded.[13]

The Czech Constitutional Court disregarded its duty under Article 267 TFEU to submit a question for a preliminary ruling by the European Court of Justice and as a non-participant in the proceedings before the European Court of Justice started by the Supreme Administrative Court, could not be invited to present its opinion. The reaction by the Czech Constitutional Court was surprising, indeed rather shocking: the Constitutional Court declared the judgment of the European Court of Justice unacceptable from the perspective of constitutional justice.[14]

However, this 'virtual' conflict between the Czech Constitutional Court and the European Court of Justice did not arise again. A peaceful solution, reflecting the specific circumstances of the particular case, was found–assisted by the fact that, later on, the differences between pension levels between Czechia and Slovakia diminished, so that fears of discrimination no longer had any foundation.

[13] Case C-399/09 *Marie Landtová* ECLI:EU:C:2011:415 (judgment of 22 June 2011).

[14] Pl. ÚS 5/12 *Slovak pensions XVII.*

European Sovereignty in Specific Areas

Strategic Sovereignty—Aspects of Its Legal Dimension

Peter-Christian Müller-Graff

Abstract The basic questions addressed in this chapter regarding the strategic sovereignty of the European Union in its legal dimension concern the substantive content of the objective of "strategic sovereignty", the links to the primary law of the European Union and some of the main legal ramifications of the Union's striving for this objective: in particular, the requirements to concretise a global strategy and sub-strategies and to cope with diverse legal challenges in order to put in place elements of the Union's sovereignty, in particular, its energy sovereignty, its economic, trade and development assistance sovereignty and its defence sovereignty.

The strategic sovereignty of the European Union in its legal dimension formed part of the overarching question addressed in the Thirtieth Anniversary Congress of the Academy of European Law on "European Sovereignty: The Legal Dimension—A Union in Control of its own Destiny".[1] The inherent basic questions addressed in this chapter regarding this topic concern (1) the substantive content of the objective of "strategic sovereignty"; (2) the links to the primary law of the European Union; and (3) some of the main ramifications of the Union's striving for this objective.

Senior Professor for Civil Law, Trade, Company und Economic Law, European Law and Comparative Law, Faculty of Law, University of Heidelberg.

P.-C. Müller-Graff (✉)
Heidelberg, Germany
e-mail: p.mueller-graff@igw.uni-heidelberg.de

[1] This text is based on the author´s introduction to the working session on "Strategic Sovereignty" at the Thirtieth Anniversary Congress of the Academy of European Law held in Trier on 13–14 October 2022.

G. Barrett et al. (eds.), *European Sovereignty*,
https://doi.org/10.1007/978-3-031-71851-9_9

1 Strategic Sovereignty as a General Objective

"Strategic sovereignty" as a general objective requires clarification regarding its meaning. I understand the idea of "strategic sovereignty" as the willingness to uphold and capability of upholding continuously the self-defined concept of living in relation to others (as a "strategic compass"[2]). In this sense, strategic sovereignty is a permanent task and has many prerequisites: first, as regards the self-defined concept, the spiritual prerequisite of self-determination based on intellectual clarity; secondly, as regards willingness, the mental virtues of political decisiveness, willpower and persistence; and thirdly, as regards capability, the factual requirements of economic resources, the internal social support of the citizens, diplomatic skills and effective military defence capacities.

2 Links to the Treaty-Based Constitutional Law of the European Union

The above-mentioned prerequisites of concept, willingness and capacity imply manifold specific challenges regarding the idea of strategic sovereignty of the European Union as a transnational polity based on law and bound by law.[3]

2.1 Links of the Self-Defined Strategic Concept to the Union's Constitutional Law

Regarding the prerequisite of a self-defined concept of living in relation to others, it will be recalled that the Union is constitutionally bound by Article 3 para 5 TEU

> in its relations with the wider world (to) uphold and promote its values and interests and contribute to the protection of its citizens. It shall contribute to peace, security, the sustainable development of the Earth, solidarity and mutual respect among peoples, free and fair trade, eradication of poverty and the protection of human rights….[4]

Article 21 para 1 TEU prescribes, even more ambitiously, that

> the Union's action on the international scene shall be guided by the principles which have inspired its own creation, development and enlargement, and which it seeks to advance in

---

[2] See Council of the European Union (2022) *The Strategic Compass of the European Union* (Brussels, 21 March 2022).

[3] Walter Hallstein, *Die Europäische Gemeinschaft* (fifth edition, Econ 1979) 51 *et seq.*; Peter-Christian Müller-Graff, "Die Europäische Union als Rechtsgemeinschaft" in Peter-Christian Müller-Graff (ed.) *Kernelemente der europäischen Integration* (Nomos 2020) 39 *et seq.*; Claus Dieter Classen, "Perspektiven der europäischen Rechtsgemeinschaft", JZ 2023, 53 ff.

[4] Peter-Christian Müller-Graff, "Artikel 3" in Matthias Pechstein, Carsten Nowak and Ulrich Häde (eds), *Frankfurter Kommentar EUV—GRC–AEUV* (Volume I, Mohr Siebeck 2017) Rn. 43.

> the wider world: democracy, the rule of law, the universality and indivisibility of human rights and fundamental freedoms, respect for human dignity, the principles of equality and solidarity, and respect for the principles of the United Nations Charter and international law.[5]

More specific aims are listed concerning the special relationship with neighbouring countries (Article 8 TEU).[6] Hence, the substantive narrative of the Union's self-understanding can be seen in the upholding and promotion of its intended and widely-practised enlightened way of life as laid down in its constitutional values and objective orientation. It can be understood as the conceptual core of what is meant by the word, sometimes used, of a "narrative" or "vision" for the "survival of the West".[7]

2.2 *Links of Strategic Willingness to the Union's Constitutional Law*

Law cannot substitute for real willpower. But the Union's constitutional law as a normative point of orientation for (internal and external) politics can continuously remind one of the necessity to muster political decisiveness, willpower and persistence in order to pursue the track of its genuine narrative as encapsulated in Article 2 TEU. Strategic sovereignty requires its translation into a coherent strategy.

2.3 *Links of Strategic Capability to the Union's Constitutional Law*

Law cannot substitute for factual capabilities. But due to the Union's primary law principle of conferral (Article 5 para 2 TEU) the Union is in principle empowered to contribute to the mentioned factual requirements of economic resources, citizens' support, diplomatic skills and effective military defence capacities for strategic sovereignty, although only on the basis of corresponding competences (see Sect. 3 below).

---

[5] Andreas von Arnauld (2022) "Das System der Europäischen Außenbeziehungen" in Andreas von Arnauld and Marc Bungenberg, *Europäische Außenbeziehungen* (Enzyklopädie Europarecht, Volume 12, second edition, Nomos 2022) 43 at 83 *et seq.* and 87 *et seq.*.

[6] Markus Kotzur, "Europäische Nachbarschaftspolitik" in von Arnauld and Bungenberg (n. 5) at 401 *et seq.*.

[7] Bruno Dupré, *European Strategic Sovereignty: What Place for the European Union in an Increasingly Transactional World?* (PPP 2023) 9, 15.

3 Some Main Ramifications of the Union's Striving for "Strategic Sovereignty"

Among the main ramifications of the Union's striving for "strategic sovereignty", are found the requirements to concretise a global strategy and sub-strategies (see Sect. 3.1 below) and to cope with diverse legal challenges in order to put in place the elements of the Union's sovereignty. Among the many such elements,[8] the working session which formed the basis of this chapter concentrated on legal challenges regarding three dimensions–the Union's energy sovereignty (see Sect. 3.2 below), its economic, trade and development assistance sovereignty (see Sect. 3.3 below) and its defence sovereignty (see Sect. 3.4 below).

3.1 Concretisation of Global Strategy and Sub-Strategies

The abstract primary law guidelines for the Union's external action which have been outlined require the concretisation of a global strategy to define and realise an adequate geopolitical place[9] as well as fitting sub-strategies, in particular *regional* sub-strategies and *subject-matter-policy* sub-strategies. Careful enlargement is part of such a strategy.

Among the necessary regional sub-strategies those directed towards the areas surrounding the European Union demand particular attention: towards the Mediterranean, the Balkans and the very east of Europe. Article 8 TEU prescribes that "the Union shall develop a special relationship with neighbouring countries, aiming to establish an area of prosperity and good neighbourliness, founded on the values of the Union and characterised by close and peaceful relations based on cooperation." Currently, the question arises as to whether this orientation also has to include a specific sub-strategy of the Union towards Russia in the sense of supporting the transformation of Russia's historically inherited autocratic and imperial system of power into an order that does not threaten the Union and its Member States, as proposed by Alexei Navalny in 2022.[10] In relation to Russia (as well as to China[11]), the Union's sub-strategy of self-assertation in "system rivalry" needs to be concretised and pursued.

The Union's abstract constitutional guidelines also require the identification of essential subject-matter policy areas for realising "strategic sovereignty" such as,

---

[8] Dupré (n. 7) at 15 mentions "space, energy, digital, transport, health". The supply of raw materials is also one of these elements.

[9] Bruno Dupré "Geo-politicisation of Europe" in Dupré (n. 7) 15.

[10] Alexei Navalny, "Wie Putin besiegt werden kann", Frankfurter Allgemeine Sonntagszeitung, 2 October 2022, 2.

[11] Moritz Rudolf, "Chancen und Risiken der Seidenstraßeninitiative" in Peter-Christian Müller-Graff (ed.), *Die Beziehungen zwischen der Europäischen Union und China* (Nomos 2017) 69 *et seq.*.

e.g., securing the supply of energy and essential raw materials, economic clout in relation to other global actors and sufficient self-defence capabilities. In all of these areas, the European Union is permanently faced with challenges. Hence the guiding question arises, under which factual and legal conditions "strategic sovereignty" of the Union has a chance of being realised in these areas–if it is to be realised at all.

3.2 Coping with Specific Legal Challenges to the Union's Energy Sovereignty

In coping with specific legal challenges to the Union's energy sovereignty the questions of (1) competences; of (2) the principle of consistency; of (3) the relation to the Energy Community; and of (4) the link to the European Atomic Energy Community arise.

3.2.1 Competences of the Union

In a Union based on law, the first concern has to be directed to the question of the extent to which the Union has competences to promote energy sovereignty. At first glance, Article 194 para 2 TFEU, in conjunction with Article 194 para 1 lit. b TFEU, seems to be pivotal in this respect. These two provisions confer upon the Union the competence that the European Parliament and the Council, acting in accordance with the ordinary legislative procedure, "establish the measures necessary to achieve the objective" "to ... ensure security of energy supply in the Union." Ensuring security of energy supply ("*Versorgungssicherheit*") does not necessarily mean self-sufficiency, but does not exclude this form of security (if at all feasible for the Union). However, in view of the Union's competences, the objective of ensuring security of energy supply[12] is in legal tension with the Treaty's unequivocal provision that the Union's measures "shall not affect a Member State's right to determine the conditions for exploiting its energy resources, its choice between different energy sources and the general structure of its energy supply". But this statement is qualified by the wording "without prejudice" to the Union's environmental protection policy competence "to adopt measures significantly affecting" such a choice (see Article 194 para 2 sub-para 2 TFEU in conjunction with Article 192 para 2 lit. c TFEU).

Hence one main track pursued by the European Commission since 2019–namely the promotion of the so called "Green Deal"[13]–can be used and interpreted also as a

[12] The question can be left open of how far energy security or even self-sufficiency in energy can be achieved in the medium term in an industrialised member state such as Germany in view of its present daily energy mix if the use of all fossil energy sources and nuclear energy are ruled out on political grounds. (See the daily energy mix report in the Frankfurter Allgemeine Zeitung).

[13] Ursula von der Leyen, "Eine Union, die mehr erreichen will. Meine Agenda für Europa. Politische Leitlinien für die künftige Europäische Union, 2019–2024" (Brussels 2018).

path towards ensuring security of energy supply and potentially even self-sufficiency. With its aim of the "green" conversion of the modes of all economic activities in production, distribution and consumption to climate neutrality by 2050, it necessarily also comprises a concept of ensuring security of energy supply based on so-called "green energy resources". To this extent, the Union is empowered on the basis of its environmental policy competence (under Article 192 TFEU)–which is required to contribute to the pursuit of the objective, among others, "combating climate change"–to adopt measures "significantly affecting" a Member State's energy mix (the "choice between different energy sources and the general structure of its energy supply"), thereby overriding the restrictions of the energy policy competence of Article 194 para 2 sub-para 2 TFEU. Using the environmental policy competence for the purpose of promoting "green energy" resources even matches one of the objectives to be pursued on the basis of the "pure" energy policy, namely "in the context of the establishment and the functioning of the internal market and with regard for the need to preserve and improve the environment", to "promote … the development of … renewable forms of energy" (see Article 194 para 1 lit. c TFEU).

3.2.2 The Obligation of Consistency

Additional aspects of primary Union law have to be taken into consideration when ensuring security of energy supply—in particular given the constitutional obligation of the Union to ensure "consistency between its policies and activities, taking all its objectives into account" (see Article 7 TFEU). At least one group of these has to be addressed in this context: the basic principles and provisions concerning the internal as well as the external dimension of the Union's economically relevant policies: namely the general guideline regarding the adoption of an economic policy "which is based … on the internal market … and conducted in accordance with the principle of an open market economy with free competition" (see Article 119 para 1 TFEU) and the ramifications of this in a system which includes provisions that competition is not distorted in the internal market (see Protocol No. 27), the prohibition of distortions of competition by industrial policy (see Article 173 para 3 sub-para 2 TFEU), the policy of state aid supervision (see Article 107 para 3 TFEU)[14] and the pursuit of the harmonious development of world trade (see Article 206 TFEU).

---

[14] See Lennart Gau, *Die Dynamik der Kompetenzbegrenzung in der unionalen Beihilfenkontrolle* (Mohr Siebeck 2024).

The legal consequences of the obligation created by Article 119 para 1 TFEU, if applicable to energy policy should neither be overrated[15] nor underestimated.[16] The wording "in accordance with the principle" has to be understood as requiring a steady orientation favouring the promotion of freedom of choice regarding supply and demand and, thereby, towards the freedom to conduct a business (see Article 16 CFREU). On the other hand, Article 119 para 1 TFEU does not contain an absolute prohibition of any regulatory measure that interferes with free wheeling and dealing on the market and free production and distribution. Such an interpretation would already be contradicted by the legitimacy of the primary law prohibition of cartels and all the regulatory policies inherent in the two additional qualifications of the free market economy as a social market economy (see Article 3 para 3 TEU)[17] and as a highly competitive market economy (see Article 3 para 3 TEU). Indeed, the constitutional order of the economy in the Union is marked by different elements which can be distinguished according to their objective:[18] provisions guaranteeing subjective economic freedoms to act in the market,[19] provisions to protect the functioning of this system of freedoms and competition against internal perversions caused by its actors[20] as well as against externally-caused distortions of competition by public interventions,[21] provisions to protect specific public goods,[22] including provisions concerning transforming the economy towards sustainability and climate neutrality,[23] provisions concerning reaching certain sectoral or regional economic

[15] It has no direct applicability: see Case C-9/99 *Échirolles* EU:C:2000:532 (judgment of the European Court of Justice). See also Wernhard Möschel, "Regulierung und Deregulierung. Versuch einer theoretischen Grundlegung", in Andreas Fuchs, Hans-Peter Schwintowski and Daniel Zimmer (eds.), *Wirtschafts- und Privatrecht im Spannungsfeld von Privatautonomie, Wettbewerb und Regulierung, Festschrift für Ulrich Immenga zum 70. Geburtstag*, (Beck 2004) 277; Christoph Herrmann, "Artikel 119 AEUV" in Matthias Pechstein, Carsten Nowak and Ulrich Haede (eds.), *Frankfurter Kommentar EUV-GRC-AEUV* (Volume III, Mohr Siebeck 2017) note 50.

[16] The European Court of Justice in Case C-9/99 *Échirolles* EU:C:2000:532 at para 25 labels it "a general principle". See Peter-Christian Müller-Graff "The Idea of an Economic Constitution ('Wirtschaftsverfassung') in German Law", in Guillaume Grégoire and Xavier Miny (eds.), *The Idea of Economic Constitution in Europe—Genealogy and Overview* (Brill 2022) 615 at 630. Ramifications of this general principle can be seen in several primary law provisions: see Peter-Christian Müller-Graff "Festigkeits- und Elastizitätsproben des Europäischen Wirtschaftsordnungsrechts", in Florian Bien, Joachim Jickeli and Peter-Christian Müller-Graff (eds.), *Maß- und Gradfragen im Wirtschaftsrecht. Zum 80. Geburtstag von Wernhard Möschel* (Nomos 2021) 211at 217.

[17] Peter-Christian Müller-Graff (2011) "Soziale Marktwirtschaft als neuer Primärrechtsbegriff der Europäischen Union", in Peter-Christian Müller-Graff, Stefanie Schmahl and Vassilios Skouris (eds.), *Europäisches Recht zwischen Bewährung und Wandel. Festschrift für Dieter H. Scheuing*, Nomos, Baden-Baden, pp. 600 *et seq.*

[18] Peter-Christian Müller-Graff, *The Idea of an Economic Constitution* (2022) 617 at 633.

[19] E.g., Articles 6, 16 and 20 CFREU.

[20] E.g., Articles 101 and 102 TFEU.

[21] E.g., Articles 106 para 1 and 107 TFEU.

[22] E.g., Articles 114 para 3 and 168 TFEU.

[23] E.g., Article 191 para 1 TFEU.

results in the interest of the security of supply or regional economic activity,[24] provisions regarding reaching macro-economic goals[25] and provisions concerning the distribution of economic gains.[26]

Hence the legal implications of Article 119 para 1 TFEU might seem weak. However, the principle of an open market economy with free competition is not only a point of guidance to be taken into consideration in any market relevant public policy and legislation. Rather, if a regulatory measure restricts a fundamental right such as the freedom to conduct a business (see Article 16 CFREU), it requires the legal legitimisation of any of those measures by a public good in accordance with the principle of proportionality in relation to the freedom to conduct a business (see Article 52 CFREU). And even without a restriction of a fundamental right, any intervention by the Union in the system of an open market economy with free competition requires compliance with the general principle of proportionality (see Article 5 para 3 TEU). This also applies to energy policy in relation to the "energy market" (Article 194 TFEU).

The tension between Union measures and the principle of a market economy with free competition is legally even more strongly perceived in the context of industrial policy within the meaning of Article 173 TFEU. Article 173 para 3 sub-section 3 TFEU contains a prohibition on distortions of competition by industrial policy. However, the scope of this prohibition is unclear. If the functional approach used in competition law to delimit relevant markets were applied to identify the relevant competition which must not be distorted by the Union's industrial policy, then the Union's promotion of green energy by means of subsidies and legislation to the disadvantage of the competitiveness and existence of fossil energy or nuclear energy would conflict with this prohibition. But insofar as such a green energy policy is followed in pursuance of public objectives which are legitimised by primary law–such as "sustainable growth" and "climate protection"–it seems debatable whether such a policy should be considered "industrial policy" in the sense of Article 173 TFEU (which refers to "speeding up the adjustment of industry to structural changes"; "encouraging an environment favourable to initiative and to the development of undertakings"; and "fostering better exploitation of the industrial potential of policies of innovation, research and technological development"). Even if it is, restrictions on free offer and demand as regards fossil energy can be justified in accordance with the requirements of Article 52 CFREU and Article 5 para 3 TEU, thereby favouring market-conforming measures (such as certificates) or compensation.

The principle of an open market economy with free competition also has an external dimension. This is underlined by Article 206 TFEU, which aims at "the progressive abolition of restrictions on international trade". However, this does not exclude the adoption of protective trade policy measures which have as their purpose

---

[24] E.g., Article 39 para 1 lit. d TFEU; Article 91 TFEU; Articles 173, 174, 179 and 194 para 1 TFEU.

[25] Article 3 para 3 subsection 1 s. 1 TEU; Article 127 TFEU.

[26] E.g., Articles 113, 115 and 153 TFEU.

the flanking of internal policies–i.e., which serve to accomplish internal energy policy (see Article 207 para 1 TFEU).

3.2.3 The Role of the European Atomic Energy Community

Insofar as concerns achieving European Union self-sufficiency in the supply of energy, the European Atomic Energy Community (Euratom) comes into play. Although Euratom is an independent international organisation, all (and only) Member States of the Union are its members–despite the well-known debates concerning political desirability of nuclear energy and the differing positions on this in several Member States. Moreover, Euratom is connected to the EU by the same institutional framework.[27] The question arises of what contribution to the Union's security of energy supply and its self-sufficiency could legally and factually be delivered by Euratom, were this politically intended. According to the Euratom Treaty, it shall be "the task" of Euratom "to contribute to the standard of living ... by creating the conditions necessary for the speedy development and growth of nuclear industries."[28] Hence this constitutional situation poses no obstacles to a European strategy of securing its "energy sovereignty" by way of promoting nuclear industries within the Union. Nor is this barred by the primary law of the Union.

3.2.4 The Role of the Energy Community

Pondering on the Union's energy sovereignty triggers the question of whether the Energy Community as an independent international organisation founded by the EU and nine Balkan States in 2005[29] can or should legally be bound to contribute to this objective. According to Article 1 of its founding Treaty, its task is "to create a legal and economic framework in relation to Network Energy" (constituted by "the electricity and gas sectors" falling within the scope of Directive (EU) 2019/944[30] and Directive 2009/73/EC[31] for several objectives: creating "a stable regulatory and market framework capable of attracting investment in gas networks, power generation, and transmission and distribution networks"; creating "a single regulatory space for trade in Network Energy"; enhancing "the security of supply of the single regulatory space by providing a stable investment climate"; improving "the environmental situation in relation to Network Energy and related energy efficiency"; fostering "the use of renewable energy"; and developing "Network Energy market competition on

---

27 Article 106 Euratom Treaty.

28 Jürgen Grunwald, "Europäische Atomgemeinschaft" in Armin Hatje and Peter-Christian Müller-Graff (ed.), *Europäisches Organisations- und Verfassungsrecht* (Enzyklopädie Europarecht, Volume 1, second edition, Nomos 2022) 1247 at 1250.

29 For the text see OJ 2015 L 198/15.

30 OJ 2019 L 158/125.

31 OJ 2009 L 211/94.

a broader geographic scale." In this target polygon, the emphasis of the Community's intended main activities can be understood as being basically twofold: on the one hand the extension of the EU internal energy market rules and principles to the participating Balkan countries and beyond on the basis of a legally binding framework,[32] and, on the other hand, the enhancement of the security of energy supply in the single regulatory space.[33] In this way the Energy Community can, both in law and in fact, serve to contribute to the Union's energy sovereignty.

3.3 Specific Challenges in Economic, Trade and Development Assistance Sovereignty

The very basis of the Union's strategic sovereignty is its stable economic prosperity. This is the backbone of the intended well-being of the peoples of the Union (see Article 3 para 1 TEU) and of the Union's and its Member States' capacity for financing the material prerequisites of its strategic sovereignty: in particular payments for necessary essential imports (such as energy, rare earth elements, semiconductors or medicaments as long as self-sufficiency, if desired, is not achieved); the transformation of the economy into a sustainable and climate-neutral mode of production, distribution and consumption; the fostering of the economic and social development in third countries; and the funding of the physical and digital equipment for reliable defence (in accordance with the maxim *vis pacem, para bellum*). Again, there are internal and external aspects in Union law concerning meeting the inherent challenges to economic and trade sovereignty.

3.3.1 Functioning Internal Market Within the Union's Constitutional (Economic) Order

The elementary basis of the Union is its functioning internal market within the Union's constitutional (economic) order.[34] While Article 3 para 1 TEU proclaims as "the Union's aim … to promote peace, its values and the well-being of its peoples", the Union's pivotal basic operative objective is establishing and maintaining a functioning internal market within the Union's constitutional order.

---

32 Dirk Buschle, "Die Energiegemeinschaft", in Hatje and Müller-Graff (n. 28) 1851 at 1856.

33 Article 2 para 2 lit. c of the Euratom Treaty.

34 For the concept of the economic constitutional order in the European Union, see Peter-Christian Müller-Graff, "Europäisches Binnenmarkt- und Wirtschaftsordnungsrecht", in Peter-Christian Müller-Graff (ed.), *Europäisches Binnenmarkt- und Wirtschaftsordnungsrecht* (Enzyklopädie Europarecht, Volume 4, Nomos 2021) at 53, 61 *et seq.*. See in general regarding the idea of an economic constitution, Grégoire and Miny (n. 16).

Hence any solid realisation of concepts of the Union's strategic sovereignty depends upon the good functioning of the internal market within the Union's constitutional order. The question arises as to whether the Union is constitutionally endowed with the necessary power to keep the legal framework of the internal market in step with developing economic, social, environmental and other challenges to the attainment of the objective of a prosperous economy. The currently ongoing process of transforming the Union's economy to a sustainable and climate neutral mode of production, distribution and consumption[35] is testing the scope of the constitutional competences of the Union in this respect.[36] It seems possible to submit as a preliminary conclusion that the Union possesses rather wide legal manoeuvring space,[37] in particular its competences under Article 114 TFEU (on approximation of internal market-relevant national laws), Art. 107 para 3 TFEU (concerning state aid supervision), Article 173 TFEU (concerning industrial policy) and Article 192 TFEU (concerning environmental policy). Whether the task of continuation of Europe's economic prosperity will succeed depends less on the competences of the Union than on their careful use so as to let the market economy generate economic welfare in the light of changing challenges. However, this does not guarantee the continuation of an achieved prosperity level, if unavoidable external factors such as the increase of prices for imported energy and a lack of substituting energies or a shortage of innovation raises the costs of production and living, and cause inflation and recession.[38]

3.3.2 Trade and Development Cooperation Policies in Relation to Third Countries

The Union's strategic sovereignty is intertwined with its trade and related policies in relation to third countries (in development cooperation). These policies are marked by economic and political aspects. The Union's global importance and political weight are essentially due to the trade attractiveness of its internal market for commercial actors in third countries (affecting imports) as well as to the global trading activities of enterprises located in the Union (affecting both imports and exports) and the Union's exclusive competence for commercial policy (as to which, see Article 3 para 1 lit. e TEU). Hence, the originally disputed[39] inclusion by the Treaty of Lisbon of the common commercial policy (Article 206 et seq. TFEU) under the rubric of the principles, objectives and general provisions of the Union's external action (under Article 21 et seq. TEU) followed reasonably on this insight.

---

[35] See, e.g., Regulation (EU) 2021/1119 (OJ 2021 L 243/1); Regulation (EU) 2020/852 (OJ 2020 L 198/13); Regulation (EU) 2019/1381 (OJ 2019 L 321/1).

[36] Peter-Christian Müller-Graff, "Festigkeits- und Elastizitätsproben" (n. 16) at 212 *et seq.*

[37] *Ibid.*, 231.

[38] Dupré (n. 7) 6.

[39] See for this discussion Christoph Vedder, "Die außenpolitische Zielbindung der Handelspolitik" in Marc Bungenberg and Christoph Herrmann (eds.), *Die gemeinsame Handelspolitik der Europäischen Union, nach Lissabon*, Nomos 2011) 121.

In order to promote trade, the Union holds exclusive competence for concluding international agreements of different intensities in this respect (Article 216 et seq. TFEU). This power is used by the Union for its global outreach to an increasing degree and with increasing density in the content of the agreements.[40] The emergence of the so called "comprehensive" or "enhanced" trade agreements with their regulatory framework for free trade (shaped along the lines of regulatory topics and rules of the internal market) can be understood as the expression of a double-headed strategy: promoting a regulatory level playing field for competition with imported goods and services (thereby also protecting consumers in the Union) on the one hand and easing exports of European enterprises to respective third countries on the other hand. As an international side effect of the Union's intensive creation of legal standards for the protection of diverse public goods within the internal market (such as health, consumer self-determination, environment and climate), increasing voluntary adaptation to these standards by third countries is reported.[41] This, however, does not seem to apply to financial transactions and the banking sector, where the Union is adapting to standards set elsewhere (the International Financial Reporting Standards (IFRS) issued by the International Accounting Standards Board (IASB[42]).

The Union's Global Gateway strategy[43] fits into this overall strategy of linking commerce and politics. According to its own definition, it is "an EU plan for major investment in infrastructure around the world" aiming "to forge links and not create dependencies".[44] This programme can be based on the Union's competence for development cooperation (see Article 208 TFEU). It takes on the challenge posed by China's "One Belt One Road" strategy.[45] Insofar as private investment of European enterprises will be encouraged by the "Global Gateway" strategy, the use of the Union's exclusive competence in the area of foreign direct investment protection (see Article 207 para 1 TFEU) may prove to be supportive in the achievement of this development policy and of the global linkage approach of the Union in the interests of both the participating States and the Union. In particular, in the view of the "Global South", it may also serve to mitigate the lingering pains of the former colonialism of European states.[46]

---

[40] Peter-Christian Müller-Graff, "Legal Europeanization outside the European Union" in Kseniia Smyrnova (ed.), *Formation and Development of European Law Science in Ukraine* (Feniks 2017) 99.

[41] Anu Bradford, *The Brussels Effect: How the European Union Rules the World* (Oxford University Press 2019).

[42] See *International Financial Reporting Standards* (IFRS) (Wiley–VCH 2023).

[43] European Union (2021), Joint Communication (JOIN(2021) 30 final, Brussels).

[44] *Ibid.* 1.

[45] For the Chinese programme see Rudolf (n. 11) 69.

[46] Dupré (n. 7) 10.

3.3.3 Protection Against Foreign Economic Interference

In the shaping of the economic dimension of strategic sovereignty, unwanted foreign economic interferences and proper defence measures must also be considered.

On the level of politics, the Union is in particular faced with the task of countering the divisive effects of China's Road and Belt strategy in Europe (under the headline "16 + 1")[47] and with the challenge of overcoming dependencies in its economy on single providers connected to a hostile autocratic state such as Russia.

On the level of competences, Article 207 para 2 (in conjunction with para 1) TFEU, with its explicit mention of "measures to protect trade" confer competence on the Union in this respect. The listed forms of dumping and subsidies are only examples which do not exclude other forms of interference. Article 207 also allows for the *screening of foreign direct investments* into the Union (as to which, see Regulation (EU) 2019/452[48]) and for deliberating on the delicate question of whether restrictions are required by strategic sovereignty or, to the contrary, are counterproductively jeopardising it by barring timely imports of the newest innovations (e.g., 5G). Also *foreign subsidies* which distort the internal market can be tackled by legal measures on the basis of Article 207 para 2 TFEU (as is done e.g., by Regulation (EU) 2022/2560[49]). Article 207 TFEU can also serve as a legal basis for trade restrictive measures that promote self-sufficiency in essential sectors such as semiconductors, rare earth exploitation, active substances, medicaments, energy and nutrition. And even *investment restrictions on European enterprises* in critical third countries can be envisaged[50] at the intersection of Article 207 TFEU and Article 64 para 2 and 3 TFEU. However, as already mentioned, tensions with the principle of an open market economy (as to which, see Article 119 TFEU) and with a competitive market order (as to which, see Article 3 para 3 TEU and Article 173 para 3 TFEU) have to be taken into consideration and require convincing legitimation. Imposing sanctions (such as Regulation (EU) 2022/1903 which is directed against Russia[51]) on the basis of Article 215 TFEU) is another aspect.

3.4 Specific Challenges in Defence Sovereignty

Strategic sovereignty is hardly feasible without effective military defence capabilities. The Union and its Member States were compelled to realise on 24 February, 2022 that the expectations which may be attributed to the EU's soft power deriving

[47] Anastas Vangeli "China´s Engagement with the Sixteen Countries of Central, East and Southeast Europe under the Belt and Road Initiative" (2017) 25 (5) China and World Economy 101.

[48] OJ 2019 L 79I/1.

[49] OJ 2022 L 330/1.

[50] European Commission, *Commission Work Programme 2023* (COM (2022) 548 final) 9 ("additional tools … in respect of outbound strategic investment controls").

[51] OJ 2022 L 259I/1.

from its prosperous economy and trade as well as the attractiveness of its values and its lifestyle alone do not protect a country in Europe against a state that is willing to deploy aggressively its military power with the intention of conquering or destroying another state. The dangers of fallout from Russia's invasion of Ukraine for European Union territory have become apparent: nuclear blackmail, sabotage and attacks on critical infrastructure. The Union and its Member States also became fully aware that their own security depends on the deterrent force of NATO and hence to a decisive degree on the willingness of the USA to honour fully its Article 5 NATO-Treaty solidarity obligation[52] towards its European allies. Obviously, the European Union in its present form is no military power. However, the turning point of February 2022 brought about by Russia's war on Ukraine has sparked the question of whether the Union is at least constitutionally equipped to develop into a self-reliant military defence actor–leaving aside any doubts as to whether the achievement of such a position will in fact translate into a realistic perspective or remain purely wishful thinking.

3.4.1 The Status Quo of the Union's Constitutional Law on Security and Defence

Assessing the Union's primary (constitutional) law under the aspect of its competences in the area of security and defence directly leads into its inner categorical constitutional and substantive core.

As regards the constitutional category: while the above-discussed dimensions of energy, economy, trade and economic assistance all rest on a supranational set of primary law provisions, the security and defence dimension, although constitutionally extant (see Articles 42 to 46 TEU) as "an integral part of the common foreign and security policy" (as to which, see Article 42 para 1 TEU in conjunction with Articles 23 to 41 TEU), lacks this quality.[53] Its legal nature is shaped according to traditional international law. The Union is capable of acting, in principle,[54] only on the basis of unanimous decisions on the part of its members in the European Council (see Article 31 para 1 TEU; and for common defence Article 42 para 2 TEU) and the Council (see Article 31 para 1, and this notwithstanding the important possibility of constructive abstention; and for decisions relating to the common security and defence policy Article 42 para 4 TEU). This mirrors the fact that the monopoly on the use of force ("*Gewaltmonopol*") including military force, lies with each Member State in its territory. The role of the Commission and the European Parliament in such policy questions is limited: the Commission's role is limited to supporting the

---

[52] For this obligation see Sebastian Graf von Kielmannsegg "WEU und NATO" in Hatje and Müller-Graff (n. 28) 2045 at 2053.

[53] Von Arnauld (n. 5) 81.

[54] There is one noticeable exception: structured cooperation. The decision to establish a "permanent structured cooperation" can be taken by the Council by qualified majority (Article 46 para 2–4 TFEU).

High Representative's referrral of a question to the Council (see Article 30 TEU); the European Parlament's role is limited to being consulted by the High Representative as well as to addressing questions or making recommendations to the Council and the High Representative and debating "progress in implementing" the relevant policies (see Article 36 TEU). The Court of Justice has no jurisidiction with respect to the provisions in these policy areas with the exception of the delineation of competences (see Article 40 TEU) and the area of annulment actions brought by natural and legal persons for the purpose of reviewing the legality of decisions providing for restrictive measures (see Article 275 TFEU). In particular the assertion of non-compliance with a decision of the European Council or the Council cannot be brought before the European Court of Justice under Article 258 or 259 TFEU.

As regards the substantive core of the Union, the question can be raised as to whether common security and defence fits in the Union's economic centre of gravity at all. However, as a defensive shield, the common security and defence policy can serve not only the Union's primary law objective of promoting peace, its values and the well-being of its peoples (under Article 3 para 1 TEU)–in other words the Union's enlightened way of life as normatively incorporated in the Union's values (seen in Article 2 TEU). It also can easily be seen as a protection of the Union's permanent realisation of its four main operative objectives, among them its basic aim of upholding a functioning internal market (as to which, see Article 3 para 3 TEU), against destruction by hostile aggressors from outside.

3.4.2 Constitutional Starting Points for the Union's Defence Strategy

On this intergovernmental constitutional basis, the Union Treaty contains starting points for developing a common defence strategy. According to Article 42 para 1 TEU, "it shall provide the Union with an operational capacity drawing on civilian and military assets." The Union "may" even "use them on missions outside the Union for peace-keeping, conflict prevention and strengthening international security in accordance with the principles of the United Nations Charter." As a consequence of the Member States' monopoly on the use of force, Member States "shall make civilian and military capabilities available to the Union for the implementation of the common security and defence policy" and "shall undertake progressively to improve their military capabilities" (see Article 42 para 3 TEU). The Treaty also provides for a specialised agency, the European Defence Agency, with the task of "defence capabilities development, research, acquisition and armaments".

Moreover the Treaty also empowers the Council "to entrust the execution of a task ... to a group of Member States in order to protect the Union's values und serve its interests" (see Article 42 para 5 TEU).[55] And, under an even farther-reaching provision, the Council is also entitled to establish (by qualified majority) a "permanent structured cooperation" on notification by Member States "whose military capabilities fulfil higher criteria and which have made more binding commitments

---

55 "In groups we trust".

to one another in this area with a view to the most demanding missions" (Article 46 para 2 TEU in conjunction with Article 42 para 6 TEU). However, all these operative possibilities depend on the capabilities, readiness and willingness of the Member States.

The Treaty also contains the solidarity clause for the case that "a Member State is the victim of armed aggression on its territory". Then "the other Member States shall have towards it an obligation of aid and assistance by all the means in their power, in accordance with Article 51 of the United Nations Charter" (see Article 42 para 7 TEU). Since compliance with this obligation depends upon the willingness of the other Member States–among them the only Member State of the Union which is a nuclear power–it is hard to see, or rather speculative to envisage, that the degree of credibility and deterrence effect of this obligation in fact comes close to or could substitute for that of the solidarity clause of Article 5 of the NATO Treaty.

The repeatedly-demanded Treaty amendment of transforming the unanimity requirement for decisions of the Council and European Council in the area of the common foreign, security and defence policy into the possibility of qualified majority decisions[56] seems out of touch with the reality of the national will to keep state monopolies on the use of force. The idea of establishing a European army[57] or reviving the concept of the failed Treaty establishing the European Defence Community of 1952 appear even more dubious. Supranationalising the military is far more ambitious than maintaining the security architecture of NATO. Instead, the normative potential of existing primary law should be seriously used and, in particular, the already-existing options of constructive abstention and structured cooperation brought to life and, last but not least, a self-defined comprehensive defence compass should be developed as–for the time being–assistance to the collective security structure provided by NATO.

4 Conclusion

A final conclusion finds "sleeping beauties" for strategic sovereignty in primary law which could be awakened. If the political will leans in this direction, the institutional stabilisation of the three analysed dimensions in primary law is to be recommended. The very basis of the Union's strategic sovereignty is the requirement that the Union have the political will for unity around common values and institutions in permanent global awareness and strategic thinking with a view to shaping a comprehensive geopolitical strategy and to forging suitable economic, diplomatic and defence tools for a concept-led action for the purposes of upholding the Union's enlightened orientation of the well-being of its peoples.

---

[56] E.g., Conference on the Future of Europe *Report on the Final Outcome*, (Brussels 2022), Proposal 21.

[57] E.g., Gerd Höfer, *Europäische Armee. Vision und Utopie* (Merus 2008).

Digital Sovereignty in the European Union: Five Challenges from a Normative Perspective

Nathalie A. Smuha

1 Introduction

In recent years, the term 'digital sovereignty' has increasingly found its way into the European Union's political discourse. As with many vessels of public speech, the fact that this notion has been used to denote different things by different people has not diminished the extent of its use. But what precisely does it signify? From a legal perspective, associating the words 'sovereignty' with 'Europe' traditionally evokes the idea of the autonomy of the EU legal order. Indeed, as far back as *Costa v ENEL*, the Union has been conceptualised by the Court of Justice of the European Union (CJEU) as an independent source of law,[1] whereby EU law presents a 'legal

[1] Case 6/64, Judgment of the Court of 15 July 1964, *Flaminio Costa v ENEL,* ECLI:EU:C:1964:66:

> By creating a Community of unlimited duration, having its own institutions, its own personality, its own legal capacity and capacity of representation on the international plane and, more particularly, real powers stemming from a limitation of sovereignty or a transfer of powers from the States to the Community, the Member States have limited their sovereign rights, albeit within limited fields, and have thus created a body of law which binds both their nationals and themselves.

Assistant Professor, Faculty of Law and Criminology, KU Leuven. This article was written while the author was a postdoctoral fellow at the University of Chicago School of Law.

The author wishes to acknowledge the support of the Research Foundation Flanders (FWO) during the period when this article was written.

N. A. Smuha (✉)
KU Leuven Faculty of Law and Criminology, Leuven, Belgium
e-mail: nathalie.smuha@kuleuven.be

G. Barrett et al. (eds.), *European Sovereignty*,
https://doi.org/10.1007/978-3-031-71851-9_10

order that has the capacity to operate as a self-referential system of norms that is both coherent and complete'.[2]

European sovereignty hence implies a vision of the European Union as an autonomous agent.[3] This holds true when considering the EU as *legislating* (having the ability to adopt legislation, through the European Parliament and Council), as *adjudicating* (having the ability to engage in judicial decision-making, through the CJEU alongside national courts), as *regulating* (having the ability to regulate, through the European Commission and regulatory agencies) and as *enforcing* (having the ability to enforce EU law, whether through the European Commission or a national authority). Arguably, the fact that the EU legal order co-exists with the legal orders of its Member States complicates yet does not diminish this picture–it merely implies a delimitation of competence and jurisdiction.[4] While sovereignty is traditionally conceptualised at the level of nation-states, it has been amply applied to the European context as well, to the extent and degree that certain competences have been allocated to the European Union by its Member States. Nor is sovereignty undermined by the fact the European Union can only operate legitimately within the boundaries stipulated by human rights, democracy and the rule of law. Instead, these boundaries signify a conception of sovereignty linked to the Kantian idea of self-governance based on reason, and thus involve a deliberate choice as to the limits within which to exercise power.[5] And even though some scholars have claimed that the concept of sovereignty has become moot in light of globalisation[6] or should even be buried altogether,[7] it has also been acknowledged that 'today, in contrast, it seems that there is a move towards increasing sovereignty',[8] and that it can be seen as an elastic concept with different shades and shapes.

---

[2] Koen Lenaerts, José A Gutiérrez-Fons and Stanislas Adam, 'Exploring the Autonomy of the European Union Legal Order' (2021) 81 Zeitschrift für ausländisches öffentliches Recht und Völkerrecht / Heidelberg Journal of International Law 47, 48.

[3] On the relationship between sovereignty and autonomy, see e.g., Raf Geenens, 'Sovereignty as Autonomy' (2017) 36 Law and Philosophy 495.

[4] See e.g., Andrew Moravcsik, *The Choice for Europe: Social Purpose and State Power from Messina to Maastricht.* (UCL press 1999).

[5] See Immanuel Kant, *Groundwork for the Metaphysics of Morals* (Lara Denis ed, Thomas Kingsmill Abbott tr, Broadview 2005). See also Paul Guyer, 'Kant on the Theory and Practice of Autonomy' in Ellen Frankel Paul, Jr Miller Fred D and Jeffrey Paul (eds), *Autonomy*, vol 20 (Cambridge University Press 2003).

[6] A contemporary critique of sovereignty—sometimes also formulated as a threat—arises from the context of globalisation, which seems to undermine the Westphalian idea of the authority of the nation state, and instead points to an erosion or at least a multi-levelling of sovereignty. The 'pooling' of sovereignty by national states through the integration project of the EU is sometimes seen as an answer to this threat. While I will not discuss this critique here, the interested reader may refer to e.g., Richard Bellamy, 'Sovereignty, Post-Sovereignty and Pre-Sovereignty: Three Models of the State, Democracy and Rights within the EU' in Neil Walker (ed), *Sovereignty in Transition* (Hart Publishing 2003); Nathalie Brack, Ramona Coman and Amandine Crespy, 'Sovereignty conflicts in the European Union' (2019) 4 Les Cahiers du Cevipol 3.

[7] See e.g., Don Herzog, *Sovereignty, RIP* (Yale University Press 2020).

[8] Roxana Vatanparast, 'Data Governance and the Elasticity of Sovereignty' (2020) 46 Brooklyn Journal of International Law 1, 3.

In this paper, it is not my intention to revisit the origins of sovereignty, nor do I want to delve into the question of just how much sovereignty a supranational entity like the European Union can claim. Instead, I want to examine what we are to make of sovereignty in Europe when it is preceded by the prefix 'digital'. One could understand the notion of digital sovereignty as a sub-category of the European Union's sovereignty; a sub-category that specifically pertains to its sovereign powers *vis à vis* digital infrastructures. Simultaneously, the deployment of this notion seems to push our conception of sovereignty outwards, beyond its traditional features, towards a reality that forces the European Union to reckon with new market structures and security threats induced by the disruptive nature of digital technologies.

The digital realm hence alters and at the same time challenges the traditional notion of sovereignty, leading the 'digital' prefix to do more work than merely express a subcategory thereof. This is because digital technologies are profoundly reshaping both societies and individuals, including how we act, communicate, and think. Inevitably, this influence also extends to political institutions, and thus to the very ability to exercise sovereignty in the first place. The recent proliferation of new European Union legislation in the digital sphere—from the Digital Services Package[9] and the AI Package[10] to the Data Package[11]—can hence be seen not only as an exercise of European Union sovereignty to ensure the protection of EU values (which range from fair competition to democracy), but also as an attempt to maintain and protect its sovereignty in an evolving world. Given society's ever-increasing reliance on digital technology, one could even ask whether the concept of 'sovereignty' still has any meaning without its digital prefix.

Against this background, this paper aims to make sense of 'digital sovereignty' in the European Union by examining both its meanings and its obstacles. I start by unpacking the term through a brief exploration of its use in European discourse, and reflect on two of its dimensions that are prevalently highlighted, which I conceptualise as *economic* digital sovereignty and *normative* digital sovereignty (Sect. 2). Focusing primarily on the latter, I then examine five challenges that European digital sovereignty currently faces, and that must be tackled if the European Union wishes to maintain its ability to exercise its sovereign powers (Sect. 3). These include the significant role of private actors in the public digital sphere, interference by foreign actors, Europe's rule of law crisis, the risk of poor digital governance, and the lack of digital literacy. Finally, I offer some concluding remarks, acknowledging the difficult balances the European Union will need to strike in its digital policies (Sect. 4).

---

[9] This includes the Digital Markets Act and the Digital Services Act, both of which were adopted in 2022.

[10] This includes the AI Act (Regulation 2024/1689 of 13 June 2024) and the AI Liability Directive (which is still being negotiated at the time of writing this article, see Proposal for a Directive of the European Parliament and of the Council on adapting non-contractual civil liability rules to artificial intelligence, COM/2022/496 final).

[11] This includes the Data Governance Act (Regulation 2022/868 of 30 May 2022) and the Data Act (Regulation 2023/2854 of 13 December 2023).

2 Unpacking Digital Sovereignty in the European Union

There is no single definition of sovereignty. Like many value-laden political concepts, it has in the past been characterised as a so-called essentially contested concept.[12] This is not different when it comes to *digital* sovereignty, and in this paper I will hence not make any attempt at defining this notion. Instead, I will briefly explore how this notion is currently used in the European Union context, with the aim of unpacking the core elements of its meaning for the purpose of our analysis.

Exploring digital sovereignty

Although the term 'digital sovereignty' had already previously entered public discourse, the year 2020 seems to have marked a high point for it. It was in this year that the French President Emmanuel Macron expressly proclaimed the need to ensure digital sovereignty at European level. According to him, this implied that it was

> up to Europe to define the regulatory framework that it imposes upon itself, as it entails both the protection of individual liberties and the economic data of our companies, lying at the heart of our sovereignty and our concrete operational capacity to act in an autonomous manner.[13]

2020 was also the year in which Germany explicitly put forward digital sovereignty as a *leitmotif* of European digital policy during its presidency of the European Council, 'to ensure that, in the context of fair competition, we increase our prosperity, protect our security and uphold our values.'[14] And it was the year that Thierry Breton, then European Commissioner for Internal Market, announced several initiatives to strengthen European digital sovereignty, which he equated with 'Europe defending its strategic interests' and 'making sure that anyone who invests, operates and bids in Europe respects our rules and values.'[15]

The fact that the calls for digital sovereignty only intensified thereafter was no surprise. The COVID-19 virus, which the World Health Organization formally started

---

[12] Georg Sørensen, 'Sovereignty: Change and Continuity in a Fundamental Institution' (1999) 47 Political Studies 590; Dan Sarooshi, 'The Essentially Contested Nature of the Concept of Sovereignty: Implications for the Exercise by International Organizations of Delegated Powers of Government' (2004) 25 Michigan Journal of International Law 1107.

[13] Author's translation from French. See Emmanuel Macron, 'Discours du Président Emmanuel Macron sur la stratégie de défense et de dissuasion devant les stagiaires de la 27ème promotion de l'école de guerre' (7 February 2020) <https://www.elysee.fr/emmanuel-macron/2020/02/07/discours-du-president-emmanuel-macron-sur-la-strategie-de-defense-et-de-dissuasion-devant-les-stagiaires-de-la-27eme-promotion-de-lecole-de-guerre> accessed 1 June 2023.

[14] Germany's Presidency of the Council of the European Union, 'Together for Europe's Recovery—Programme for Germany's Presidency of the Council of the European Union' (Federal Foreign Office 2020) 8.

[15] Thierry Breton, 'Speech by Commissioner Thierry Breton at Hannover Messe' (Hannover Messe Digital Days, 20 July 2020) <https://ec.europa.eu/commission/presscorner/detail/es/speech_20_1362> accessed 1 June 2023.

calling a pandemic in March 2020, offered a grim reminder of our collective dependence on digital technologies. Never was this dependency felt more than the moment when the world practically stopped, and digital technology became our only means of communicating, not only for private, but also for professional and public ends. More importantly, however, it also underlined our dependency on the enablers and providers of digital technology and its infrastructure. Consider, for instance, the Google-Apple partnership to develop application programming interfaces and operating system-level technology to allow for Bluetooth-based contact tracing. Rapidly, governments across the world started relying on this infrastructure to manage the pandemic—and to indirectly manage the civil liberties of their citizens. Yet as Luciano Floridi points out, the same companies saw no issue in admitting that they also had the power to 'disable the system on a regional basis when no longer needed'.[16]

Evidently, this reliance on digital technology, and on the entities providing it, raised new questions in relation to state sovereignty–not only at national but also at European Union level. In her 2020 State of the Union address, Commission President Ursula von der Leyen therefore acknowledged the need to 'double down' investments in 'European tech sovereignty' so as to 'shape our digital transformation according to our own rules and values'. Concretising this ambition, in early 2021 the European Commission published a Communication titled *2030 Digital Compass: the European way for the Digital Decade.* The Communication stressed how the pandemic 'exposed the vulnerabilities of our digital space' and 'its dependencies on non-European technologies.'[17] The Communication also set out 'concrete targets' to ensure that Europe's digital ambitions would be met, hence reflecting the desire of the European Union and its Member States to take (back) control over Europe's digital future.[18] The Union is indeed not entirely helpless when it comes to protecting its digital sovereignty, and European Union institutions have been exploring several ways to address new sovereignty-related questions. In this regard, Floridi also points out that 'between companies and states, the former can determine the nature and speed of change, but the latter can control the direction of change'.[19] Companies may well be the ones developing the technology, yet states are able to draw on their sovereignty to set the boundaries within which such development ought to take place.

The ability to decide on this direction is also echoed in Larsen's use of the term digital sovereignty, which according to him 'refers to a nation's ability to control its digital destiny', while adding that this 'may include control over the entire AI supply chain, from data to hardware and software'.[20] Furthermore, some references

---

[16] Luciano Floridi, 'The Fight for Digital Sovereignty: What It Is, and Why It Matters, Especially for the EU' (2020) 33 Philosophy & Technology 369, 369.

[17] European Commission, '2030 Digital Compass: The European Way for the Digital Decade' (2021) Communication from the Commission to the European Parliament, the Council, the European Economic and Social Committee and the Committee of Regions COM/2021/118 final.

[18] *Ibid.*

[19] Floridi (n 16) 371.

[20] Benjamin Cedric Larsen, 'The Geopolitics of AI and the Rise of Digital Sovereignty' (*Brookings*, 8 December 2022) < https://www.brookings.edu/research/the-geopolitics-of-ai-and-the-rise-of-digital-sovereignty/> accessed 8 April 2023.

to digital sovereignty go beyond the state and explicitly include the role of natural and legal persons, either directly, e.g., avowing that citizens and businesses should be able to independently assert control over their relationship with digital technology, or indirectly, e.g., avowing that states must ensure to 'protect their citizens and businesses from the manifold challenges to self-determination in the digital sphere'.[21]

Lifting this to the European context, European digital sovereignty can thus be understood as the ability of the European Union–including its citizens and businesses–to decide autonomously on their relationship with (providers of) digital technology.[22] This implies the exercise of control over two entwined elements, namely (a) the direction or 'destiny' of digital technology within the European Union, and (b) the concrete digital infrastructure that enables the technology. Let me briefly discuss each of these in turn, starting with the latter.

Economic digital sovereignty

Many digital sovereignty claims pertain to control over digital infrastructure, which is typically associated with productive capabilities and economic power in the digital sphere. Let us call this *economic digital sovereignty (EDS)*, or the ability of the European Union to control the production factors of digital technologies and their underlying infrastructure. It is in this context that the European Union's dependency on (foreign) technology actors is often problematised. Consider, for instance, the 2023 Opinion of the European Economic and Social Committee on Digital Sovereignty, which in its first paragraph states that

> despite significant progress to enhance the EU's digital sovereignty, there is still heavy reliance on non-EU-based tech companies. This is limiting the EU's leadership and strategic autonomy in the digital world, and in turn limiting the EU's economic growth potential.[23]

Think also of Commissioner Breton's above-mentioned speech, in which he stated that 'to be ahead of the curve, we need to develop suitable European infrastructures allowing the storage, the use, and the creation of data-based applications or Artificial Intelligence services. I consider this as a major issue of Europe's digital sovereignty.'[24] In other words, the European Union must limit its dependency on, and the influence of, technology actors in the US and China and bolster its own means of technology production. Concerns in this regard range from Europe's economic competitiveness and security, and its geopolitical position, to the general welfare of its constituents.

---

[21] Julia Pohle and Thorsten Thiel, 'Digital Sovereignty' (2020) 9 Internet Policy Review. Having analysed several digital sovereignty claims, Pohl and Thiel suggest these can be classified based on whether they seek to enhance self-determination by states, companies or individuals.

[22] The terms digital sovereignty, data sovereignty and technological sovereignty are sometimes used distinctly (see e.g., Fig. 1, page 2 of Annegret Bendiek and Isabella Stürzer, 'Advancing European Internal and External Digital Sovereignty. The Brussels Effect and the EU-US Trade and Technology Council' (2022) 20 SWP Comment 1.). However, I use the first term as also encompassing the latter two.

[23] Opinion of the European Economic and Social Committee on Digital Sovereignty: a crucial pillar for EU's digitalisation and growth 2023 (2023/C 75/02).

[24] Breton (n 15).

As a result, the European Union has been drawing on areas in which its legal competences are strongest–from internal market law to competition law–in order to take measures aimed at enhancing its economic digital sovereignty.[25] The European Chips Act is a case in point.[26] This regulation, which was proposed by the Commission in February 2022 and entered into force in September 2023, sets up the Chips for Europe Initiative in order to reinforce the Union's competitiveness, resilience and innovation capacity in the semiconductor industry. Concretely, it establishes a framework to financially support manufacturing facilities to ensure security of supply, and it creates a monitoring mechanism for the semiconductor value chain in order to respond to disruptions of the supply of semiconductors that have an impact on the proper functioning of the internal market.[27] Other examples are European Union initiatives concerning data and data governance,[28] network connectivity,[29] edge and cloud computing[30] and cybersecurity.[31]

Importantly, the European Union also clearly acknowledged the importance of these initiatives beyond the economy, and has highlighted their links with core European Union values, such as fundamental rights and democracy. By gaining more control over the production of digital technology and its infrastructure, the Union aims to increase its grip over the normative direction that digital technology is taking. This direction is also clearly expressed in the Parliament and Council Decision on the Digital Decade Policy Programme 2030, which expresses as one of its primary objectives in Article 3, 'promoting a human-centred, fundamental-rights-based, inclusive, transparent and open digital environment where secure and interoperable digital technologies and services observe and enhance Union principles, rights and values and

---

[25] See also Dennis Broeders, Fabio Cristiano and Monica Kaminska, 'In Search of Digital Sovereignty and Strategic Autonomy: Normative Power Europe to the Test of Its Geopolitical Ambitions' [2023] Journal of Common Market Studies 1, 5.

[26] Regulation (EU) 2023/1781 of the European Parliament and of the Council of 13 September 2023 establishing a framework of measures for strengthening Europe's semiconductor ecosystem and amending Regulation (EU) 2021/694 (Chips Act).

[27] The legal basis of the EU's Chips Act rests on two sets of provisions, namely Articles 173(3), 182(1) and 183 TFEU as regards the regulation's goal to accelerate the semiconductor production of the Union's industry, and Article 114 TFEU as regards its goal of creating a harmonised legal framework for increasing the Union's resilience and security of supply.

[28] For instance, the European Data Strategy of February 2020, which formed the basis of initiatives such as the Data Governance Act (Regulation 2022/868 of 30 May 2022) and the Data Act (Regulation 2023/2854 of 13 December 2023). To a certain extent, the General Data Protection Regulation (Regulation 2016/679 of 27 April 2016) also fits in this list, as it not only sets limitations but also seeks to enable the flow of personal data.

[29] For instance, the Gigabit Infrastructure Act, adopted in 2024 (Regulation (EU) 2024/1309 of the European Parliament and of the Council of 29 April 2024 on measures to reduce the cost of deploying gigabit electronic communications networks, amending Regulation (EU) 2015/2120 and repealing Directive 2014/61/EU).

[30] For instance, the launch of the European Alliance for Industrial Data, Edge and Cloud in July 2021, which builds on the European data strategy and the Declaration on European Cloud signed by EU Member States in October 2020.

[31] For instance, the Cybersecurity Act (Regulation 2019/881 of 17 April 2019).

are accessible to all, everywhere in the Union'. The economic is hence inherently intertwined with the normative.

Normative digital sovereignty

In the light of the above, claims about asserting the European Union's digital sovereignty not only extend to controlling digital technology and its infrastructure as such (for instance to reduce Europe's dependence on foreign providers thereof), but also allude to the self-determination of Europe's digital 'destiny' through norm-setting: by expressing the values that digital technology providers should abide by and the conditions to which technology should be subjected, Europe can shape how technology will shape its society. Hence this is often associated with legal powers and competences, or the capacity to set autonomously rules on digital technology and its providers. Let us call this *normative digital sovereignty (NDS)*, or the ability of the European Union to control the normative framework within which digital technologies operate in Europe. As noted above, within the European Union legal order, this framework can be shaped through legislative, adjudicative, regulatory and enforcement actions. Importantly, however, it encompasses an array of normative instruments going well beyond mere binding legislation, also including, for instance, soft law initiatives.

Accordingly, in addition to relying on its economic power, Europe can adopt norms or requirements for the design, provision and use of technology. To the extent that those norms also affect technology providers that are established outside the European Union, Europe can seek to impose its normative framework beyond its own constituents, and hence try to ensure that the digital technology that it is dependent on—even if foreign—nevertheless complies with its values. This has influentially been described by Anu Bradford as the so-called 'Brussels effect'.[32] Many of the European Union initiatives mentioned above are in fact hybrid in scope:[33] while they may focus primarily on norm-setting, they typically also have a strong economic undertone, given that the legal basis typically concerns Article 114 TFEU's internal market harmonisation.

The AI Act is a good example of this.[34] It establishes a harmonised legal framework for AI systems that are placed on the Union market to ensure they 'are safe and respect existing law on fundamental rights and Union values'.[35] Building on the *Ethics Guidelines for Trustworthy AI* developed by the Commission's High-Level

[32] Anu Bradford, *The Brussels Effect: How the European Union Rules the World* (Oxford University Press 2020).

[33] Broeders, Cristiano and Kaminska (n 25) 9.

[34] Regulation (EU) 2024/1689 of the European Parliament and of the Council of 13 June 2024 laying down harmonised rules on artificial intelligence and amending Regulations (EC) No 300/2008, (EU) No 167/2013, (EU) No 168/2013, (EU) 2018/858, (EU) 2018/1139 and (EU) 2019/2144 and Directives 2014/90/EU, (EU) 2016/797 and (EU) 2020/1828 (Artificial Intelligence Act). The AI Act relies on Article 114 TFEU as its legal basis and, more limitedly, Article 16 TFEU as concerns the specific rules it contains around the processing of personal (biometric) data in law enforcement.

[35] *Ibid*, Explanatory Memorandum.

Expert Group on AI in 2019,[36] the AI Act's primary aim is to set out a vision for Europe's AI 'destiny', ensuring that it is compatible with respect for fundamental rights, democracy and the rule of law by imposing a set of requirements on the provision and use of such systems. Clearly, this aim is not an ideal match with the product-safety regulation approach that was proposed to achieve it (and, unsurprisingly, the AI Act has not been spared from criticism).[37] That said, the AI Act can also be seen as a prime example of Europe making use of its regulatory power to impose its vision through a comprehensive set of rules that will have extra-EU effects, thus potentially gaining a first-mover competitive advantage in the race to AI regulation.[38] Moreover, at the same time, the Commission has been careful to stress that the enhanced legal certainty which the AI Act will generate will also benefit the economic development and uptake of AI in Europe. Normative direction-setting aims may well be at the forefront of the regulation, yet one of its explicit objectives also concerns the facilitation of investment and innovation in AI, for instance through the establishment of regulatory sandboxes in all Member States.

Economic and normative digital sovereignty can hence be seen as two sides of the same coin.[39] Critics have sometimes even blamed the European Union for relying on its legislative powers to compensate for its lack of economic power in the digital sphere, with China and the US being portrayed as *producing* technology, and Europe merely *regulating* it. Yet regardless of Europe's digital sovereignty standing, its constitutional obligation to adhere to human rights, democracy and the rule of law also means it must respect and protect these values across its digital policies. In other words, the Union's objective of expanding its economic digital sovereignty must not

---

[36] Nathalie A Smuha, 'The EU Approach to Ethics Guidelines for Trustworthy Artificial Intelligence' (2019) 20 Computer Law Review International 97.

[37] See e.g., Nathalie A Smuha and others, 'How the EU Can Achieve Legally Trustworthy AI: A Response to the European Commission's Proposal for an Artificial Intelligence Act' (Social Science Research Network 2021) <https://papers.ssrn.com/abstract=3899991>; Michael Veale and Frederik Zuiderveen Borgesius, 'Demystifying the Draft EU Artificial Intelligence Act' (2021) 22 Computer Law Review International 97; Nathalie A Smuha, 'Beyond the Individual: Governing AI's Societal Harm' (2021) 10 Internet Policy Review; Jeremias Adams-Prassl, 'Regulating Algorithms at Work: Lessons for a "European Approach to Artificial Intelligence"' (2022) 13 European Labour Law Journal 30.

[38] Nathalie A Smuha, 'From a "Race to AI" to a "Race to AI Regulation": Regulatory Competition for Artificial Intelligence' (2021) 13 Law, Innovation and Technology 57.

[39] One could also perceive the economic dimension as normative since economic policies are inevitably underpinned by an implicit or explicit normative vision of society.

stand in the way of–but rather should be conducive to–the protection of the European Union's core values as listed in Article 2 TEU.[40]

3 Five Challenges for European Digital Sovereignty

In the sections above, I have conceptualised European digital sovereignty as the European Union's ability to decide autonomously on its relationship with digital technology, both economically and normatively. This implies the ability to control the production factors of digital technologies and their underlying infrastructure, as well as the normative framework within which such technologies operate. Currently, this ability is threatened by various challenges, which the Union will need to tackle if it wishes to safeguard and maintain its digital sovereignty. Without the pretention of being exhaustive, in this section I examine five challenges in particular, focusing primarily on the normative dimension of digital sovereignty. Two of these challenges are *external* to the European Union, namely the significant role of private power in the public digital sphere (3.1) and malicious interference by foreign actors (3.2). Three of them are *internal*, namely Europe's so-called rule of law crisis (3.3), the risk of poor digital governance (3.4), and a lack of digital literacy (3.5).

3.1 Private Power in the Digital Public Sphere

Digital technology and the infrastructure that enables it is almost exclusively in the hands of private companies. A handful of these companies are denoted as 'big tech' or 'tech giants', in light of their dominant or quasi-dominant position in various areas of the tech industry, from artificial intelligence to cloud computing, e-commerce and social networking.[41] Essentially, these private actors make vital choices about the design of the technologies that shape our world in a multitude of ways. Decisions as to

[40] This appears to be explicitly acknowledged in the European Declaration on Digital Rights and Principles for the Digital Decade, signed by the Parliament and Council in December 2022. See The European Parliament, the Council and the Commission, 'European Declaration on Digital Rights and Principles for the Digital Decade' (2022) <https://digital-strategy.ec.europa.eu/en/library/european-declaration-digital-rights-and-principles> accessed 29 July 2023. Recital 6 of the Declaration's Preamble states that the

> EU way for the digital transformation of our societies and economy encompasses in particular digital sovereignty in an open manner, respect for fundamental rights, rule of law and democracy, inclusion, accessibility, equality, sustainability, resilience, security, improving quality of life, the availability of services and respect of everyone's rights and aspirations.

[41] See in this regard Damian Tambini and Martin Moore, *Regulating Big Tech: Policy Responses to Digital Dominance.* (Oxford University Press 2022).

which capabilities, limitations and thus affordances digital technologies should have, are riddled with normative implications. Consider, for instance, choices regarding the order and shape in which information is being shown to us on social media platforms, the content that is filtered on chatbots, the security measures implemented to prevent hacks or data leaks, the datasets on which AI systems are trained, or the ability to engage in end-to-end encrypted communication.

These digital technologies permeate our daily lives not only at the individual level, but also at the level of companies, organisations, public institutions and governments–all of which depend on them. Accordingly, decisions surrounding their operations and functioning have direct and indirect impacts on society at large, including in ways that we are not yet able to discern. Private actors hence also exercise considerable influence on the public sphere, without, however, being bound by the conditions that typically direct public action, such as the requirement to act in the public interest and the need to justify one's actions. In liberal democracies, justifications typically stem from a legal norm that was democratically decided upon and that grants certain competences. However, when it comes to big tech, decisions with normative implications are being taken by people who work in the interest of the private company that hired them, and without democratic input, even though it affects the public at large. It is hence no surprise that large tech companies are being called 'quasi-sovereign' given the extent of their power.[42] Interestingly, regulators are also treating the heads of these companies as they would treat heads of state.[43]

Moreover, when the European Union (or any other regulator, for that matter) seeks to deploy its normative digital sovereignty to reign in the power of these companies, these efforts must grapple not only with an inherent asymmetry of information, but also with billions of dollars that the same companies are spending to lobby against restrictive regulations that would undermine their power.[44] Yet in a less overt manner, these companies also influence European Union norms by framing the role of their technologies within a positive narrative of progress, ingenuity, and public interest—through marketing, advertising and other initiatives–which in turn affects public opinion as well as policy initiatives around those technologies.

Furthermore, even when hard law has been adopted, it is clear that legislation has its limits. For instance, over six years after its entry into force, experience with the

---

[42] See for instance Broeders, Cristiano and Kaminska (n 25) 2.

[43] For instance, a scroll through the Twitter feed of Sam Altman (CEO of Open.AI) between April and June 2023, shows him having one high-level meeting after another with heads of state, as well as the President of the European Commission, all eagerly posing next to him for a formal picture.

[44] For instance, during the AI Act's negotiations Open AI has been called out for lobbying for the watering down of certain requirements in the Act, as reported by Billy Perrigo, 'Exclusive: OpenAI Lobbied E.U. to Water Down AI Regulation' *Time* (20 June 2023) <https://time.com/6288245/openai-eu-lobbying-ai-act/> accessed 22 June 2023. For another example, see reporting around the efforts to weaken the Digital Markets Act before its finalisation: Natasha Lomas, 'Report Reveals How Big Tech Lobbied to Weaken EU Rules' *TechCrunch* (22 April 2022) <https://techcrunch.com/2022/04/22/google-facebook-apple-eu-lobbying-report/> accessed 22 June 2023.

GDPR has shown that its safeguards are being underenforced.[45] Even when investigations are carried out and infringements of European Union competition law or data protection law are found, the size of the fines that are imposed barely makes a difference for companies whose annual revenues are higher than the GDP of several countries. Some have therefore called for the creation of publicly-funded alternatives to private tech infrastructures or 'digital public infrastructures'.[46] The fact that many of these companies are established outside Europe—and hence might be more difficult to bring within Europe's jurisdiction, despite their effect on the European public sphere—has also inspired calls for the establishment of European-based big tech platforms.[47] Yet regardless of their place of establishment, large private actors in the digital sphere will continue posing a significant challenge to the European Union's ability to decide autonomously on its digital fate. And while the Union has been adopting and negotiating a series of new regulations that aim to tighten its control over that fate, only time will tell how effective these rules will be in the event private tech companies would prefer not to abide by them.

3.2 *Interference by Foreign Entities*

A second challenge emanates from outside the European Union's borders, and arises when foreign entities deliberately interfere with Europe's digital sovereignty. Such interference is neither new nor confined to the European Union. Russia has, for instance, been accused of interfering both with the US elections of 2016[48] and with the UK's Brexit referendum[49] which took place in the same year, as well as

---

[45] See e.g., Estelle Masté, 'Four Years under the GDPR: How to Fix Its Enforcement' (Access Now 2022) <https://www.accessnow.org/wp-content/uploads/2022/07/GDPR-4-year-report-2022.pdf> accessed 29 June 2023.

[46] Ethan Zuckerman, 'The Case for Digital Public Infrastructure' (The Knight First Amendment Institute at Columbia University 2020) <http://knightcolumbia.org/content/the-case-for-digital-public-infrastructure> accessed 25 June 2023.

[47] Jean-François Bobier and others, 'Can Europe Create Its Own Deep-Tech Giants?' (Boston Consulting Group 2022) <https://www.bcg.com/publications/2022/how-can-europe-build-deep-tech-leaders> accessed 25 June 2023.

[48] United States Senate, 'Report of the Select Committee on Intelligence—Russian Active Measures Campaigns and Interference in the 2016 US Election' (2020) <https://www.intelligence.senate.gov/sites/default/files/documents/Report_Volume1.pdf> accessed 29 June 2023. See also Kathleen Hall Jamieson, *Cyberwar: How Russian Hackers and Trolls Helped Elect a President: What We Don't, Can't, and Do Know* (Oxford University Press 2020).

[49] This accusation is more contentious, and the UK government was criticised for not duly investigating such interference. See also Mark Landler and Stephen Castle, '"No One" Protected British Democracy From Russia, U.K. Report Concludes' *The New York Times* (21 July 2020) <https://www.nytimes.com/2020/07/21/world/europe/uk-russia-report-brexit-interference.html > accessed 29 June 2023.

alleged attempts to interfere in European Union Member States.[50] A 2016 Joint Communication by the European Commission and the High Representative of the Union for Foreign Affairs and Security Policy underlined an increase in security challenges—particularly in the form of hybrid threats, described as

> the mixture of coercive and subversive activity, conventional and unconventional methods (i.e., diplomatic, military, economic, technological), which can be used in a coordinated manner by state or non-state actors to achieve specific objectives while remaining below the threshold of formally declared warfare.[51]

These activities range from blatant cyber-attacks on digital (critical) infrastructure to the initiation of mis- and dis-information campaigns and (social) media manipulation. Evidently, foreign meddling with the European Union's digital and political infrastructure undermines the Union's digital sovereignty. While securing resilience against such threats is primarily a Member State responsibility, the Union is increasingly seeking to coordinate and consolidate Member State efforts in this context.[52] Evidently, a vulnerability in one Member State leads to the vulnerability of the European Union as a whole. This also led the European Parliament to set up a Special Committee on Foreign Interference in all Democratic Processes in the European Union, including Disinformation (INGE) in June 2020. The mandate of this Committee was renewed in March 2022 (ING2), with a final report adopted in June 2023 calling for 'a coordinated strategy to increase the EU's resilience to foreign interference and information manipulation and protect the 2024 European elections.'[53]

When Russia invaded Ukraine in February 2022, this not only destabilised the global 'order' that had been taken for granted by many, but it also served as a chilling reminder that such threats are not limited to cyberspace. Moreover, it exposed even more clearly Europe's vulnerability when it comes to physical infrastructures that enable digital technology. If gas pipelines can be sabotaged, are undersea internet cables next?[54] And if so, how can these be protected? The fact that these cables—on which the internet traffic of virtually the entire world depends—are operated largely by private companies, does not make things easier.

---

[50] See Erik Brattberg and Tim Maurer, 'Five European Experiences with Russian Election Interference' (Carnegie Endowment for International Peace 2018).

[51] European Commission and High Representative of the Union for Foreign Affairs and Security Policy, 'Joint Communication to the European Parliament and the Council: Joint Framework on Countering Hybrid Threats—a European Union Response' (2016) JOIN (2016) 18 final.

[52] See e.g., also High Representative of the Union for Foreign Affairs and Security Policy, 'Joint Report to the European Parliament and the Council on the Implementation of the Joint Framework on Countering Hybrid Threats—a European Union Response' (European Commission 2017).

[53] European Parliament, 'Foreign Interference: MEPs Call for Urgent Protection of 2024 European Elections' (6 January 2023) <https://www.europarl.europa.eu/news/en/press-room/20230524IPR91908/foreign-interference-meps-call-for-urgent-protection-of-2024-european-elections> accessed 24 June 2023.

[54] Mark Scott, 'Will Russia Attack Undersea Internet Cables Next?' *POLITICO* (29 September 2022) <https://www.politico.eu/article/everything-you-need-to-know-about-the-threat-to-undersea-internet-cables/> accessed 24 June 2023.

It should be stressed that the threat of foreign interference is certainly not limited to Russia. Malicious cyber activities directed against European Union institutions and European companies have also emanated from China,[55] leading the Parliament's ING2 Special Committee to focus on both Russian and Chinese interference. Furthermore, beyond (cyber) attacks and informational warfare campaigns, foreign actors have other tools to influence the European Union's digital sovereignty. Consider, for instance, European companies' reliance on Chinese digital technology, which can lead to infrastructural vulnerabilities by facilitating surveillance practices.[56] Likewise, China's data regulations can be seen against the same background. As Kokas persuasively argues, China protects its digital borders by controlling data and tech infrastructure and meticulously adopted laws 'that enshrine direct government access to corporate data, both domestically and internationally', thus facilitating so-called 'data-trafficking'.[57] This affects not only individuals but also companies and institutions whose data is being 'trafficked'. Accordingly, through norm-setting, China is exercising its own digital sovereignty to enlarge its grip over foreign entities. Another example concerns the European Union's criticism of Chinese court rulings that prevent European companies from protecting their intellectual property rights for technological innovations.[58] These tensions show the inherent link between economic and normative digital sovereignty, as they are largely fuelled by the differences in the underlying societal value-systems. Moreover, the global rise in authoritarian tendencies[59] makes it likely that clashes in value-systems will continue to threaten Europe's digital sovereignty.

The European Union is not entirely defenceless against these threats. The Commission has sought recourse to dispute resolution mechanisms to enforce the rights of European Union companies,[60] and has adopted several initiatives to limit its dependency on foreign technologies. Moreover, various regulations have been

---

[55] 'China: Declaration by the High Representative on Behalf of the European Union Urging Chinese Authorities to Take Action against Malicious Cyber Activities Undertaken from Its Territory' *Council of the European Union* (19 July 2021). See also Stuart Lau, 'Europe Joins US to Condemn Cyberattacks from China' *POLITICO* (19 July 2021) <https://www.politico.eu/article/europe-us-condemnation-china-state-sponsored-cyberattacks/> accessed 24 June 2023.

[56] See e.g., Clothilde Goujard, 'Time to Ban TikTok, EU Lawmakers Tell Governments' *POLITICO* (2 June 2023) <https://www.politico.eu/article/time-ban-tiktok-kaspersky-huawei-eu-parliament-lawmakers/> accessed 25 June 2023; Samuel Stolton and Laurence Cerulus, 'Belgian Intelligence Puts Huawei on Its Watchlist' *POLITICO* (28 March 2023) <https://www.politico.eu/article/belgian-intelligence-huawei-watchlist-espionage-china-eu-nato/> accessed 25 June 2023.

[57] Aynne Kokas, *Trafficking Data: How China Is Winning the Battle for Digital Sovereignty* (Oxford University Press 2022) 2.

[58] European Commission, 'EU Challenges China at the WTO to Defend High-Tech Sector' (Brussels, 18 February 2022) <https://ec.europa.eu/commission/presscorner/detail/en/ip_22_1103> accessed 25 June 2023.

[59] Freedom House, 'Freedom in the World 2022: The Global Expansion of Authoritarian Rule' (2022) <https://freedomhouse.org/sites/default/files/2022-02/FIW_2022_PDF_Booklet_Digital_Final_Web.pdf> accessed 1 August 2022.

[60] E.g., before the WTO, see European Commission, 'EU Challenges China at the WTO to Defend High-Tech Sector' (n 58).

adopted precisely to better protect the Union's constituents. The General Data Protection Regulation (GDPR), for instance, establishes important safeguards against trafficking in individuals' data.[61] Furthermore, since October 2020, the Foreign Direct Investment Regulation applies.[62] In determining whether a foreign investment merits screening, the Regulation considers the investment's effect on, *inter alia*, 'critical technologies and dual use items (including artificial intelligence, robotics, semiconductors, cybersecurity, quantum, aerospace, defence, energy storage, and nuclear technologies, nanotechnologies and biotechnologies)' and on 'access to or the ability to control sensitive information'.[63] In addition, the Commission is currently mulling over a ban on European companies developing certain sensitive technologies abroad,[64] just as it is urging Member States to disallow certain foreign companies from participating in their 5G telecoms networks out of security concerns.[65] Finally, as a response to Russia's invasion of Ukraine, the European Union also managed to adopt several heavy sanction packages with the aim of weakening Russia's ability to finance and continue the war. Many of these sanctions explicitly targeted the digital sector, including for instance the imposition of technology export controls.[66] These examples demonstrate the Union's ability to target foreign countries that threaten its values. At the same time, the effectiveness of these efforts depends greatly on the strength of the European Union's own (economic) digital sovereignty, the sovereignty of its 'allies', and the way in which other countries and institutions are positioning themselves in this arena.

[61] European Parliament and Council, Regulation (EU) 2016/679 of the European Parliament and of the Council of 27 April 2016 on the protection of natural persons with regard to the processing of personal data and on the free movement of such data, and repealing Directive 95/46/EC (General Data Protection Regulation) 2016 1. See also Zuzanna Gulczyńska, 'A Certain Standard of Protection for International Transfers of Personal Data under the GDPR' (2021) 11 International Data Privacy Law 360.

[62] Regulation (EU) 2019/452 of the European Parliament and of the Council of 19 March 2019 establishing a framework for the screening of foreign direct investments into the Union (OJ L 79I, 21 March 2019, pp. 1–14).

[63] *Ibid*, Article 4.

[64] Jakob Hanke and Barbara Moens, 'EU Looks to Ban Companies from Making Sensitive Tech in China' *POLITICO* (20 June 2023) <https://www.politico.eu/article/eu-ban-companies-make-sensitive-tech-china/> accessed 25 June 2023.

[65] Reuters, 'China Slams EU Ban on Huawei, ZTE Demands Equal Treatment' *Reuters* (16 June 2023) <https://www.reuters.com/business/media-telecom/china-firmly-opposes-huawei-ban-by-some-eu-countries-2023-06-16/> accessed 25 June 2023.

[66] See in this regard Michael Adam and Sanne Keijer, 'Sanctions on the Russian Digital Sector: How Effective Are They?' (European Parliamentary Research Service 2023). June 2023 marked the adoption of the 11th sanction package against Russia, see 'Press Release: EU Adopts 11th Package of Sanctions against Russia for Its Continued Illegal War against Ukraine' *European Commission* (Brussels, 23 June 2023) <https://ec.europa.eu/commission/presscorner/detail/en/ip_23_3429> accessed 23 June 2023.

3.3 *Europe's Rule of Law Crisis*

The rise in authoritarian tendencies is not confined to countries outside Europe. Over the past decade, several European Union Member States have taken actions that weakened human rights protections, undermined the democratic process and eroded the rule of law. From the adoption of laws that blatantly discriminate against people of a different sexual orientation[67] and judicial reforms that undermine the separation of powers,[68] to obstructions of civil society organisations and independent media outlets[69]— collectively, these developments are seen as a 'rule of law crisis' within the European Union.[70] The EU's digital sovereignty thus faces an important threat that emanates from within the European Union legal order. When the very Member States that make up the Union decide to ignore or violate EU law, or to undermine its primacy, this weakens Europe's ability to maintain its autonomy, including when it comes to its relationship with digital technology.

Crucially, however, the European Union seems to treat concerns linked to digital technologies as separate from concerns linked to its rule of law crisis, despite the fact that the former can exacerbate the latter. Scholars have increasingly been mapping the harms that can arise from the ubiquitous use of automated decision-making systems, especially in the public sphere. These encompass, *inter alia*, the risk of bias and discrimination, wide-spread manipulation, mass-surveillance and privacy infringements, and the erosion of the rule of law.[71] Yet at the same time, the European Union is (financially) encouraging Member States to digitalise and automate its

67 See in this regard Katinka Linnamäki, 'Not in Front of the Child: Illiberal Familism and the Hungarian Anti-LGBTQ+ "Child Protective Law"' (2022) 10 Politics and Governance 16.

68 See also Anna Śledzińska-Simon, 'The Rise and Fall of Judicial Self-Government in Poland: On Judicial Reform Reversing Democratic Transition' (2018) 19 German Law Journal 1839.

69 European Federation of Journalists, 'Hungary Dismantles Media Freedom and Pluralism' (European Federation of Journalists 2019) <https://europeanjournalists.org/blog/2019/12/03/new-report-hungary-dismantles-media-freedom-and-pluralism/> accessed 29 June 2023; 'Hungarian Civil Society Raises Alarm over NGO Law Change' (*Euractiv*, 22 April 2021) <https://www.euractiv.com/section/justice-home-affairs/news/hungarian-civil-society-raises-alarm-over-ngo-law-change/> accessed 5 September 2022.

70 JHH Weiler, 'Europe in Crisis—On Political Messianism, Legitimacy and the Rule of Law' [2012] Singapore Journal of Legal Studies 248; Laurent Pech and Kim Lane Scheppele, 'Illiberalism Within: Rule of Law Backsliding in the EU' (2017) 19 Cambridge Yearbook of European Legal Studies 3.

71 Mireille Hildebrandt, 'Algorithmic Regulation and the Rule of Law' (2018) 376 Philosophical Transactions of the Royal Society A: Mathematical, Physical and Engineering Sciences 20,170,355; M Brkan, 'Artificial Intelligence and Democracy' (2019) 2 Delphi—Interdisciplinary Review of Emerging Technologies 66; Gabbrielle M Johnson, 'Algorithmic Bias: On the Implicit Biases of Social Technology' (2021) 198 Synthese 9941; Francesco Ragazzi and others, 'Biometric & Behavioural Mass Surveillance in EU Member States' (Report for the Greens/EFA in the European Parliament 2021) <http://extranet.greens-efa.eu/public/media/file/1/7297> accessed 16 February 2022. See also Nathalie A. Smuha, *Algorithmic Rule By Law: How Algorithmic Regulation in the Public Sector Erodes the Rule of Law* (Cambridge University Press, forthcoming at the time of writing this article).

public services.[72] And in the new AI act, barely any distinction is made between requirements imposed on high-risk systems used by private companies and those used by governments. For virtually all systems, no prior verification by an independent entity is needed to assess whether the requirements are met before the system is used. Member States' police forces and migration authorities are hence able to 'self-assess' the compatibility of their AI systems with the AI Act's requirements.[73]

Admittedly, an independent national supervisory authority can carry out *ex post* compliance controls. Moreover, when it comes to the use of facial recognition systems by law enforcement authorities in public places–an extremely sensitive application given its significant impact on several human rights–the suggested additional safeguard consists of 'pre-judicial approval' of the technology's use.[74] What is, however, the value of a pre-judicial approval if the executive branch of a Member State continuously seeks to capture the judiciary and undermines its impartiality? What is the value of *ex post* control by a supervisory authority if that authority's independence cannot be guaranteed? And even if both the judiciary and the supervisory authority would nevertheless carry out their functions in an impartial and independent manner–how much damage can a government cause to human rights, democracy and the rule of law by deploying AI systems at scale in a way that fosters illiberal and authoritarian ends, before its actions are challenged?

These two sets of problems should hence not be seen in isolation from each other. The European Union's ability to decide autonomously its digital course risks being undermined if it cannot be ensured that Member States will actually abide by its digital policies. Moreover, given the mutual trust that underpins the European Union legal system, all Member States are adversely affected when one Member State shies away from its commitments under European Union law and is no longer worthy of such trust. In addition, this also affects the European Union's external position, as its geopolitical strength–including when it comes to digital matters–hinges on its unity. Accordingly, if the European Union wishes its digital policies to succeed, both internally and externally—it is crucial that it gets a better grip on this threat from within.

Admittedly, some European Union institutions have made attempts to tackle these concerns. The European Parliament adopted several resolutions against Hungary[75]

---

[72] The EU recovery plan, designed to 'rebuild a post-COVID-19 Europe', explicitly includes a pillar on 'digital transformation' that Member States need to integrate in their recovery and resilience plans to receive a financial contribution.

[73] See also Smuha and others (n 36) 37.

[74] In the AI Act, pre-judicial approval was introduced as a safeguard against law enforcement's arbitrary reliance on (real-time) remote biometric identification.

[75] See for instance 'European Parliament Resolution of 1 June 2023 on the Breaches of the Rule of Law and Fundamental Rights in Hungary and Frozen EU Funds' (European Parliament 2023) (2023/2691(RSP)) <https://www.europarl.europa.eu/doceo/document/TA-9-2023-0216_EN.html> accessed 28 June 2023.

and Poland,[76] asking the Commission and the Council to take action. The Commission also brought these Member States before the European Court of Justice for rule of law and human rights infringements.[77] It also recently launched the conditionality mechanism against Hungary, which allows the Union to target breaches of the rule of law that affect or seriously risk affecting the sound financial management of the budget or the protection of the Union's financial interests.[78] The Court of Justice has issued several judgments[79] condemning Member States' actions that were incompatible with protection of the rule of law, as has the European Court of Human Rights in Strasbourg.[80] Nevertheless, concerns remain. Furthermore, the values of liberal democracy are inherently fragile in all countries, especially given the increase in populism. Their protection and realisation should hence be considered as a continuous work in progress, which should be pursued in all domains of European Union action. It is hence crucial for the Union to contextualise this internal threat also within the sphere of its digital policies.

3.4 Poor Digital Governance

A fourth challenge stems from the risk that the European Union will use its norm-setting power in an inadequate manner, thereby foregoing the protection of its constituents against the adverse effects that digital technologies can generate. If its existing or upcoming digital regulations are deficient, incomplete or ineffective,

---

[76] See for instance European Parliament, 'European Parliament Resolution of 17 September 2020 on the Proposal for a Council Decision on the Determination of a Clear Risk of a Serious Breach by the Republic of Poland of the Rule of Law (COM(2017)0835—2017/0360R(NLE))'; 'European Parliament Resolution of 21 October 2021 on the Rule of Law Crisis in Poland and the Primacy of EU Law' (European Parliament 2021) (2021/2935(RSP)).

[77] See for instance European Commission, 'Commission Refers Hungary to the Court of Justice of the EU over Violation of LGBTIQ Rights' *European Commission—European Commission* (Brussels, 15 July 2022) <https://ec.europa.eu/commission/presscorner/detail/en/ip_22_2689> accessed 28 June 2023; European Commission, 'The European Commission Decides to Refer Poland to the Court of Justice of the European Union for Violations of EU Law by Its Constitutional Tribunal' *European Commission—European Commission* (Brussels, 15 February 2023) <https://ec.europa.eu/commission/presscorner/detail/en/ip_23_842> accessed 28 June 2023.

[78] European Commission, 'Proposal for a Council Implementing Decision on Measures for the Protection of the Union Budget against Breaches of the Principles of the Rule of Law in Hungary' (European Commission 2022) COM (2022) 485 final.

[79] See e.g., Laurent Pech and Dimitry Kochenov, 'Respect for the Rule of Law in the Case Law of the European Court of Justice: A Casebook Overview of Key Judgments since the Portuguese Judges Case' (SIEPS 2021) <https://www.sieps.se/en/publications/2021/respect-for-the-rule-of-law-in-the-case-law-of-the-european-court-of-justice/> accessed 29 July 2023.

[80] See in this regard also Elisabeth Steiner, 'The Rule of Law in the Jurisprudence of the European Court of Human Rights' in Werner Schroeder (ed), *Strengthening the Rule of Law in Europe: From a Common Concept to Mechanisms of Implementation* (Hart Publishing 2016); Robert Spano, 'The Rule of Law as the Lodestar of the European Convention on Human Rights: The Strasbourg Court and the Independence of the Judiciary' (2021) 27 European Law Journal 211.

or if Member States fail to implement them duly, the role of digital technology in European society will evolve in a way that was not desired, or that is incompatible with the European Union's values. In essence, through poor digital governance, the European Union could also undermine its own digital sovereignty. It is hence not enough for the European Union to adopt legislative initiatives in the digital sphere, but it is essential that those initiatives are robust, evidence-based, and capable of steering digital technology in the direction that guarantees their compatibility with human rights, democracy and the rule of law. To concretise the risk of poor digital governance, let me provide an example of the consequences that may follow from poor AI regulation.

At the time of writing of this paper, the European Parliament and the Council just finalised negotiating the abovementioned AI Act, setting out the conditions under which AI systems can be placed on the market or put into service in the European Union. These negotiations are took place amidst tensions between those who fear that a strict approach to AI regulation might harm innovation and undermine the benefits it can generate, and those who maintain that strict rules are indispensable to protect European Union values against AI's risks. What happens if it turns out that this balance was not struck in an appropriate manner? Let us imagine that the new AI governance framework would have erred on the side of the former, foregoing any imposition of stringent transparency and accountability rules for AI providers and users, and instead relying on voluntary codes of conduct. This would severely undermine our ability to assess whether the organisations that deploy AI systems are abiding by European Union law—including EU non-discrimination legislation and data protection regulations–thus diminishing the EU's digital sovereignty.

Moreover, AI systems are also being increasingly used to enforce (European Union) law, by 'translating' legal rules into code to enable algorithmic regulation (whether by governments, for instance in public administrations, or by companies, for instance in the context of AI-enabled content moderation). Without a proper AI governance mechanism, it will be impossible to verify whether a translation has occurred in a manner that is compatible with European Union law. Nor will it be possible to ensure that governments are not somehow relying on those systems to surveil and control their population in a way that is incompatible with EU norms.[81] More generally, the risk is not merely the fact that an array of intrusive AI applications—from facial recognition systems to predictive policing and manipulative chatbots—will be rolled out in all domains of our lives and affect human rights. The main danger is that this roll-out will prove irreversible as AI systems become an inextricable part of existing infrastructures. High investments, path dependencies, and the gradual habituation of these systems across the population will lead to their societal entrenchment, even if undermining our individual and collective autonomy, and thus also our sovereignty.[82]

---

[81] See in this regard also Marvin van Bekkum and Frederik Zuiderveen Borgesius, 'Digital Welfare Fraud Detection and the Dutch SyRI Judgment' (2021) 23 European Journal of Social Security 323.

[82] See in this regard Karen Yeung, 'Why Worry about Decision-Making by Machine?' in Karen Yeung and Martin Lodge (eds), *Algorithmic Regulation* (Oxford University Press 2019); Karen

The European Union legislator created a unique opportunity to decide upon Europe's AI future—one that will be difficult to revisit now that the AI Act is adopted. Despite uncertainties about the evolution of the technology, despite the information asymmetries between AI developers and regulators, and despite the lack of a proper understanding of the technology's (long term) impact on society, the European Union was forced to take a stance on AI's governance and ensure that the normative framework it puts in place aligns with its goals and values. This has not been an easy task, especially in the light of the Union's desire also to foster the technology's development within its borders and reduce dependencies on foreign technology providers. Yet given the rapid and widespread implementation of ever more powerful AI systems, there is little time for regulatory experimentation that can help ensure a regulatory race to the top, since not (yet) regulating is also a choice, and one that the European Union could ill afford.[83] It hence needed to rely on its vast experience with (other technology) regulation to ensure an approach that is both pungent and flexible in protecting its digital fate, and only time will tell whether the AI Act will succeed in fulfilling those aims.

3.5 *Lack of Digital Literacy*

The final challenge I wish to highlight concerns the need for an appropriate level of digital literacy within the European Union. After all, to exercise digital sovereignty, one must have an understanding of what digital technologies are, how they function, what their capabilities and limitations are, and how they affect society. This holds true for regulators at national and European Union level that adopt digital policies, but it is equally important for citizens, who must be able to express their informed opinion, within a democratic process, regarding the type of digital future they envisage for society. Studies have for instance found a positive correlation between digital literacy and online political engagement.[84] In essence, digital literacy can be seen as a precondition for digital sovereignty.

Yeung, 'Responsibility and AI—A Study of the Implications of Advanced Digital Technologies (Including AI Systems) for the Concept of Responsibility within a Human Rights Framework' (Council of Europe 2019) DGI(2019)05.

[83] Smuha, 'From a "Race to AI" to a "Race to AI Regulation"' (n 38) 81.

[84] Kahne, Nam-Jin Lee and Jessica Timpany Feezell, 'Digital Media Literacy Education and Online Civic and Political Participation' (2012) 6 International Journal of Communication 1; See also Joseph Kahne and Benjamin Bowyer, 'Can Media Literacy Education Increase Digital Engagement in Politics?' (2019) 44 Learning, Media and Technology 211; Yunrong Li and Gang Li, 'The Impacts of Digital Literacy on Citizen Civic Engagement—Evidence from China' (2022) 3 Digital Government: Research and Practice 1.

According to Eurostat, in 2021 only 54% of people in the European Union aged 16 to 74 had basic overall digital skills.[85] Digital skills in this context refer to information and data literacy skills, communication and collaboration skills, digital content creation skills, safety skills and problem-solving skills.[86] To increase this number, the Commission launched the Digital Education Action Plan, aimed at improving 'digital literacy, skills and capacity at all levels of education and training and for all levels of digital skills'.[87] While education remains primarily a Member State competence, especially as regards the content of educational programs and their organisation, the Commission has encouraged coordinated actions at the level of the European Union, from the exchange of best practices to supporting cooperation in the educational realm.

Importantly, digital literacy includes, but goes beyond, digital skills. It also implies the ability to think critically about and engage with digital technologies, and to understand their (adverse) effects on individuals and society. Regarding AI literacy, for instance, the High-Level Expert Group on AI noted that this covers

> fostering the understanding of AI systems more generally (including a basic understanding of machine learning and reasoning), but also raising awareness of data protection rights, an understanding of how (personal) data can be used, the implications of digital tracking, and the importance of issues such as fairness, explainability, transparency, robustness of AI systems, and knowledge of these topics.[88]

The lack of such understanding stands in the way of participating in public debates, which are increasingly taking place in the digital sphere. Yet it also diminishes people's ability to realise the impact that digital technology might have on their lives. This, in turn, diminishes their ability to formulate their views on which impact they deem compatible with societal values, and their ability to urge political representatives to take proper action.

Finally, ensuring digital literacy is not only crucial in order to *adopt* but also to *enforce* the digital regulations through which the European Union is exerting and protecting its digital sovereignty. The AI Act, for instance, hinges on the development of standards through which compliance with its requirements can be assessed and compared, from AI fairness to transparency.[89] Developing such standards requires an understanding both of the technical aspects of the technology and of its effects

---

[85] 'How Many Citizens Had Basic Digital Skills in 2021?' (Eurostat 2022) <https://ec.europa.eu/eurostat/web/products-eurostat-news/-/ddn-20220330-1> accessed 26 June 2023.

[86] *Ibid*. To be classified as having 'basic overall digital skills', a person must be able to carry out at least one activity related to each of those areas.

[87] European Commission, 'Communication from the Commission to the European Parliament, the Council, the European Economic and Social Committee and the Committee of the Regions: Digital Education Action Plan 2021–2027—Resetting Education and Training for the Digital Age' (2020) SWD (2020) 209 final. The first such plan was adopted in January 2018 as part of the initiative to establish a European Education Area.

[88] High-Level Expert Group on AI, 'Policy and Investment Recommendations for Trustworthy AI' (European Commission 2019) 10 <https://digital-strategy.ec.europa.eu/en/library/policy-and-investment-recommendations-trustworthy-artificial-intelligence>.

[89] According to Recital 61 of the Commission's proposal for an AI Act,

on individuals and society, including for instance how the technology might affect fundamental rights. There is therefore a need for people with multidisciplinary skills to ensure that the AI Act's aspired-to safeguards are effectively implemented.[90] Similarly, Member States need to appoint supervisory authorities that can verify compliance with the AI Act's requirements.[91] Yet apart from needing financial resources, such authorities will only be able to properly carry out their tasks if they also have the necessary *human* resources with sufficient competences and skills. To secure their digital sovereignty also over the longer term, EU institutions and Member States alike will need to step up their efforts and augment Europe's digital literacy sooner rather than later.

4 Conclusions

The European Union has put digital sovereignty increasingly high on its agenda. The ubiquity of digital technologies in all domains of society has prompted concerns about the level of control we still have over our relationship with them, and over their effects on individuals, companies and institutions–for better and for worse. Strengthening digital sovereignty is thus seen as a means to secure such control, and in particular to maintain autonomy over Europe's digital 'destiny'. The scale at which these technologies function and our increased dependency on them has given the matter a sense of urgency.[92] As the Commission and the High Representative noted in a recent Communication on this subject,

> the global pandemic, Russia's illegal and unprovoked war in Ukraine, hostile economic actions, cyber and infrastructure attacks, foreign interference and disinformation and a global increase in geopolitical tensions have exposed risks and vulnerabilities in our societies, economies and companies that did not exist only a few shorts year ago.[93]

In this paper, I have sought to unpack the notion of digital sovereignty in the European Union through an exploration of its use in European discourse. While digital sovereignty is elastic and knows various dimensions, a dual thread seems

standardisation should play a key role to provide technical solutions to providers to ensure compliance with this Regulation. Compliance with harmonised standards as defined in Regulation (EU) No 1025/2012 of the European Parliament and of the Council 54 should be a means for providers to demonstrate conformity with the requirements of this Regulation.

[90] See in this regard also the example in Francesco Sovrano and others, 'Metrics, Explainability and the European AI Act Proposal' (2022) 5J 126.

[91] See Article 70 and following of the AI Act.

[92] See also Madiega Tambiama, 'Digital Sovereignty for Europe' (European Parliamentary Research Service 2020) EPRS Ideas Paper.

[93] European Commission and High Representative of the Union for Foreign Affairs and Security Policy, 'Joint Communication to the European Parliament, the European Council and the Council on "European Economic Security Strategy"' (European Commission 2023) JOIN (2023) 20 final.

to run across many of its conceptions, namely the ability to control the production factors of digital technologies and their underlying infrastructure (*i.e.,* economic digital sovereignty) and the ability to control the normative framework within which such technologies operate (*i.e.,* normative digital sovereignty). Focusing primarily on the latter, I then examined five challenges that the Union must tackle to secure its sovereignty ambitions in the digital realm. Yet the economic and the normative are intrinsically intertwined, and the question remains to which extent the European Union can impose its values on digital technology (providers) without also ramping up its global digital market share.

Without a doubt, the regulatory choices and investments that the Union will adopt during this 'digital decade' will be determinative of Europe's digital fate for decades to come. A delicate balance will need to be struck between the potential for innovation and protective regulation, between economic gains and individual rights, and between international cooperation and strategic independence. There is no single way to govern digital technologies, and only time will tell if the course adopted by the European Union will generate the effects intended. Yet as long as Europe bears in mind the constitutional boundaries of its sovereignty–namely the need to protect human rights, democracy and the rule of law–there is hope that it can harness technology in a way that not only safeguards but even fosters the very values that ground its legal order.

Failing Better? Member State Sovereignty Concerns and the European Union's Inability to Create a Durable Fiscal Policy

Gavin Barrett

> *"Ever tried. Ever failed. No matter. Try again. Fail again. Fail better."*
> *Samuel Beckett, Worstward Ho!*

1 Introduction

The purpose of this chapter is to reflect briefly on the role of sovereignty concerns in the development of European fiscal policy. It is the argument of this chapter that such concerns have marked the shape of economic and monetary union from the very beginning, that they have had a restrictive effect on the development of the currency union and that even now they continue to play a major retarding role and indeed seem likely to continue to do so. It might well be countered that sovereignty concerns always exist on any occasion on which it is sought to transfer national competences to EU level. Yet such concerns appear to have carried particular weight in the policy field of EMU, since (and as shall be seen in more detail in the text below):

(i) Member States have only ever committed themselves to the mere coordination of fiscal policy, rather than giving even shared (much less exclusive) competence to the EU in this field;

Professor of Law, Jean Monnet Professor of European Constitutional and Economic Law, Sutherland School of Law, University College Dublin.
The author acknowledges the valuable research assistance provided by Marie-Hélène de Bairéid in the writing of this chapter.

G. Barrett (✉)
Dublin, Ireland
e-mail: gavin.barrett@ucd.ie

G. Barrett et al. (eds.), *European Sovereignty*,
https://doi.org/10.1007/978-3-031-71851-9_11

(ii) enforcement of any such coordination was–strikingly–first sought to be outsourced to the (foreseeably) dubious efficiency of the markets rather than being entrusted in a meaningful and operational form to the EU;

(iii) when a (merely preventive and corrective) role was conferred by legislation on the EU, this was first done in a narrowly-focused and enduringly ineffective form, involving non-automatic legal sanctions, the final decision on which was carefully left to the Council (in which Member State interests are represented) rather than the Commission (in which the interests of the EU as a whole are meant to prevail). In practice, no sanctions have ever been applied by the Council (despite supposed reforms and scope-broadening changes over the years to the relevant rules). No Member State has ever yet been fined or penalised for budgetary misbehaviour. The net effect of this is that even when power has been given to the EU to enforce fiscal discipline, the Member State representatives in Council have shown no interest in deploying it, effectively negating much of the effect of a sovereignty transfer in this area;

(iv) there has been a failure to develop a permanent fiscal policy along the lines of anything seen in national federal entities involving a large central budget resourced independently of the Member States. While there have been significant recent steps which may ultimately lead in this direction, they have been stipulated to be temporary in nature and have tended to be permeated with intergovernmentalism and unanimity voting requirements.

All of this is gone into in more detail in the text that follows, however. In order to gain an understanding of fiscal policy within the Economic and Monetary Union, it is important to remember that this Union is effectively divided into two separate aspects.[1] In the first place, there is the field of monetary policy which is both harmonised and an exclusive competence of the European Union.[2] In contrast, when it comes to economic policy–usually interpreted in the EMU context as meaning fiscal policy (essentially the powers to tax, spend and borrow)–the role of the European Union is, as already mentioned, merely to *coordinate*. Thus Article 5 TFEU provides that "the Member States shall coordinate their economic policies within the Union…Specific provisions shall apply to those Member States whose currency is the euro." Unlike monetary policy therefore, economic policy has remained the preserve of the Member States rather than of the European Union, even if the Member States have agreed that it should be coordinated to some degree at EU level.[3]

The division between monetary and economic policy is not quite as watertight as this may make it sound. The European Central Bank has engaged in several major programmes, which have at the very least skirted the borderline between fiscal

---

[1] See for a very readable introduction to this area, Michele Chang, *Economic and Monetary Union* (Palgrave Macmillan, 2016), chapter 2.

[2] Article 3(1) TFEU provides that "the Union shall have exclusive competence in the following areas… (c) monetary policy for the Member States whose currency is the euro".

[3] For a useful introduction to the law of economic and monetary union, see, *Alicia Hinarejos,* Economic and monetary union, chapter 19 of Steve Peers and Catherine Barnard, *European Union Law* (4th edition, Oxford University Press 2023), chapter 19.

policy and monetary policy. These have included the Outright Monetary Transactions Programme,[4] followed by, for example, the Bank's massive quantitative easing programmes. Notwithstanding the very real effects that these programmes have had on the economies of Eurozone States, however, they have both been held by the European Court of Justice to fall under the rubric of monetary rather than fiscal policy.[5] In the *Gauweiler* case, in particular, the European Court of Justice noted that that in order to determine whether a measure fell within the area of monetary policy it was appropriate to refer principally to the objectives of that measure.[6] The fact that the Outright Monetary Transactions programme might also be capable of contributing to the economic stability of the euro area did not call that assessment into question: a monetary policy measure could not be treated as equivalent to an economic policy measure merely because it might have indirect effects on the eurozone economy.[7] Similarly, in the *Weiss* ruling, the Court of Justice upheld the legality of the secondary markets public sector asset purchase (quantitative easing) programme.[8] Given these findings but also because of the constraints of space, it is not proposed to deal with such ECB initiatives further in this chapter. However, this is not to say that the Outright Monetary Transactions and quantitative easing programmes have not had major fiscal policy implications, for they clearly have. Indeed, their implications may be said to have stretched beyond the merely economic into the political or even constitutional, since the economic relief they provided may be said to have relieved what would otherwise have been far greater pressure on Member States to abandon their sovereignty concerns and endow the European Union with a fiscal capacity of a

---

[4] Rather remarkably, this was never activated but its mere announcement was of major political and economic significance. See Alicia Hinarejos, "The Legality of Responses to the Crisis", chapter 41 of Fabian Amtenbrink and Christoph Herrmann (eds.), *The EU Law of Economic and Monetary Union* (Oxford University Press, Oxford, 2019) at 1368 *et seq.*. See also Vestert Borger, "The transformation of the ECB in sovereign bond markets", Chap. 2 of Thomas Beukers, Diane Fromage, and Giorgio Monti, *The New European Central Bank: Taking Stock and Looking Ahead* (Oxford University Press 2022).

[5] *See* the decisions of the European Court of Justice in Case C-62/14 *Gauweiler and Others* and Case C-493/17 *Weiss* EU:C:2015:400.

[6] See para. 46 of the ruling of the Court, relying on its earlier ruling to that effect in Case C-370/12 *Pringle* EU:C:2012:756, paragraphs 53 and 55.

[7] See paras. 51–52 of the ruling of the Court.

[8] Case C-493/17 *Weiss and Others* ECLI:EU:C:2018:1000. See especially para. 61 of the ruling in which the Court observed that

> it should be recalled that a monetary policy measure cannot be treated as equivalent to an economic policy measure for the sole reason that it may have indirect effects that can also be sought in the context of economic policy (see, to that effect, judgments of 27 November 2012, *Pringle*, C-370/12, EU:C:2012:756, paragraph 56, and of 16 June 2015, *Gauweiler and Others*, C-62/14, EU:C:2015:400, paragraph 52).

kind more comparable to that which has tended to be seen in more long-established federal structures.[9]

2 European Union Fiscal Policy—A System and its Several Iterations

The EU's framework of fiscal policy rules has undergone several iterations since (and indeed during) the birth of Economic and Monetary Union. These iterations have supposedly sought to ensure fiscal coordination between states participating in the monetary union and to ensure the stability of national budgets, something regarded as a precondition for the stability of the single currency. In practice, however, to the extent to which they have involved coordination, they have operated largely as a merely political process of peer pressure, since the Member States appear to have been steadfastly disinterested in deploying the legal procedures that they themselves had set up for the enforcement of fiscal rules.

Various stages in the evolution of this framework can be identified:

(i) the adoption of the effective constitution of Economic and Monetary Union in the primary law of the then European Community in the Maastricht Treaty (which entered into force in 1993)—largely along the lines of the proposals in the Delors Report of 1989[10];

(ii) the revisiting of the issue of fiscal policy in the Amsterdam European Council conclusions in June 1996[11]—in other words, after the Maastricht settlement but prior to the advent of the so-called third (and final) stage of EMU—and the subsequent adoption of secondary legislation constituting the so-called Stability and Growth Pact (SGP) in line with the European Council conclusions[12];

(iii) the shuddering blow to the credibility of the Pact brought about at the behest of Germany and France in November 2003, through the organisation of a blocking minority in Council to prevent the censure of those States for breach of the Pact's terms, a step which the Court subsequently refused to interfere with,[13]

---

[9] See for some reflections on this topic, Alicia Hinarejos, "Fiscal Union by Other Means? The ECB and the Courts", Chap. 10 in Alicia Hinarejos and Robert Schütze, *EU Fiscal Federalism: Past, Present, Future* (Oxford University Press 2023).

[10] Report of the Committee for the Study of Economic and Monetary Union (European Community, Luxembourg, April 1989).

[11] See Resolution of the European Council on the Stability and Growth Pact (Amsterdam, 17 June 1997) (OJ C 236 2.08.1997).

[12] Namely Council Regulation (EC) No 1467/97 of 7 July 1997 on speeding up and clarifying the implementation of the excessive deficit procedure (OJ L 209 2.08.1997); and Council Regulation (EC) No 1466/97 of 7 July 1997 on the strengthening of the surveillance of budgetary positions and the surveillance and coordination of economic policies (OJ L 209 2.08.1997).

[13] See Case C-27/04 *Commission v Council* EU:C:2004:436 (Judgment of the Full Court, 13 July 2004).

and the subsequent relaxation of the terms of the Pact in 2005, rendering it more flexible and discretionary[14];

(iv) the amendment of the Pact in various ways (including broadening its ambit and purportedly improving its enforcement mechanism, by the 2011 'six-pack' of legislative measures[15] and the 2013 'two-pack'[16]) in response to the economic and banking crises which shook the EU from 2008 onwards, accompanied by the adoption of the Fiscal Stability Treaty;

(v) the adoption of the potentially revolutionary fiscal model constituted by the (for now purely temporary) Next Generation EU initiative in 2021,[17] at the same

---

[14] See Council Regulation (EC) No 1055/2005 of 27 June 2005 amending Regulation (EC) No 1466/97 on the strengthening of the surveillance of budgetary positions and the surveillance and coordination of economic policies (OJ L 352 M 31.12.2008); and Council Regulation (EC) No 1056/2005 of 27 June 2005 amending Regulation (EC) No 1467/97 on speeding up and clarifying the implementation of the excessive deficit procedure (OJ L 174, 7.7.2005), the effects of which are examined in Antonio Estella, "EU Fiscal Coordination", Chap. 6 of Hinarejos and Schütze (n. 9) at 152–156.

[15] Consisting of Regulation (EU) No 1175/2011 of the European Parliament and of the Council of 16 November 2011 amending Council Regulation (EC) No 1466/97 on the strengthening of the surveillance of budgetary positions and the surveillance and coordination of economic policies (OJ L 306, 23.11.2011); Council Regulation (EU) No 1177/2011 of 8 November 2011 amending Regulation (EC) No 1467/97 on speeding up and clarifying the implementation of the excessive deficit procedure (OJ L 306, 23.11.2011); Regulation (EU) No 1173/2011 of the European Parliament and of the Council of 16 November 2011 on the effective enforcement of budgetary surveillance in the euro area (OJ L 306, 23.11.2011); Council Directive 2011/85/EU of 8 November 2011 on requirements for budgetary frameworks of the Member States (OJ L 306, 23.11.2011); Regulation (EU) No 1176/2011 of the European Parliament and of the Council of 16 November 2011 on the prevention and correction of macroeconomic imbalances (OJ L 306, 23.11.2011); and Regulation (EU) No 1174/2011 of the European Parliament and of the Council of 16 November 2011 on enforcement measures to correct excessive macroeconomic imbalances in the euro area (OJ L 306, 23.11.2011).

[16] Consisting of Regulation (EU) No 473/2013 of the European Parliament and of the Council of 21 May 2013 on common provisions for monitoring and assessing draft budgetary plans and ensuring the correction of excessive deficit of the Member States in the euro area (OJ L 140, 27.5.2013); and Regulation (EU) No 472/2013 of the European Parliament and of the Council of 21 May 2013 on the strengthening of economic and budgetary surveillance of Member States in the euro area experiencing or threatened with serious difficulties with respect to their financial stability (OJ L 140, 27.5.2013).

[17] NextGeneration EU was put in place via the adoption of a series of interlocking legal measures: Council Regulation (EU) 2020/2094 of 14 December 2020 establishing a European Union Recovery Instrument to support the recovery in the aftermath of the COVID-19 crisis (OJ L 433I, 22.12.2020); Council Regulation (EU, Euratom) 2020/2093 of 17 December 2020 laying down the multiannual financial framework for the years 2021 to 2027 (OJ L 433I, 22.12.2020); Council Decision (EU, Euratom) 2020/2053 of 14 December 2020 on the system of own resources of the European Union and repealing Decision 2014/335/EU, Euratom (OJ L 424, 15.12.2020); Regulation (EU) 2021/241 of the European Parliament and of the Council of 12 February 2021 establishing the Recovery and Resilience Facility (OJ L 57, 18.2.2021); Regulation (EU, Euratom) 2020/2092 of the European Parliament and of the Council of 16 December 2020 on a general regime of conditionality for the protection of the Union budget (OJ L 433I, 22.12.2020); and the Interinstitutional Agreement between the European Parliament, the Council of the European Union and the European Commission on budgetary discipline, on cooperation in budgetary matters and on sound financial management, as

time as the amended Stability and Growth Pact was suspended for the duration of the COVID-19 crisis (a suspension later prolonged by a further year into 2024 to cope with the effects of the Russian invasion of Ukraine);[18] and finally
(vi) the current proposals (not yet adopted at the time of writing of this chapter) seeking to modify the amended Stability and Growth Pact rules in anticipation of their resurrection, now that the COVID-19 crisis has passed.

However, none of these iterations of the fiscal policy framework has proved enduring. Furthermore, the presently mooted changes, which seem likely to form the next iteration of the fiscal framework of EMU do not self-evidently appear to be the final word on the topic. It is worthwhile considering the various stages identified above in somewhat more detail in the text that follows.[19]

3 In the Beginning: the Maastricht Treaty Arrangements on Fiscal Policy

The agreement to pool monetary sovereignty which formed such a significant part of the Maastricht Treaty signed in 1992 was indisputably a major step for Member States, and involved a very considerable pooling of sovereignty in and of itself. However, the extent of the sovereignty that Member States were willing to share in the 1990s had very definite limits. It has always been broadly accepted that a monetary union cannot exist independently of provisions regarding participant states' fiscal policy: hence, for example, an excessively loose fiscal policy can destroy confidence in a currency, as the markets may come to fear that debts will be paid off by turning on the printing presses. Yet Member States, perhaps already feeling they had ceded enough to the European Union by envisaging and facilitating a single currency stepped back at Maastricht from drawing what were arguably the full consequences of monetary union and from making extensive provisions in the fiscal sphere.

Under the original design of Economic Monetary Union, as this emerged from the Maastricht Treaty, the policy of the European Union was thus to leave fiscal policy largely to the Member States, subject to the rigours of market discipline, subject, as we have already seen, to a vague commitment to coordination seen in Article 5

---

well as on new own resources, including a roadmap towards the introduction of new own resources Interinstitutional Agreement of 16 December 2020 between the European Parliament, the Council of the European Union and the European Commission on budgetary discipline, on cooperation in budgetary matters and on sound financial management, as well as on new own resources, including a roadmap towards the introduction of new own resources (OJ L 433I, 22.12.2020). See more generally Federico Fabbrini, *EU Fiscal Capacity* (Oxford University Press 2022), Chap. 4.

[18] See János Allenbach-Ammann, "EU fiscal rules to be suspended for another year", Euractiv, 23 May, 2022.

[19] For a good analysis of EU fiscal coordination from the pre-Maastricht era up to the six-pack and two-pack reforms, see Estella (n. 14). For the impact of COVID-19 and the Ukraine conflict, see Fabbrini (n. 17).

TEU,[20] and a few substantive rules, outlined in the text below. This policy of non-intervention was reinforced by various articles in the Treaty, such as the Article 123 TFEU[21] prohibition on monetary financing and the Article 125 TFEU 'no bailout' rule, the purport of both of which was that if Member States behaved in a fiscally irresponsible manner, they would be subject to the full rigours of the market, and neither the European Union nor its Member States (or so the Treaty signalled) would intervene.

The idea was thus that the markets would ultimately be responsible for ensuring fiscal discipline. Strikingly, the Member States at Maastricht permitted hardly anything by way of substantive regulation of their fiscal behaviour to be inserted in the Treaties. As has been observed of the (to date, still largely unamended) Treaty rules on EMU,

> there are few substantive rules, with fiscal governance being mainly defined in terms of procedures for EU surveillance of Member States' policies. Beyond the general principle that Member States should 'regard their economic policies as a matter of common concern' (Article 121(1) TFEU), ensuring 'compliance' with the guiding principles of 'stable prices, sound public and monetary conditions and a sustainable balance of payments' (Article 120 and Article 119(3) TFEU), the only provision in the Treaty that comes close to a substantive fiscal rule is that Member States 'shall avoid excessive government deficits' (Article 126(1)).[22]

Article 126 TFEU was supplemented by the associated Protocol (No 12) on the Excessive Deficit Procedure annexed to the Treaties, Article 1 of which laid down the famous reference values of 3% for the ratio of government deficits to GDP and 60 % for the ratio of government debt to GDP. Even this excessive deficits/debts rule would need to be subsequently extensively elaborated upon by secondary legislation in order to make it in any way workable. An enforcement mechanism for it was lacking in the Maastricht settlement and, notwithstanding the various evolutions in European Union fiscal policy examined in the text below, an *effective* such mechanism has remained lacking right up to the present day. At Maastricht, even if the Member States were willing to concede in theory that monetary union could not leave them with an entirely free fiscal hand, they remained unwilling to concede to the European Union much more than the benefit of several vague and non-committal generalisations in this regard. The waves of European regulation therefore began (as they would later continue) by washing impotently against the largely rock-solid face of state sovereignty.

The failure to provide for proper enforcement of agreed fiscal discipline standards was not the only lacuna in the Economic and Monetary Union. In most fiscal unions, the loss of tools such as the power to devalue a currency and the power to control interest rates tends to be compensated for by a centralised budget, financed in some

---

[20] See further Alicia Hinarejos, *The Euro Area Crisis in Constitutional Perspective* (Oxford University Press, Oxford, 2015) 121.

[21] The post-Lisbon numbering of these articles is used in this chapter, but the content of the relevant provisions corresponds very closely with the original provisions.

[22] Lucio Pench, "The new Stability and Growth Pact: Innovation and Continuity in the Light of Next Generation EU", (Rebuild Centre Working Paper No. 14, 2024) at 2.

shape or form by taxation revenue sourced independently of the Member States. Asymmetrical shocks impacting on a particular area or participant state in such a currency area (normally a state) can be compensated for in such currency unions by reductions in the tax take to the centre and by increases in social welfare provision from the centre–effectively involving a transfer of resources from other areas of the currency union. Yet the size of the European Union's budget has remained pitifully small in comparison to federal states such as the United States, Canada, Australia, Germany or Belgium. Moreover, such revenue as the European Union receives tends to be constituted in the main (even if not exclusively) by direct member state contributions, which are hard fought over, and politically controversial in most, if not all, Member States. Member State governments will normally be anxious to assure their electorates that they are not the paymasters of the Union and increases in contributions tend to be fiercely resisted. Yet the same States–ever sovereignty conscious–have equally resisted the creation of a new centralised fiscal authority with independent powers of taxation and expenditure.

4 Fiscal Policy Revisited: the Stability and Growth Pact

The hands-off design of fiscal policy that emerged from the Maastricht Treaty negotiations did not endure even until the advent of full economic and monetary union. The Member States quickly had second thoughts regarding the adequacy of the fiscal arrangements they had agreed, and revisited the Maastricht settlement, even while leaving the Treaty provisions embodying the original settlement unchanged.

Hence after the adoption of the Treaty provisions on EMU at Maastricht, but before the entry into force of full economic and monetary union most of a decade later, and largely influenced by German concerns that strict fiscal discipline be exercised by EMU participant States, the Member States adopted the so-called 'Stability and Growth Pact' (which, notwithstanding its name, always far concerned fiscal stability much more than growth). Introduced in 1997, the Pact provided legislative underpinning for the Treaty rules on excessive debts and deficits.[23] It also sought to streamline fiscal governance obligations and to promote stability-oriented monetary policies. The Pact involved both a so-called Preventive Arm and a so-called Corrective Arm. *The Preventive Arm* had the effect that the Commission and Council gained authority to monitor Member State budgets, requiring detailed reports on national budget management strategies aiming for a budget "close to balance or in surplus".[24] Fiscal policy was to be conducted by Member States in a sustainable manner over the medium term. Member States were required to achieve and maintain a medium-term budgetary objective (specific to each country and taking into account each country's individual economic and budgetary position) which provided a safety margin against

[23] See further Jean-Paul Keppenne, "Fiscal rules", Chap. 3 of Federico Fabbrini and Marco Ventoruzzo (eds.), *Research Handbook on EU Economic Law* (Edward Elgar 2019).

[24] See generally Regulation 1467/97 (n. 12).

the risk of breaching the 3% deficit threshold. Following surveillance, the Council was to offer recommendations to the state, signalling that it should persist with a national plan or take corrective action if deviations persisted or worsened. A failure in preventive measures would trigger the "corrective" phase of the SGP.

The Corrective Arm elaborated on the Treaty's 'Excessive Deficit Procedure' (EDP) system.[25] Under this, as has been seen, if a Eurozone State's government deficit (broadly speaking) exceeded the reference value of 3% of GDP or its government debt exceeded the reference value of 60% of GDP, it would be considered to have an excessive deficit or debt. The European Commission would assess the situation and make recommendations to the Member State to correct the excessive deficit or debt. The Council was given a window to impose sanctions after notice. Regulation 1467/97 favoured non-interest-bearing deposits as initial sanctions, convertible to fines if deficits persisted after two years, intensifying pressure for compliance.

Notwithstanding the carefully-crafted system provided for in the Stability and Growth Pact, the Pact has from the outset been largely enforced at the political level, rather than any other. It has essentially been a system of fiscal discipline based on two elements–first, Member State peer pressure (allied to domestic political considerations), and secondly, the threat of loss of market confidence.[26] The extent to which this has translated into prudent national fiscal policy has unsurprisingly in the light of this varied from one State to another, as well as over time.[27]

A striking feature of the Stability and Growth Pact was how little scope it left for judicial enforcement. Its provisions were never held to be directly effective, in other words, to confer rights which national courts must enforce. European-level courts also find themselves on the sidelines: the Member States excluded the possibility of either Commission or Member State prosecutions for violations of the excessive debt procedure under Arts. 258 and 259 TFEU.[28] Moreover, judicial review by individuals of the excessive debt procedure was–predictably–excluded by the Court itself because of what was held to be their lack of direct concern.[29]

---

[25] Article 126 TFEU.

[26] The loss of market confidence frequently comes late but it can strike with extraordinary force. A relatively recent example was seen following the fiscally reckless mini-budget introduced by the United Kingdom during the short-lived premiership of Liz Truss, which led to the collapse of sterling in the currency markets, a precipitous fall in gilt prices, rocketing UK government bond yields and the threaten of pension fund insolvencies. (See Richard Partington, "The mini-budget that broke Britain—and Liz Truss", The Guardian, 20 October 2022.) The political impact of all this was sufficient to force Truss to resign as prime minister.

[27] See the observations in this regard in Fitch, "Effectiveness of the EU's Redesigned Fiscal Rules Remains Uncertain", 23 March 2024.

[28] See Article 126(10) TFEU, which provides that "The rights to bring actions provided for in Articles 258 and 259 may not be exercised within the framework of paragraphs 1 to 9 of this Article".

[29] See Case T-215/11 *ADEDY and Others v Council of the European Union* EU:T:2012:627 (Order of the General Court of 27 November 2012). This concerned actions for annulment concerning decisions addressed to Greece with a view to its remedying a situation of excessive deficit. The actions were held inadmissible by reason of what was held to be an absence of direct concern on the part of the litigants.

In practice, and notwithstanding appearances, then, this was a Pact that left Eurozone states a very wide amount of discretion. Sovereignty therefore very much remained at State level. As Pench has concisely summarised

> the Treaty does not give to the EU the power to directly interfere with national budgets and EU fiscal rules cannot be enforced via the Court of Justice. This makes EU fiscal governance more akin to a form of organised peer pressure than genuine supranational decision-making.[30]

Even such European-level peer pressure as existed had its limits reflected in wide Commission and Council discretion: at every step of the way, the system was designed to ensure that the Commission might well propose–but the Council would decide, with a failure to decide not being actionable under Article 265 TFEU. Thus when the Commission proposed sanctions for both Germany in 2002 and France in 2003 in respect of their fiscal misbehaviour, these countries engineered the creation of a blocking minority within the Council of the European Union to prevent any sanctions being applied to them. Although the Commission challenged this before the European Court of Justice in *Commission v Council*,[31] it did not succeed in this action. In essence, the Court held that the Council had not been guilty of any actionable failure to act by reason of its failure to adopt the recommendations of the Commission. The unfortunate result of this was to put an end to the operation of the Stability and Growth Pact as a means of ensuring fiscal discipline at least insofar as this was supposed to happen through the operation of the Pact's own enforcement provisions.

A second flaw in the Stability and Growth Pact was its excessively narrow focus on deficit and debt limits. This failing would come home to roost when the sovereign debt crisis arrived relatively undetected by a Union unable to drag its attention away from the siren-like fascination apparently generated by the issue of debts and deficits.

5 The 2005 Relaxation of the Stability and Growth Pact

Successively, with the agreement on the Maastricht Treaty provisions and then the Stability and Growth Pact, regulation of fiscal coordination in the EU could be characterised as having become increasingly strict. Increasingly strict provisions on enforcement meant little without the will to enforce them however–and that such a lack of will existed was highlighted by the circumstances that led to the ruling in *Commission v. Council.*[32] The next iteration of the fiscal policy framework of the European Union–the 2005 relaxation of the Stability and Growth Pact–went in the opposite direction to the earlier ones. Legislation was adopted in that year in the shape of Regulation 1055/2005,[33] bringing notable changes to the Pact's Corrective

[30] Pench (n. 22) 26.

[31] Case C-27/04 *Commission v Council* EU:C:2004:436.

[32] Case C-27/04 *Commission v Council* EU:C:2004:436.

[33] Council Regulation (EC) No 1055/2005 of 27 June 2005 amending Regulation (EC) No 1466/97 on the strengthening of the surveillance of budgetary positions and the surveillance and coordination of economic policies (OJ L 174, 7.7.2005, 1–4).

Arm, but also essentially confirming the relaxed approach that had been taken by the Member States to the enforcement of fiscal rules,[19] and reflecting in turn political pressure from France and Germany, which had failed to comply with the Pact from 2003 on, and were not inclined to see themselves punished for this.

The combination of the political unwillingness within the Council to apply sanctions and the relaxation of the rules to reflect a more relaxed approach had as an unfortunate consequence a breakdown in fiscal discipline among the Member States. Greece in particular was guilty of particularly egregious breaches in this respect which came to light when the government changed in Greece and the new government–in order to politically embarrass its predecessor–revealed that the latter been communicating incorrect figures concerning debt and deficit levels to the other Member States.[34] This immediately, however, triggered panic in the bond markets concerning Greek debt, necessitating the financial rescue of that country.

The EU response to the financial crisis that began with Greece, but would come to concern other countries including Ireland, Portugal, Cyprus (all of whom would enter EU-IMF bailout programmes) but also Spain and Italy, had several facets. These included the construction of temporary bailout mechanisms followed by a permanent bailout mechanism in the form of the European Stability Mechanism,[35] as well as the creation of a European Banking Union. It is however its implications for fiscal policy that concern us here.

6 The Six-Pack, the Two-Pack and the Fiscal Stability Treaty

The fiscal policy implications of the combined economic and banking crisis at European level which began in 2008 included the adoption, in 2011, of the so-called Six-Pack of legislation and in 2013 of the so-called Two-Pack of legislation which had the collective effect of both broadening and deepening the Stability and Growth Pact.[36] Broadening the Pact included the introduction of a Macroeconomic Imbalance Procedure, the scope of which went beyond merely looking at debt and deficit limits and whether these had been breached. Deepening it involved providing for more stringent enforcement and heftier sanctions and preventing these sanctions from being avoided by the assembly of a blocking minority in Council. Instead, from now on, a reverse majority rule would apply within the Council, with the result that

---

[34] See for one account of this, Jean Pisani-Ferry, *The Euro Crisis and its Aftermath* (Oxford University Press 2014) at 8 *et seq.*

[35] See concerning the European Stability Mechanism, Menelaos Markakis, "The Reform of the European Stability Mechanism: Process, Substance and the Pandemic" (2020) 47 Legal Issues of Economic Integration 359; and Jean-Victor Louis, "The unexpected revision of the Lisbon Treaty and the establishment of a European Stability Mechanism" in Diamond Ashiagbor, Nicola Countouris and Ioannis Lianos, *The European Union after the Treaty of Lisbon* (Cambridge University Press 2012), chapter 11.

[36] See the measures listed in ns. 15 and 16. See for further discussion, Estella (n. 14) 149.

sanctions could be adopted under the Stability and Growth Pact, unless a qualified majority was assembled in *opposition* to those sanctions.[37]

In addition to the reforms to the Six-Pack and the Two-Pack, a Fiscal Stability Treaty was also adopted, further strengthening the fiscal framework. The Treaty included several key provisions: its core was the so-called 'fiscal compact' according to which somewhat stricter fiscal rules were introduced, including the introduction of the notion of structural deficits. Member States had to adhere to the so-called balanced budget Rule, and thus maintain a balanced budget or surplus with an annual 'structural deficit' not exceeding 0.5% of the gross domestic product (GDP). In addition, they had to follow the so-called debt brake rule by reducing public debt exceeding 60% of GDP at an average rate of one-twentieth per year. The Treaty also enhanced surveillance and coordination of economic policies among Member States.[38]

The original attempt to constitutionalise the Fiscal Stability Treaty by including it in the European Union treaties failed, thanks to (somewhat opportunistic) opposition to this from the United Kingdom and the Czech Republic. The Fiscal Stability Treaty was thus adopted as an intergovernmental treaty, rather than as an amendment to the TFEU. The original idea that it require the introduction of a balanced-budget rule into the constitutions of the various Member States also failed. However, only a very much watered-down provision of this requirement was ultimately included.[39]

For all their purported strictness, the reforms which have just been described did not appear to work according to their own terms: in the face of fiscal misbehaviour, no sanctions were ever applied under the reformed rules: indeed the Commission never even proposed their application to the Council, apparently knowing better than to propose sanctions that would never be accepted. Although it can be countered that Member States have at least striven in practice to comply with at least some of the Pact's strictures, this appears to have been more the result of peer pressure than the enforcement of rules effecting the transfer of any economic sovereignty to EU level. Beyond apparent Member State unwillingness to contemplate the Stability and Growth Pact's enforcement according to its own terms, other problems also affected the Pact.

Its one-size-fits-all approach, in other words, its failure to differentiate between states, and across-the-board application of the Treaty reference values of requiring public debt to be below 60% of GDP and the budget deficit to be below 3%[40]–requiring tougher consolidation the more a State fell short–meant the Pact's prescriptions could be seen both as unrealistic and as potentially counterproductive. They might, for example, encourage poor policy outcomes such as procyclical budgets and

---

[37] See for a detailed analysis of the provisions of the Six Pack and Two Pack, Estella (n. 14) 149.

[38] Treaty on Stability, Coordination and Governance in the Economic and Monetary Union 2013.

[39] Article 3(2) of the Treaty now merely requires "provisions of binding force and permanent character, preferably constitutional, or otherwise guaranteed to be fully respected and adhered to throughout the national budgetary processes".

[40] See Article 1 of Protocol (No 12) on the Excessive Deficit Procedure. See also M. Sandbu, "*A new start for Europe's stability and growth pact*", Financial Times, 31 December 2023.

reductions in needed public investments.[41] Thus even where the Pact had an impact, its effect on public finances has not always been viewed positively.

On top of all of this, the Pact was also regarded as too complex: in practice, better compliance has tended to be seen with the Pact's deficit rules than its requirements regarding debt, in part because the former were clearer and easier to understand. From 2017 to 2019, indeed, it must be acknowledged that violations of the deficit criterion were rare, even if this came about as a result of favourable refinancing conditions and a sustained period of uninterrupted growth, rather than any road-to-Damascus-like change of heart regarding fiscal policy on the part of Member States.[42]

Viewed in the round, Eurozone States' records of compliance with the Stability and Growth Pact until its eventual suspension in 2020 can be described as having been weak. Notwithstanding this, however, and as has already been noted, no sanctions for violation of the Pact's requirements were applied. Long-term increases in public debt ratios diverged, rising in the absence of adequately built-up fiscal buffers. Yet, nervous of exacerbating growing deflationary tendencies, the Commission held back from deploying the excessive deficit procedure.[43] Overall, prior to COVID-19, deficits were reduced, but debts were not.[44] Ultimately the revised rules were to be suspended with the onset of the pandemic itself–a step showing their unsuitability of the normal regime in the event of economic crises–and remained suspended until shortly before the publication of this book.

7 COVID-19 and the Suspension of Aspects of the Stability and Growth Pact

On 23 March 2020, the budgetary requirements imposed by the Stability and Growth Pact (if not the actual procedures) were suspended by the Council acting on a Commission proposal under that Pact's general escape clause.[45] The excessive debt

---

[41] Sandbu (n. 40).

[42] See for some useful background in this regard, Klaus-Jürgen Gern,Stefan Kooths and Ulrich Stolzenburg, *When and How to Deactivate the SGP General Escape Clause? Fiscal Surveillance after the Break* (European Parliament (PE 651.376, Economic Governance Support Unit, Directorate-General for Internal Policies of the European Parliament, December 2020).

[43] Fitch (n. 27) 1.

[44] Assisted however by improved economic conditions. See Pench (n. 22) 4. See more generally European Commission, *Economic governance review report on the application of Regulations (EU) No 1173/2011, 1174/2011, 1175/2011, 1176/2011, 1177/2011, 472/2013 and 473/2013 and on the suitability of Council Directive 2011/85/EU* (Communication from the Commission to the European Parliament, the Council, the European Central Bank, the European Economic and Social Committee and the Committee of the Regions (COM/2020/55 final).

[45] See European Commission, *Communication from the Commission to the Council on the activation of the general escape clause of the Stability and Growth Pact* (COM(2020) 123 final, Brussels, 20 March 2020). The clause, introduced as part of the 'Six-Pack' reform of the Stability and Growth Pact in 2011, is set out in Articles 5(1), 6(3), 9(1) and 10(3) of Regulation (EC) 1466/97 and Articles 3(5) and 5(2) of Regulation (EC) 1467/97. Note also European Commission, *2020*

procedure was effectively also suspended, this time by means of a policy of avoiding taking any decision to place member states in the procedure in the light of the exceptional economic certainty. This latter effective suspension was maintained until the end of 2023.[46] The idea of both of these suspensions was to allow Member States to take the necessary measures to restart their economies in the wake of the COVID-19 pandemic (and also to finance the green and digital transitions),[47] and subsequently to deal with the economic impact of Russia's invasion of Ukraine. Although the suspensions were generally regarded as the correct approach to take, one particular result of this revival of more or less unrestricted Member State sovereignty in the fiscal field was foreseeable in the particular economic context: debts and deficits ballooned, creating in turn an impetus for a reinstatement of the Pact in some shape or form.

8 Proposals for a Revised and Reformed Stability and Growth Pact

The post-COVID-19 process of revival of the Stability and Growth Pact in amended form took considerable time, and indeed at the time of writing of this chapter, was not entirely complete, and culminated only shortly before the publication of this book. That new rules should be envisaged does not come as much of a surprise: the existing ones had been rightly criticised on grounds that included that they were "ineffective, too complex and often encouraged bad economic policy like procyclical budgets and skimping public investments".[48] As we have seen, the sanctions envisaged for non-compliance were never applied. And more tellingly, the rules simply did not in practice lead to fiscal buffers being sufficiently rebuilt in the wake of sovereign debt and banking crises to prevent widespread and long-term increases in national debt ratios.[49]

The legislative history of reconstituting the Stability and Growth Pact in remodelled form was as follows. Following on European Commission orientations for reform of the EU economic governance framework published back in November 2022, Commission legislative proposals aimed at revising the Stability and Growth

European Semester: Country-specific recommendations (COM(2020) 500 final, Brussels, 20 May 2020, Communication to the European Parliament, the European Council, the Council, the European Central Bank, the European Economic and Social Committee, the Committee of the Regions and the European Investment Bank) at 5. See for further useful discussion here, Gern, Kooths and Stolzenburg (n. 42) and note more generally J. Angerer and A. Zoppè, *Thematic Digest: "When and how to deactivate the SGP general escape clause?"* (PE 659.625, Economic Governance Support Unit, Directorate-General for Internal Policies of the European Parliament, February 2021).

[46] See Pench (n. 22) 5–6.

[47] *Ibid.*

[48] See Sandbu (n. 40).

[49] See Fitch (n. 27) 3.

Pact were put forward in April 2023.[50] These consisted, specifically, of two draft regulations aimed at replacing (in the case of the preventive arm) and amending (in the case of the corrective arm) the Stability and Growth Pact plus a draft amending directive concerning the requirements for Member State budgetary frameworks.[51] Among the objectives of these original proposals were the twin aims of simplifying the operation of the Stability and Growth Pact and making its operation less numerically-based and more country-specific. A key idea was that nationally-decided trajectories should now determine the application of the Pact rather than numerical rules: an approach which would differentiate between Member States and would increase the discretion of non-highly indebted Member States in deciding upon expenditure priorities. (Surveillance was to be simplified: indeed, for *low*-debt Member States, the anticipated result of the proposals has been described as being that "the prescriptions of the preventive arm of the [Pact] effectively cease to exist and what is left is only the [excessive deficit procedure] for breach of the 3% of GDP deficit threshold".[52] For high and low-debt states alike, once national plans were in place, the idea was that only one observable indicator would matter–the net expenditure path.) Additionally, the possibility of extension (subject to conditions relating to reforms and investment) of the period for adjusting the debt-levels of high-debt Member States was also foreseen.[53]

The fundamental debate over these proposals would end up being between more heavily-indebted states (including both Italy and France) which had sought more flexibility in the rules and more 'frugal' states like Germany less keen on changes to the original pact, which continued to insist on the need for fiscal discipline (notwithstanding the enforcement failures which had marked the original and indeed the Pact as revised after the banking and sovereign debt crises).

By late December 2023, Council agreement in principle was reached on both the corrective arm regulation and the budgetary frameworks directive (leaving only the mere need to consult the European Parliament regarding both). Just prior to the publication of this book, on 29 April 2024, both measures were adopted by the Council and entered into force the next day.[54] Late December 2023 also saw a mandate for

---

[50] See generally on the original proposals, Fabien Amtenbrink and Jakob de Haan, "The European Commission's approach to a reform of the EU fiscal framework: a legal and economic appraisal" (2023) 48(4) EL Rev 422.

[51] See, more precisely, Proposal for a Regulation of the European Parliament and of the Council on the effective coordination of economic policies and multilateral budgetary surveillance and repealing Council Regulation (EC) No 1466/97 (COM(2023) 240 final, Brussels, 26.4.2023); Proposal for a Council Regulation amending Regulation (EC) No 1467/97 on speeding up and clarifying the implementation of the excessive deficit procedure (COM(2023) 241 final, Brussels, 26.4.2023) and Proposal for a Council Directive amending Directive 2011/85/EU on requirements for budgetary frameworks of the Member States (COM(2023) 242 final, Brussels, 26.4.2023).

[52] Pench (n. 22) 26.

[53] *Ibid* 7.

[54] See "Economic governance review: Council agrees on reform of fiscal rules" (Council press release of 21 December 2023), and see now Council Regulation (EU) 2024/1264 of 29 April 2024 amending Regulation (EC) No 1467/97 on speeding up and clarifying the implementation of the excessive deficit procedure (OJ L, 30 April 2024) and Council Directive (EU) 2024/1265 of 29 April

negotiating with the European Parliament on the preventive arm regulation. A subsequent marathon sixteen-hour trilogue in February 2024 led to a provisional political agreement between Parliament and Council representatives concerning this.[55] This provisional political agreement on the preventive arm then went back to both institutions for a formal vote of approval (after having first secured approval in Coreper[56] and the Economic Affairs Committee[57]). Just prior to the publication of this book, more precisely on 29 April 2024, the preventive arm regulation was duly adopted and entered into force the following day. [58] Although there appeared to be an expectation that the new rules would really only apply fully from 2025, with 2024 more in the nature of a period of transition.[59]

A few words may be added to what has already been said about the proposed measures. A first point is that the proposals to amend the preventive arm and the corrective arm of the Stability and Growth Pact are quite different.

The *preventive arm* of the Pact—the part amended by recourse to the ordinary legislative procedure (i.e., co-decision by Council and Parliament)[60]–is seeing quite significant changes. One of the main innovations, as already noted, is the proposed differentiated approach–allowing country-specific multi-annual fiscal trajectories–thus taking into account the varying public debt levels, the economic challenges and the fiscal positions of the individual Member States. The *modus operandi* is to be that each Member State will prepare and publicly submit to the Commission a medium-term fiscal structural plan–covering four or five years (*i.e.* the length of the national legislative period)–whereby it commits to a fiscal trajectory that ensures sustained gradual debt reduction and details its fiscal policy, reforms and investments.[61] (In the case of Member States with a government debt exceeding 60% of GDP or a

2024 amending Directive 2011/85/EU on requirements for budgetary frameworks of the Member States (OJ L, 30 April 2024). Both measures entered into force on 30 April 2024, with the Member States required to implement Directive 2011/85/EU by 31 December 2025.

[55] See "Economic governance review: Council agrees on reform of fiscal rules" (Council press release of 21 December 2023) and see Europe Daily Bulletin No. 13348, 13 February 2024.

[56] In the case of the Council of the European Union.

[57] In the case of the European Parliament.

[58] See now Regulation (EU) 2024/1263 of the European Parliament and of the Council of 29 April 2024 on the effective coordination of economic policies and on multilateral budgetary surveillance and repealing Council Regulation (EC) No 1466/97. See also Council of the European Union, "Economic governance review: Council and Parliament strike deal on reform of fiscal rules" (Press Release, 10 February 2024).

[59] See Anon., "Revision of Stability Pact, MEPs secure an investment-friendly provision from EU Council", Agence Europe Daily Bulletin, 13 February 2024 and Anon., "EU agrees on complicated new spending rules describe by Left as tool for austerity", Journal. i.e.,10 February 2024.

[60] See Proposal for a Regulation of the European Parliament and of the Council on the effective coordination of economic policies and multilateral budgetary surveillance and repealing Council Regulation 1466/97 (COM(2023) 240 final, Brussels, 26 April 2023).

[61] The period is extendable to seven years if certain national reforms and investments (which may include Recovery and Resilience Facility investments) e.g., improving growth potential and supporting fiscal sustainability are effected. For a more detailed examination of the preparation and submission of these plans, see Proposal for a Regulation of the European Parliament and of the Council on the effective coordination of economic policies and multilateral budgetary surveillance

government deficit exceeding 3% of GDP, this, however, will be preceded by the transmission by the Commission of a risk-based 'reference trajectory' (expressed in terms of multiannual net expenditure) designed to indicate how government debt can be put on a plausibly downward trajectory or else stays below 60% of GDP over the medium term and the projected government deficit be brought below 3% of GDP and maintained at that level.[62]) The Council will then adopt a recommendation setting the net expenditure path of each Member State (and supposed to serve as a single indicator[63]) based on the national medium-term fiscal-structural plan,[64] and the Member States incorporate this into their plans. A control account will record deviations from the country-specific net expenditure paths.[65] The system is thus one which is likely to involve intense dialogue with Member States.[66]

The changes to the *corrective arm* of the Stability and Growth Pact[67] are less substantial, and generally aimed at ensuring coordination (e.g,. as regards definitions) with the changes to the preventive arm. Hence, to take one example, the actions required to be taken under the excessive deficit procedure have been reformulated into changes in net expenditure. The scale of the sanctions is reduced from the present level (although fines are to be cumulative). However, the previously pertaining processes and timelines will continue to exist for the excessive deficit procedure.[68] The procedure for the adoption of the changes envisaged to the corrective arm is also different to that regarding the changes to the preventive arm–it involves merely the consultation of the European Parliament, with the aim being that the reforms will be adopted in Council at the same time as the changes to the preventive arm (which must be agreed with the Parliament).

---

and repealing Council Regulation (EC) No 1466/97 (COM(2023) 240 final, Brussels, 26.4.2023) at 10 *et seq.*

[62] In requirements which seem likely both to sharpen this requirement but perhaps also to create a certain lack of clarity, each reference trajectory will need to comply with a debt sustainability safeguard (ensuring it decreases debt) and a deficit resilience safeguard (involving a safety margin which is below the deficit reference value of 3% of GDP, the aim here being to create fiscal buffers).

The net expenditure path in the plan need not correspond with that in the reference trajectory but sound data-driven economic arguments explaining any higher expenditure path must be provided.

[63] This approach seems calculated to reduce reliance on the less certain criterion of an economy's cyclical position.

[64] Essentially, this can consist of an endorsement of the national plan, a request for revisions or the implementation of the reference trajectory. If the adjustment period has been extended, this recommendation will also endorse reform and investment commitments which underlie the extension.

[65] This may improve transparency around compliance assessments.

[66] Although this is not entirely innovatory in itself—the point has been made that adjustment programmes already involved substantial dialogue between Member States and the Commission under the previous Stability and Growth Pact regime. (See Fitch (n. 27) 3.) Pench has suggested the idea here however is of replicating the experience of the more intense Member State-Commission contacts during the preparation of the Recovery and Resilience Plans. (Pench (n. 22) 14.

[67] Note that this arm is of particular relevance to high-debt states, because of the risk for them of being made the subject of the excessive deficit procedure on grounds of an excessive debt.

[68] See for a detailed analysis, Pench (n. 22) 19 *et seq.*

Overall, at least two criticisms can be made of the proposed reforms. The first is that of excessive complexity. The new model of budgetary discipline in the Eurozone has something of the air of the proverbial horse designed by a committee. In other words, the virtue of simplicity (possessed by the original proposals) is gone. The introduction of medium-term fiscal structural plans, for example, might have been used to simplify matters. Instead, however, the determined opposition of Germany and other 'frugal' states meant that the old numerical approach was not abandoned, but rather added to the proposed new approach.[69] A more complex structure has thus taken the place of the Commission proposals' original simplified approach (even if it retains the core elements of the original proposals of a medium-term focus, increased Member State ownership of the process and the idea of more gradual change in indebtedness). This has not helped clarity–one commentary has noted that it is unclear how the relevant rules will change how the Pact operates, noting that the excessive deficit procedure will still use structural deficit-based targets and the Pact as a whole will still use multiple targets.[70] There is also plenty of scope for disagreement regarding, for example, what constitute permissible adjustment period extensions and plan revisions[71] Pench, however, while giving a somewhat mixed review to the reforms on this basis, at least praises what he argues is the simplification they will bring to the surveillance process, summarising that.

> the draft legislation agreed by the Council traduces in part the original spirit of the reform, by introducing numerical safeguards over and above the constraints justified by debt sustainability, which risk compromising the national ownership of the plans, specifically, by high-debt Member States. However, the reform greatly simplifies surveillance, at least in two respects: for low-debt Member States, the prescriptions of the preventive arm of the SGP effectively cease to exist and what is left is only the EDP for breach of the 3% of GDP deficit threshold; for all Member States, once the plans are in place, there is only a single observable indicator that matters for compliance, the net expenditure path.[72]

In noting that the numerical rules will remain, it is also only fair to acknowledge that there will be real change, in that the numerical rules that remain under the Pact will be more relaxed than those that previously pertained.[73] Countries will be allowed

---

[69] I.e., using e.g., expenditure paths and control accounts. An approach which led to the new regime being opposed (unsuccessfully) by the Greens/European Free Alliance and the Left group in the European Parliament. (See Europe Daily Bulletin (Europe Daily Bulletin (No. 13348, 13 February) 2.)).

[70] See the comments in this regard in Fitch (n. 27). Thus, to take one example, and as already noted, it is envisaged that Commission reference trajectories will need to comply with both a debt sustainability safeguard and a deficit resilience safeguard. (See "Economic governance review: Council agrees on reform of fiscal rules" (Council press release of 21 December 2023) 4.

[71] See Pench (n. 22) 14.

[72] *Ibid* 26.

[73] Thus Sandbu points out that the notorious one-twentieth rule—which demanded debt ratio reductions of one-twentieth of the excess above 60 per each year, implying a reduction of 5% of GDP per year for Greece, 4% for Italy and 3% for France, Spain, Portugal and Belgium—will now be gone. Additionally, the medium-term requirement for structural near-balance will give way to a need for countries with a public debt exceeding 90% of GDP to reduce their deficit to 1.5% and countries

to bring down excessive debt at a slower pace for over four to seven years[74] and will benefit from a certain number of exemptions[75] which also allow for a more gradual approach to cutting back.[76] That much said, it seems far from guaranteed that the economic effect of the new rules will be beneficial even if they are adhered to. The rules will in any case clearly have an effect that varies from state to state, imposing a particularly harsh burden on states such as Spain which are heavily burdened– but very little on Germany which already imposes a remarkably harsh budgetary discipline on itself domestically.

The second criticism which can be made is the more fundamental one of the improbability that the new rules will ever actually be properly enforced. (In this sense, the insistence on a continued numerical approach by the frugal states may end up proving to have been counterproductive.) The problem with the Stability and Growth Pact has never been Member States insisting on sovereignty at the point of norm design, but at the point of norm implementation. In practice, Member States have always adopted a fallback position that *in extremis* the rules will be ignored. Going by past Member States behaviour, there is every danger that any "additional constraints in the design of the rules may be offset by a reduced commitment in their implementation by Member States and their enforcement by the Commission and the Council".[77] Moreover, envisaged potential negative consequences for a Member State found, as they will now be capable of being, in non-compliance at an earlier stage

with a public debt of 60–90% of GDP to reduce it below 2%. Thus there will be more room for deficit spending under the new rules. (See Sandbu (n. 40) 2.).

[74] Thus they may apply for an extension of the four-year fiscal adjustment period to a maximum of seven years if they execute investments and reforms that improve their potential for resilience and growth, address agreed EU priorities—such as digital, green, social or defence investment—and support fiscal sustainability. (See "Economic governance review: Council agrees on reform of fiscal rules" (Council press release of 21 December 2023) 3. Some concerns have been expressed that in practice, this may lead to weakened public debt sustainability. (See Fitch (n. 27) 3).

[75] Thus, and as noted, protecting reforms and investments in strategic areas such as digital, green, social or defence expenditure and allowing some room for counter-cyclical policies. (*Ibid.*, 4.) This was a demand made by countries led by France, which did not however secure the exemption for investment spending that many of them had wanted. This failure to make greater allowance for investment-related expenditure has been criticised. See Anon., "EU agrees on complicated new spending rules decried by Left as tool for austerity", Journal.ie, 10 February 2024 and Sandbu (n. 40).

[76] See P. Tamma and M. Arnold, "EU agrees long-delayed reform of fiscal rules", Financial Times, 10 February 2024.

[77] Pench (n. 22) 27.

of the Excessive Deficit Procedure[78] will include early fines, suspension of European Structural and Investment Funds or Recovery and Resilience Facility funds and exclusion from ECB purchases of their government securities under the Transmission Protection Mechanism.[79] Such extensive consequences naturally raise doubts concerning the prospect of either the Commission or the Council ever deploying the Procedure.[80] It is thus far from clear that the adoption of the new rules will result in any improvement in compliance or in enforcement–many factors will be at work pulling States in the opposite direction. (Tellingly, the highly indebted states appear to have traded the acceptance of relative strictness in the new rules in exchange for short-term flexibility–i.e., seeing their implementation effectively delayed and negotiating transitional arrangements to avoid rising interest costs and post-pandemic recovery expenditure being caught by the new rules.[81] This is not the way one should approach a system of rules if one really expects them to have staying power.[82] Noticeably too, even before the new rules enter into force, doubts are already being expressed as to whether Italy (and to a lesser extent, France) will be able to comply with the new limits.[83] And even if this is possible, it seems in any case somewhat improbable that France, for example, which has never felt any need to adhere rigidly to the demands of the Pact before now, will alter its position in the wake of the amendments to the Pact now. The fundamental problem may be that although the Member States are willing now (as in the past) to accept ostensibly legally-binding rules, they are generally not yet ready in reality to surrender sovereignty in this area beyond the constraints put on them by the combination of peer pressure on the part of other States, domestic political pressures and market forces.

---

[78] Under the corrective arm of the revised Pact, insofar as concerns the *debt*-based excessive debt procedure, the Commission—which, as already noted, will monitor the evolution of a Member State's expenditure each year with a control account which will make possible tracking upward and downward deviations from the trajectory that has been agreed for net budgetary expenditure—will now issue a report (triggering the excessive deficit procedure) when (i) the ratio of government debt to GDP exceeds the reference value, when (ii) the headline deficit is not close to being in balance or in surplus and (iii) where the monitored deviations exceed 0.3% annually or 0.6% over several years.

The excessive deficit procedure when opened on the basis of the deficit criterion will remain unchanged: the corrective net expenditure path must be consistent with a minimum annual structural adjustment of at least 0.5% of GDP. (See "Economic governance review: Council agrees on reform of fiscal rules" (Council press release of 21 December 2023) 4 and Europe Daily Bulletin (No. 13348, 13 February) 2.).

[79] Pench (n. 22) 25–26.

[80] *Ibid* 27.

[81] See Sandbu (n. 40).

[82] *Ibid.*

[83] See Martin Arnold, Giuliana Ricozzi and Amy Kazmin "Italy commits to cut deficit despite soaring cost of tax credits", Financial Times, 9 April 2024.

9 Next Generation EU and the Prospect of the Creation of a Permanent Centralised Fiscal Capacity

Up until this point, this chapter has concerned itself with a model of fiscal sovereignty that sees decision-making power as residing at the national level, subject to such restrictions imposed at European Union level as are perceived to be necessary. Such a model was all that Member States were willing to envisage at Maastricht and in its immediate aftermath (i.e., at the time of the adoption of the Stability and Growth Pact). And yet this model is a controversial one: other approaches to sovereignty are possible.[84]

What can be seen as a new stage in the evolution of the fiscal framework of the European Union came about with the onset of the COVID-19 crisis. Some of the early responses of the Union to the economic consequences of the pandemic have already been seen in this chapter, including the deployment of the escape clause in the Stability and Growth Pact.[85] Also notable in the EU's early reaction was the use of the EU Solidarity Fund and the EU Structural and Investment Funds to render economic assistance. (One should also not forego mention in this context of the ECB Pandemic Emergency Purchase Programme which ultimately saw the Frankfurt-based institution commit to purchase government bonds and commercial paper in the amount of €1.85 trillion. This was unavoidably of major economic significance, since it ensured purchasers would be found for the huge volume of bonds issued to pay for COVID-19-related recovery measures. It was, however, nonetheless a monetary policy measure from the perspective of EU law and therefore is not further examined in this chapter.[86]) A number of explicitly economic measures were also engaged in by the EU, including the deployment of the European Stability Mechanism to support national financing of healthcare measures, and the establishment of the SURE initiative[87] which sought to enable the Commission to transfer up to €100

---

[84] See for an excellent discussion of the choices available, Alicia Hinarejos *The Euro Area Crisis in Constitutional Perspective* (Oxford University Press 2015) Chap. 10, and by the same writer, "Fiscal Federalism in the European Union: Evolution and Future Choices for EMU" (2013) CMLRev 1621. See also Fabian Amtenbrink and Menelaos Markakis, "Never Waste a Good Crisis: on the Emergence of an EU Fiscal Capacity", Chap. 7 in Hinarejos and Schütze (n. 9).

[85] With other aspects, as we have seen, including the liberalisation of the state aid regime, the use of the EU Solidarity Fund and the EU Structural and Investment Funds to render assistance. See more generally on the response of the EU to the economic side of the crisis e.g., Gavin Barrett, "Coronavirus and EU Law: Driving the Next Stage of Economic and Monetary Union?", and Richard Crowe, "The EU Recovery Plan: New Dynamics in the Financing of the EU Budget", Chaps. 3 and 6, respectively in Gavin Barrett, Jean-Philippe Rageade, Diana Wallis and Heinz Weil, *The Future of Legal Europe: Will We Trust in It?* (Springer 2021); and Fabbrini (n. 17) Chaps. 3–5.

[86] See by way of analogy, Case C-493/17 *Weiss* EU:C:2019:1046. Note that the European Investment Bank (EIB) also established an investment scheme, albeit in the much smaller amount of €40 billion. (See Fabbrini (n. 17) 43 *et seq.*) and a €25 billion pan-European guarantee fund.

[87] Short for European instrument for temporary Support to mitigate Unemployment Risks in an Emergency.

million to the greatly-stressed national unemployment insurance regimes in the form of loans.[88]

Towering in importance above all other fiscally-related initiatives by the Union in the COVID-19 period, however, is the 2021 Next Generation EU recovery fund which was designed to permit the rebuilding of Member State economies post-COVID-19 with deference to EU digital, environmental and social inclusion priorities. Proposed by the Commission and agreed upon in principle in modified form after a marathon five-day long European Council meeting on 21 July 2020, Next Generation EU took its final shape as a €750 billion system of loans (of up to €360 billion) and grants (of up to €390 billion). What was radically new about Next Generation EU (apart from its scale) was the idea that it would be financed by EU borrowing in the financial markets. These borrowings would be repaid over a thirty-year period leading up to 2058 through EU own resources—which were envisaged as involving new EU taxes. It thus involved a significantly new approach to the deployment of fiscal resources to what had previously been seen, even if one envisaged by the Member States as being temporary in nature.

The relatively complex legal mechanics of this initiative have been well explained elsewhere,[89] but included (a) the creation of an EU Recovery Instrument establishing the fund and its overall financial scope and objectives;[90] (b) an Own Resources Decision, *inter alia,* conferring the power on the Commission to issue common debt so as to finance Next Generation Europe;[91] (c) a Recovery and Resilience Facility, *inter alia,* setting out what Member States ought to seek to achieve using Next Generation resources;[92] and (d) an inter-institutional agreement between Parliament, Council and Commission to work towards introducing own resources designed to repay the borrowing used to finance Next Generation Europe–which were foreseen as possibly including national contributions calculated on the weight of non-recycled plastic packaging waste, as well as resources deriving from a carbon border adjustment mechanism, a digital levy, a financial transaction tax and a financial contribution

[88] See Council Regulation (EU) 2020/672 of 19 May 2020 on the establishment of a European instrument for temporary support to mitigate unemployment risks in an emergency (SURE) following the COVID-19 outbreak (OJ L 159, 20.5.2020, pp. 1–7).

[89] See e.g., Fabbrini (n. 17) p. 48.

[90] See Council Regulation (EU) 2020/2094 of 14 December 2020 establishing a European Union Recovery Instrument to support the recovery in the aftermath of the COVID-19 crisis (OJ L 433I, 22.12.2020, pp. 23–27).

[91] See Council Decision (EU, Euratom) 2020/2053 of 14 December 2020 on the system of own resources of the European Union and repealing Decision 2014/335/EU, Euratom (OJ L 424, 15.12.2020, p. 1–10). See further Ana Belén and Macho Pérez, "The Own Resources Decision (ORD) & EU public finances" (Rebuild Working Paper, February 2024).

[92] See Regulation (EU) 2021/241 of the European Parliament and of the Council of 12 February 2021 establishing the Recovery and Resilience Facility (OJ L 57, 18.2.2021, p. 17–75). For a detailed overview of the Recovery and Resilience Facility, see Stefania Baroncelli, "The Recovery and Resilience Facility" (Rebuild Working Paper, January 2024).

linked to the corporate sector or a new common corporate tax base.[93] A conditionality regime targeting behaviour undermining the rule of law was also more or less simultaneously introduced.[94] The EU's Multi-annual Financial Framework–of which Next Generation EU was to form an additional component–also needed to be adjusted.[95]

Next Generation EU undoubtedly involved an unprecedented step in EU-level fiscal policy. Yet the question of just how radical the departure should actually be regarded as having been remains unclear. Moreover, at least some Member States seem eager that any concession of sovereignty to the European Union involved be confined to the most limited possible, particularly in terms of being a temporary rather than a permanent initiative.

Those espousing the view that Next Generation EU is of lasting major significance include Fabbrini, who has described the approval of Next Generation EU as "a paradigm change for the EU architecture of economic governance", and asserted that "the process of European integration has experienced during COVID-19 an unprecedented leap forward, with the EU now enjoying fiscal powers which would have been unthinkable until recently". The same writer has seen Next Generation Europe as having "greatly rebalanced the original asymmetry of EMU, endowing it with a fiscal capacity, i.e., an integrated public budget that the EU can use to stabilise the economy during a cyclical crisis and to invest in European public goods".[96]

Also taking the view that there has been transformational change, albeit from a somewhat different perspective, is Panasci, who has argued that the adoption of Next Generation EU has altered the European economic constitution, moving the EU economic governance paradigm from rule-based fiscal integration to discretion-based fiscal intervention, displacing 'strict conditionality' and the mutually reciprocal insurance logic which she sees as having characterised financial transfers between Member States in favour of income equalisation between them, with Article 125 TFEU (the famous 'no bailout' provision seen as forming a key part of EMU's

---

93 See Interinstitutional Agreement between the European Parliament, the Council of the European Union and the European Commission on budgetary discipline, on cooperation in budgetary matters and on sound financial management, as well as on new own resources, including a roadmap towards the introduction of new own resources Interinstitutional Agreement of 16 December 2020 between the European Parliament, the Council of the European Union and the European Commission on budgetary discipline, on cooperation in budgetary matters and on sound financial management, as well as on new own resources, including a roadmap towards the introduction of new own resources (OJ L 433I, 22.12.2020, pp. 28–46). See in particular Annex II thereto, Entitled "Interinstitutional Cooperation on a Roadmap towards the Introduction of New Own Resources".

94 Regulation (EU, Euratom) 2020/2092 of the European Parliament and of the Council of 16 December 2020 on a general regime of conditionality for the protection of the Union budget (OJ L 433I, 22.12.2020, p. 1–10).

95 See Council Regulation (EU, Euratom) 2020/2093 of 17 December 2020 laying down the multi-annual financial framework for the years 2021 to 2027 (OJ L 433I, 22.12.2020, p. 11–22) as subsequently amended.

96 Fabbrini (n. 17) 65 and also 98 where he describes Next Generation EU as making "the EU more akin to a federal regime such as that of the US, in which the central government has a fiscal capacity to stabilise the economy and support Member States in fiscal crisis".

economic constitution) no longer seen as precluding redistribution via EU financial intervention.[97]

Finally, further taking the view that enduring change has been seen–but with a more critical perspective on this–are Leino-Sandberg and Ruffert, who have characterised Next Generation EU as having involved the creation of a permanent fiscal capacity—but without a robust EU legal fundament.[98]

Ultimately, only time will tell if the model of Next Generation EU will indeed prove to be enduringly influential. Even now, however, and without necessarily going as far as any of the above commentators, it can certainly be asserted that Next Generation Europe has involved major innovation in at least two ways. In the first place, it has involved borrowing on an unprecedentedly large scale so as to finance both grants and loans to Member States, facilitating expenditure to attain common goals agreed at EU level. The other significant change relates to its governance:[99] as Pench notes, the Recovery and Resilience Facility creates "a new type of performance-based conditionality tying financial support to the implementation of reforms and investments planned by Member States in line with broad policy objectives set at EU level."[100] Fabbrini's conclusion is that

> overall, what emerges is a new system of economic governance in which the EU defines the strategic objectives, designed to strengthen the ecological and digital transition, inclusive growth, and economic resilience, and the Member States commit to reach these priorities as a condition to receive significant amounts of EU funds over time.[101]

The model *is* certainly a new one. And to date, it has been successfully deployed in combating the economic effects of COVID-19.[102] But, as has been noted, its acceptability as an enduring model has not been established. Moreover, although the politically comparatively easy tasks of agreeing to set it up, of borrowing to fund it and of disbursing its payments have been undertaken, Member States notably left the rather more difficult task of funding the repayments to a future date–and completion

---

[97] Maria Antonia Panasci, "Unravelling Next Generation EU as a Transformative Moment: from Market Integration to Redistribution" (2024) 61 CMLRev 13 esp. at 52 *et seq.*

[98] Païvi Leino-Sandberg and Matthias Ruffert, "Next Generation EU and its constitutional ramifications: a critical assessment" (2022) 59 CMLRev 433 at 472.

[99] See here Jonathan Zeitlin, David Bokhorst and Edgars Eihmanis, "Governing the RRF. Drafting, Implementing and Monitoring National Recovery and Resilience Plans as an Interactive Multilevel Process" (Recovery Watch, June 2023).

[100] Pench (n. 22) 4.

[101] Federico Fabbrini, "Fiscal policy in times of crises: an analysis of EMU constitutional framework" (European Parliament, Directorate-General for Internal Policies, Policy Department for Citizens' Rights and Constitutional Affairs (PE 753.369) September 2023) 18.

[102] Notwithstanding considerable negative publicity regarding large-scale frauds perpetuated in various Member States concerning Next Generation EU funding. (See e.g., Nektaria Stamouli, "Fraud-busters swoop on Greek contracts involving €2.5B of EU recovery funds", Politico, 10 April 2024.) Sound financial management, and finding the correct balance between macroeconomic performance and the protection of EU financial interests have had to be a focus point from the outset of the architects of Next Generation EU. See Pauline Thinus and Paul Dermine, "Financial Oversight: Internal and External Control Authorities" (Rebuild Working Paper, February, 2024).

of the task of agreeing how this should be done has proven notably lacking in success thus far.[103]

The Russian invasion of Ukraine on 24 February 2024 provided a further opportunity to assess the willingness of Member States to see the emergence of a more fiscally sovereign EU, although admittedly in a policy area–namely foreign affairs, defence and security–which is dominated by intergovernmentalism. The fiscal response of the European Union to this war was essentially two-pronged.[104] On the one hand, the Member States created the European Peace Facility in March 2021.[105] The sums involved in this were not insignificant: the Facility was eventually provided with a financial ceiling of more than €17 billion for the period 2021–2027.[106] Nonetheless, it cannot on this account be described as involving any major shift in sovereignty: indeed one commentator has memorably described the Facility as "exhibit A of intergovernmentalism in the EU".[107] Any significant decisions concerning it are taken by unanimity,[108] and a Member State can avoid contributing to an operation by abstaining in the Council vote on that operation.[109] Moreover, the Facility, an off-budget instrument,[110] is financed by direct transfers by each EU Member State paid every year, based on its estimated annual budget. Member State control is thus everywhere.

The other significant instrument in this area is the Macro-Financial Assistance Instrument, which has involved the issue of €18 billion of debt to provide financial relief to Ukraine, to support its reconstruction and prepare it for EU membership.[111]

---

[103] Thus far, we have seen only the introduction of a levy paid by EU Member States on foot of plastic packaging waste generated in national territory and not recycled. (See Council Decision (EU, Euratom) 2020/2053 of 14 December 2020 on the system of own resources of the European Union and repealing Decision 2014/335/EU, Euratom (OJ L 424/1, 15.12.2020); and Council Regulation (EU, Euratom) 2021/770 of 30 April 2021 on the calculation of the own resource based on plastic packaging waste that is not recycled, on the methods and procedure for making available that own resource, on the measures to meet cash requirements, and on certain aspects of the own resource based on gross national income (OJ L 165/15, 11.5.2021). For a good summary of present situation in this respect (accompanied by a policy suggestion), see Pascal Saint-Amans, "Broader border taxes: a new option for European Union budget resources" (Policy brief, Bruegel, 21 March 2024).

[104] For the non-fiscal response, which was significant, see Fabbrini (n. 17), Chap. 6.

[105] See Council Decision (CFSP) 2021/509 of 22 March 2021 establishing a European Peace Facility, and repealing Decision (CFSP) 2015/528 (ST/5212/2021/INIT) (OJ L 102, 24.3.2021).

[106] See "European Peace Facility", website of the European Commission at https://fpi.ec.europa.eu/what-we-do/european-peace-facility_en (accessed 5 April 2024).

[107] Fabbrini (n. 101) 28.

[108] By the Facility Committee which has a representative from each Member State. See Article 11(1) and (14) of Council Decision (CFSP) 2021/509.

[109] Although it is then required to make an additional contribution to other assistance measures. See generally Article 5 of Council Decision (CFSP) 2021/509.

[110] Necessarily so, since Article 41(2) TEU prohibits 'expenditure arising from operations having military or defence implications' from being charged to the EU budget.

[111] See Regulation (EU) 2022/2463 of the European Parliament and of the Council of 14 December 2022 establishing an instrument for providing support to Ukraine for 2023 (macro-financial assistance+).

(PE/71/2022/INIT OJ L 322, 16.12.2022, p. 1–14).

Macro-Financial Assistance is more intergovernmental than Next Generation EU since the debt is not backed up by the EU budget, but rather by the 26 EU Member States other than Viktor Orban's Hungary.[112] However, if Macro-Financial Assistance is not supranational in nature, it veers at least somewhat more in this direction than does the European Peace Facility, as it involves the issuance of common debt. Payments made under it are in the form of loans.[113] Fabbrini has asserted, not unreasonably, that the Ukraine war confirms that external threats are one of the strongest drivers of the consolidation of centralised powers in federalised union of states.[114] He has also argued that the EU's response to the Ukraine war has revealed a trend towards consolidating a centralised fiscal capacity at the EU level of government, and also (referring to Macro-Financial Assistance) to resort to funding mechanisms analogous to those used during the COVID-19 pandemic—in other words SURE and Next Generation EU (which he regards as "legally engineering a constitutional transformation in the EU architecture of economic governance"[115]). The fact remains however that Member States have retained a stranglehold of unanimity voting requirements in this area, with each expansion in fiscal capacity generally requiring amendments to the Own Resources Decision and the Multi-Annual Fiscal Framework. (The Ukraine measures are in any case located in the CFSP and CSDP policy fields, where unanimity voting is in any case the normal rule, and supranational institutions like the Court of Justice and the Commission are largely excluded, leaving decision-making to the Member States.) All initiatives to date have moreover been framed as once-off, temporary measures. The Member States, if they wish to create a permanent fiscal capacity or more generally to exempt decision-making in this field from being crippled by unworkable voting and institutional arrangements, need to reform the Treaty rules.[116] Whether the Member States will be willing to do this, however—a step that would entail a significant shift in sovereignty—remains far from certain: as Amtenbrink has pointed out (referencing also the challenge of dealing with *Bundesverfassungsgericht* case-law here), in particular "German politicians may find that they have limited legal leeway and little to profit in political terms from abolishing the well-established standoffish attitude towards the establishment

[112] Hungary effectively blocked any amendment to the EU's Multiannual Financial Framework (with Hungary using the unanimous vote needed for the adoption of this as a chance to apply pressure—to put matters at their mildest—on other Member States into allowing Hungary to escape the imposition of conditionality on completely unrelated additional EU funding for that State).

[113] Article 4(1) of Regulation (EU) 2022/2463.

[114] Fabbrini (n. 101) 33.

[115] *Ibid* 32.

[116] In particular, Article 122 TFEU, used as a legal basis for temporary measures like SURE and Next Generation EU, may not stretch to an analogous but more permanent fiscal capacity (and is arguably too intergovernmental a Treaty basis for this in any case, excluding, as it does, a role for the European Parliament). See here Fabian Amtenbrink, "The COVID-19 pandemic and fiscal union: the case for the establishment of a permanent supranational fiscal shock absorption capacity and important lessons to be learned from SURE and Next Generation EU" (Rebuild Working Paper, February 2024) at 11 *et seq.*. See also Francesco Saraceno, Jérôme Creel, Nicolas Leron, Sandrine Levasseur, Frédéric Allemand, *Making Next Generation EU a permanent tool* (Recovery Watch, March 2023).

of a more robust supranational fiscal capacity."[117] A strong case for creating a permanent robust supranational fiscal shock absorption capacity can nonetheless certainly be made out in a context which includes a pitifully small own resources ceiling of 1.4% of the EU's gross national income and the decidedly mixed picture that exists of avoidance of excessive debts and deficits on the part of Member States, and hence a limited ability on their part to absorb fiscal shocks. Arguments for such a fiscal capacity include the risks of contagion when regional or country-specific shocks occur and of euro area-wide economic shocks; the contribution a permanent shock absorption capacity could provide to financial stability in the EU, and the contested current role of thc ECB as a crisis manager.[118]

10 Conclusion

It has been seen in this chapter that in practice, even if not in the letter of the law, Member States have insisted upon retaining control over national fiscal policy, with the prospect of their collaborating in the imposition of sanctions for fiscal misbehaviour on any of their number being so apparently remote that in recent times no such sanctions have even been proposed by the Commission. The very recent reactivation of the Stability and Growth Pact may possibly bring improvements to the fiscal regime but it is by no means clear it will result in any fundamental change to the situation that has pertained up to now.[119]

If the Member States have been unenthused by the prospect of the European Union deploying its powers as the disciplinary authority of the economic union, they have, over the years, tended to show an equal lack of enthusiasm regarding the other alternative of creating a permanent centralised budgetary authority with resources of its own. Concerns about fiscal sovereignty led to the agreement on Next Generation EU being limited to an arrangement which is purely temporary in nature in preference to a proposal to create a permanent centralised budgetary authority analogous to that seen in other federal arrangements. (The failure to create such an arrangement may fairly be linked with the reluctance to agree upon an own resources strategy appropriate to the needs of today's European Union, which may

[117] *Ibid* at 8. See in this regard now the *Bundesverfassungsgericht* ruling in Cases 2 BvR 547/21 and 2 BvR 798/21, *Own Resources,* (judgment of 6 December 2022) and the commentary thereon by Paul Dermine and Anna Bobić, "Of Winners and Losers: A Commentary of the *Bundesverfassungsgericht ORD* Judgment of 6 December 2022" (2024) EUConst 1 at 10, in which these authors note that "the *Bundesverfassungsgericht*...used this case to provide its own blueprint, by introducing a detailed set of conditions applicable to the EU's borrowing operations and try to set the tone of the Union's future fiscal and budgetary trajectory".

[118] *Ibid* at 3 *et seq.*. Note now the proposal for EU defence bonds to fund investment in European defence and security. See Anon., "President Michel calls for 'defence bonds' at EDA Annual Conference 2023", European Defence Agency website, 30 November 2023.

[119] See more generally, Fabien Amtenbrink and Jakob de Haan, "The European Commission's approach to a reform of the EU fiscal framework: a legal and economic appraisal" (2023) 48(4) EL Rev 422.

in turn be legitimately linked with another failure to share sovereignty, the failure to agree to majority voting concerning the European Union budget.) As regards Next Generation EU, quite worryingly, there has also been a failure to date to agree on a repayment strategy for the enormous sums borrowed under this programme. While hopes exist that Next Generation EU marks the beginnings of real change at EU level regarding centralised fiscal capacity, it is far from impossible that it will prove to have been an ephemeral supernova of fiscal centralisation rather than have involved a permanent shift. Time alone will tell. At least a new model has been pioneered.

As has been seen, fiscal policy has undergone many iterations–enough indeed for one writer to have described the EU system of fiscal governance as 'completely unstable' and to have decried the 'never-ending spiral of change'.[120] And yet, ironically, such instability may be due to a constant–that of Member States consistently failing to grasp the nettle of what is actually needed in the context of Economic and Monetary Union: a greater and more permanent transfer of sovereignty. Perhaps the greatest dilemma the European Union faces for the future, is deciding on whether it wishes to change to the more centralised, federalised approach towards fiscal policy exhibited on a temporary basis in the measures adopted to remedy the effects of the COVID-19 economic crisis, or whether the presently-mooted more moderate reforms to the reformed Stability and Growth Pact are as far as the Member States wish to go. At the present time, at least in terms of what they are saying, it seems as if the horizon of the Member States' ambitions tends more in the direction of limited reforms to the Stability and Growth Pact. And yet more ambitious and optimistic takes (such as that of Fabbrini) may ultimately prove correct. Notably shrewd observers such as Sandbu have hinted that right now (and particularly as the next seven-year budget cycle draws near) one might more profitably watch what Member States do than what they say. Moreover, Next Generation EU seems, broadly speaking, to have worked and to be bringing about necessary changes: in other words, the economic convergence required to see both the Single Market and the single currency (and more broadly the European Union as a whole) succeed seems to be happening as a result of Next Generation EU, as beneficiary States show higher growth rates. Moreover, Next Generation EU's novel system of conditionality (whereby financial support to Member States is linked to the execution of reforms or investments in line with broad EU policy objectives) is also seen to have worked. Certainly, even as the phenomenon of COVID-19 fades into the rear view mirror, policies to advance the green transition; digital transformation; economic cohesion, and health, economic, social and institutional resilience remain both as vital as ever and incapable of being achieved simply by simple reliance on market forces.[121]

This chapter has been concerned with the difficulties that have been experienced in transferring legal sovereignty in fiscal matters to European level. As has been seen, these have been and continue to be considerable. One irony in all of this may be noted, which is that notwithstanding the ongoing opposition of the Member States to

---

[120] Estella (n. 14) 169–170.

[121] See generally Martin Sandbu, "The EU's recovery fund is already shaping its future", Financial Times, 7 April 2024.

the transfer of legal powers to EU level and–where the Member States agree to their transfer–to their effective enforcement, any such opposition to such transfers and enforcement has in practice (as has been argued elsewhere by this writer and others) concealed a real transfer of *political* power, and national power to adopt a budget has been subjected to European-level constraints. It might be that such constraints are political rather than legal in nature and operate via the non-legal means of inter-state peer pressure but they appear nonetheless to be in some degree influential.[122] It seems ironic that rather than entirely blocking a shift in power to EU level, enduring opposition to the transfer of legal sovereignty to European level in fiscal matters may well simply have operated to change the form in which some transfer of power has taken place, (a) ensuring that European power operates mainly in the form of constraints on national discretion rather than in the form of an independent federal-level fiscal policy; and additionally (b) seeing to it that the enforcement of such constraints has operated on the political rather than the legal plane. However, as the latest reforms to the Stability and Growth Pact and the EU response to COVID-19 (in the shape, in particular, of SURE and Next Generation EU) have shown, legal change is also occurring. Only time will tell if the latest reforms to the Stability and Growth Pact on the one hand, and the precedent set by Next Generation Europe and the response to the Ukraine crisis on the other, will see lasting transfers in fiscal competence follow on the heels of recent developments.

The way ahead is not straightforward. Sovereignty concerns appear to have had a retarding effect on the development of the currency union and even now to be continuing to play a major role concerning the shape of EMU. It should also be noted that although what has been under discussion in this chapter has been fiscal sovereignty, the question of political sovereignty is intimately linked to this, since more centralised fiscal sovereignty is arguably a *sine qua non* for the creation of a more politically sovereign Europe. Europe faces ever more challenges demanding collective responses. Whether Member States can provide such responses will depend on their willingness to overcome concerns about sovereignty, including in the fiscal policy field, and to embrace the necessary changes–which will include Treaty changes. Whether they are prepared to show such willingness remains to be seen.

[122] See in this regard Gavin Barrett, "The Eurozone: Meeting the Challenge of Representative Democracy?" (2018) 40 Journal of European Integration 249 at 254–255; and Ben Crum, "Parliamentary Accountability in Multilevel Governance: What Role for Parliaments in Post-Crisis EU Economic Governance." (2018) 25 Journal of European Public Policy 268 at 269, where that writer argues that while the economic crisis of 2008 onwards did not lead member states to actually transfer economic competences to the European level, it did lead them to succumb to a much-reinforced system of surveillance, and that although the eventual right to adopt the budget is preserved at national level, governments' economic decisions have been increasingly constrained at European level.

About the Next Generation EU Recovery Plan

Margarida Marques

Abstract This chapter discusses the Next Generation EU Recovery Plan. Written by a Member of the European Parliament, it is a contribution intended to bring a political perspective into the discussion, and not necessarily a technical one.

Written as it is by a Member of the European Parliament, this contribution is intended to bring a political perspective into the discussion, not necessary a technical one. In fact, the writer's academic background is in mathematics in the form of statistics and operational research rather than that of a law professor. Similarly, the writer has had a long career in national and European public administration–but provides this contribution as a politician, rather than as an academic or as an official of one of the European Union institutions.

Shortly after the COVID-19 pandemic struck the European Union, the European Parliament and the European Council made fighting the coronavirus pandemic and its immediate consequences a political priority for the Union. The Parliament and the Council tasked the Commission to

> start to prepare the measures necessary to get back to a normal functioning of our societies and economies and to sustainable growth, integrating inter alia the green transition and the digital transformation, and drawing all lessons from the crisis. This will require a coordinated exit strategy, a comprehensive recovery plan and unprecedented investment.[1]

In May 2020, the European Parliament demanded an ambitious recovery package worth €2 trillion, linked to the next European Union Multiannual Financial Framework (MFF), and built on the European Union budget. If one asks why the Parliament

[1] Joint statement of the Members of the European Council, Brussels, 26 March 2020 (OR. en) available online at <https://www.consilium.europa.eu/media/43076/26-vc-euco-statement-en.pdf> accessed 31 January 2024.

Member of the European Parliament, Vice-Chair of the Committee on Budgets (2019–2024).

M. Marques (✉)
Brussels, Belgium
e-mail: margarida.marques@europarl.europa.eu

G. Barrett et al. (eds.), *European Sovereignty*,
https://doi.org/10.1007/978-3-031-71851-9_12

sought this, the answer is that the European Parliament is a budgetary authority, but one with a twist to distinguish it from traditional parliaments: the European Parliament has competence only on the expenditure part of the European Union budget, not on the revenue side. Under Article 311 of the Treaty on the Functioning of the European Union, very explicitly, competence on the revenue part of the Budget—i.e., the creation of a system of own resources for financing the Budget–is a Council decision that "shall not enter into force until it is approved by the Member States in accordance with their respective constitutional requirements"–which, for the most part, means approval by Member States with ratification by national parliaments. Thus on this issue, we have clarity about sovereignty belonging to Member States' national parliaments.

On the expenditure side of the Budget, Article 312 of the Treaty on the Functioning of the European Union applies. This provides for the Multiannual Financial Framework, which is designed to ensure that Union expenditure develops in an orderly manner and within the limits of its own resources. Here, the European Parliament has a say. Parliament is also part of the annual budgetary exercise.

When the Commission put forward a proposal to establish a €750 billion European Union recovery instrument, Next Generation EU, on top of a revised 2021–2027 Multiannual Financial Framework worth €1.1 trillion, it was a partial answer to what the European Parliament wanted. In fact, it is an instrument outside the European Union budget but anchored in the European Union budget; a debt line was created to ensure the payment of the interest i.e., the cost of servicing the debt.

The financing of the instrument would come from funds borrowed on the markets by the Commission on behalf of the European Union–the first time this dimension would exist–while a mix of new and already-planned instruments under the European Union budget would channel expenditure, combining grants (proposed to be to the value of €500 billion) and loans (proposed to be to the value of €250 billion).

Next Generation EU relates to various legislative proposals, in which Parliament is involved to varying extents, depending on the issue at stake. Such proposals include:

1. the revised 2021–2027 Multiannual Financial Framework–where Parliament's consent is required;
2. the own resources system–where consultation of Parliament is required for the decision and the consent of Parliament is required for its implementing measures; and
3. the sector-specific legislation governing a number of European Union budgetary instruments–where co-decision applies as part of the ordinary legislative procedure.

Within the Next Generation EU package, a specific proposal was made–using Article 122 of the Treaty on the Functioning of the European Union (TFEU) as a legal basis–to create the European Union recovery instrument via a Council Regulation, with a view to activating the empowerment to borrow. Article 122 TFEU provides the European Union with the possibility of establishing measures appropriate to the economic situation, to be decided upon in a spirit of solidarity between Member States. This is not the Community method. Instead, Article 122 brings the decision to the more intergovernmental forum of the Council. Nor is the European Parliament involved in this legislative procedure, which requires a qualified majority in Council. (Article 122 TFEU had already been used in the context of the immediate response to the COVID-19 crisis in order to establish the European instrument for temporary support to mitigate unemployment risks in an emergency (SURE).)

In practice, this Council Regulation is the basic act that created the external assigned revenue–based on Article 21(5) of the EU Financial Regulation[2]–for Next Generation EU and allocated the resources from the borrowing operations to a number of European Union budgetary instruments. The original proposal was that grants (including financial instruments and provisioning for guarantees) would channel two thirds of the resources (€500 billion) through the European Union budget while loans to Member States would get the remaining one third (€250 billion).

But the question may be asked who in the end created Next Generation EU and where the sovereignty lies?

In the European Council of July 2020–the longest in the history of the European Council–the heads of state or government reached political agreement to give to European citizens, families, enterprises, societies and Member States alike, an effective and concreate answer to the crisis, and one which was very different from what had been seen with the financial crises of 2008 to 2010. The European Council adopted a package worth €1,824.3 billion, combining the new Multiannual Financial Framework and the recovery instrument. Although the volume of Next Generation EU was kept at €750 billion, as proposed by the Commission, the mix of grants (at €390 billion, down from the €500 billion in the proposal) and loans (at €360 billion, up from the €250 billion in the proposal) was changed. The time available for commitments was shortened by one year (to 2021–2023 instead of 2021–2024) by the European Council. The resources for the Recovery and Resilience Facility (RRF) were increased to €672.5 billion (of which loans were to amount to €360 billion and grants to €312.5 billion).

In addition to the Recovery and Resilience Facility, various other European Union budgetary instruments received additional resources from Next Generation EU.[3] However, the cuts to the grant component reduced the degree of strengthening that Next Generation EU had been planned to provide to such EU budgetary instruments as Horizon Europe and the Just Transition Fund. Furthermore, the idea of a Solvency Support Instrument was dropped by the European Council.

The European Parliament welcomed the idea of a recovery fund–something Parliament itself had pushed for–deeming its creation an historic move for the European Union. This involved new *de facto* deficit spending. Nevertheless, since it was adopted on the basis of Article 122 and by the European Council alone, Parliament called for Parliament's full democratic involvement in the recovery instrument, noting that

---

[2] As to which, see European Commission, Directorate-General for Budget, *Financial regulation applicable to the general budget of the Union—July 2018* (Publications Office, 2021) available online at <https://data.europa.eu/doi/10.2761/985939> accessed 19 December 2023.

[3] Namely, REACT-EU (€47.5 billion); Horizon Europe (€5 billion); InvestEU (€5.6 billion); rural development (€7.5 billion); the Just Transition Fund (€10 billion); and RescEU (€1.9 billion).

the legal basis chosen for it did not give a formal role to elected Members of the European Parliament, and deploring the reduction of the grant component in the final agreement.

Beyond this, Parliament did not accept the European Council political agreement on the Multiannual Financial Framework, expressing instead its readiness to engage in constructive negotiations with the Council to improve the settlement. A final Multiannual Financial Framework agreement was subsequently reached in November 2020 after trilateral negotiations. This new inter-institutional agreement on budgetary matters ensures greater involvement of the European Parliament as one arm of the budgetary authority in the governance of Next Generation EU.

On 14 December 2020, the Council adopted the regulation establishing the European Union Recovery Instrument. Here again the question of sovereignty reared its head–since it was only in June 2021 that the instrument became operational, following on the ratification of the new own resources decision by all Member States.

The fact that Next Generation EU was created as a temporary measure to address a specific crisis had a specific context, namely, the COVID-19 pandemic, and the lack of cash flow in Member States to address immediate needs. However, one can argue that the approach has proven successful, that it should become permanent and that it should continue exist in order to provide European Union-wide solutions and increase the Union's capacity to respond. Arguably, this could be the embryo of the solution to future capacity needs.

Let us now turn to the future of economic governance and its link to Next Generation EU. Since the COVID-19 pandemic, European Union political discourse has been based on resilience, and more specifically, on becoming more resilient to new crises. Next Generation EU–and especially the Recovery and Resilience Facility–became a milestone along the European Union´s pathway towards ensuring resilience during the COVID-19 crisis. But new crises continue to unfold one by one: more recently, we have seen the Ukrainian conflict, the energy crisis and the inflation spiral. It is not so long since the International Monetary Fund mooted that a complete shut-off of Russian gas to Europe, a resurgence of COVID-19 and a possible financial crisis in China were looming on the horizon.

We cannot continue to delay the discussion of creating a common fiscal capacity in the European Union in order to be able to tackle the effects of another major and unexpected crisis. This is an essential pillar, needed to reinforce a fragile and vulnerable Economic and Monetary Union. But a common fiscal capacity would also meet the need to have a rainy day fund, or last resort financial source, that can immediately support governments, households and companies.

As has been seen in the discussion above, the new temporary instruments created during COVID-19 (such as SURE, REACT EU, Next Generation EU and the Recovery and Resilience Facility) are an inspiration and opportunity. After over two years, these instruments can also be labelled as milestones and should be adapted and made permanent in the European Union´s toolbox for dealing with new crises.

As this writer has argued for a long time, SURE should serve as a model for focusing on short term and targeted interventions–helping families and companies to tackle rising energy costs, for example–and the Recovery and Resilience Facility as a model for a more long-term investment capacity to support structural investments in Europe–building a real strategic autonomy, including energy autonomy, for example.

Nowadays, the SURE model is probably the instrument that attracts the highest degree of consensus among Member States, but ambitions need to be raised higher than this. A robust European Union fiscal capacity is needed in order to respond to unforeseen events and to invest in European Union strategic priorities. In the meantime, the European Commission published its proposals for the new economic governance rules in April 2023.[4]

One of the positive aspects of the new package was the confirmation that the Recovery and Resilience Facility would be used a blueprint for the governance of the new economic framework, something the Parliament requested in its report on the reform of the fiscal rules and economic governance[5] in July 2021. Under Commission proposals which were subsequently adopted and entered into force in April 2024, Member States will have multi-year national fiscal plans to reduce debt at a rate agreed with the Commission, whereby more fiscal space for strategic investments and reforms can be negotiated. As is the case under the Recovery and Resilience Facility, there will be regular progress checks. The Commission and the Council will approve commitments to reforms and investments in national plans provided by the Member States.

With the Recovery and Resilience Facility serving as an inspiration for governance of the economic framework, some steps have been taken in the direction of a more robust and ambitious economic governance. The publication of a joint article by Commissioners Gentiloni and Breton, calling for joint mutualised tools and a budgetary response at European level to tackle the energy crisis in a manner similar to that deployed during the COVID-19 pandemic, is also a clear sign that the tide is also turning within the Commission.[6] A permanent fiscal capacity like the Recovery and Resilience Facility is crucial in order to promote investments focused on achieving real convergence on European political priorities like strategic autonomy or the climate or digital transition, with clear criteria and achievable targets

---

[4] See Proposal for a Regulation of the European Parliament and of the Council on the effective coordination of economic policies and multilateral budgetary surveillance and repealing Council Regulation (EC) No 1466/97 (Brussels, 26.4.2023 COM(2023) 240 final 2023/0138 (COD)) available online at <https://eur-lex.europa.eu/legal-content/EN/TXT/?uri=CELEX%3A52023PC0240> accessed 31 January 2024. This new economic governance framework—as to which, see now Regulation (EU) 2024/1263 of the European Parliament and of the Council of 29 April 2024 on the effective coordination of economic policies and on multilateral budgetary surveillance and repealing Council Regulation (EC) No 1466/97—was adopted, and entered into force on 30 April 2024. <https://eur-lex.europa.eu/eli/reg/2024/1263/oj> accessed 21 October 2024.

[5] See paragraph 57 of the European Parliament own-initiative (INI) Report, "The review of the macroeconomic legislative framework for a better impact on Europe's real economy and improved transparency of decision-making and democratic accountability" available online at <https://www.europarl.europa.eu/doceo/document/TA-9-2021-0358_EN.pdf> accessed 31 January 2024.

[6] Editors' note: this was published as an op-ed in several European newspapers. See e.g., Thierry Breton and Paolo Gentiloni, "Nur eine europäische Antwort kann Industrie und Bürger schützen", *Frankfurter Allgemeine Zeitung,* 3 October 2022.

being linked to the disbursements. This is the most efficient way to secure national ownership from Member States and gain the trust of all contributors.

The Recovery and Resilience Facility is an innovative instrument that provides substantial economic policy firepower to drive economic reforms through the use of positive incentives and to ensure coherence between investment and reforms in Member States and between national and European Union objectives. The joint borrowing is also an innovative step in order to have quickly available sufficient resources to confront any sudden crisis and give confidence to international investors.

We must also learn lessons from Next Generation EU for European economic governance:

- the Recovery and Resilience Facility has provided the incentive to implement reforms and investments in line with national and European policies. Indeed, the Facility has provided the–much-needed–incentive for the implementation of Country-Specific Recommendations and is already working to this end, with well-defined interim goals and objectives;
- the Recovery and Resilience Facility Regulation has provided the framework for the approval, review and implementation of national reform and investment plans;
- the Regulation has established the power relations between the Commission, the Member States and the Council;
- the Regulation has brought about closer cooperation and trust between national governments and European institutions;
- the Regulation has created a scrutiny function for the European Parliament;
- the Regulation has contributed to increasing mutual trust;
- national parliaments, social and regional partners have obtained increased relevance through the preparation and implementation of national reform and investment plans;
- the Regulation has promoted greater alignment of priorities and challenges at national and European level.

In view of the high levels of investment which will be required in the years to come, the European Union fiscal framework should play an appropriate role in incentivising national public investment and reforms, in particular ensuring coherence between investment and reforms in Member States and between national and European Union objectives.

If it is sought to be ambitious, one could also look at the Recovery and Resilience Facility and Next Generation EU as a model to change the paradigm and create a new generation of European Union budgets post-2027. The last crises have shown that the European Union budget is not fit to address crises. The €2 trillion firepower of the new Multi-annual Financial Framework, Next Generation EU, and in particular the Recovery and Resilience Facility, cannot be allowed to become a missed opportunity.

Arguably, a golden opportunity exists to review and improve the European Union's economic and budgetary governance. The European Union must be provided with suitable means to address its priorities and cope with unforeseen challenges, in order to meet the rising expectations of European Union citizens, not only in the short term but in the long run.

The unprecedented magnitude of COVID-19 forced an unprecedented response from all institutions responsible for political decisions. For the current multiple crisis–the subjects of which range from Ukraine to energy, from inflation to the after-effects of COVID-19–and which has implications which are much more uncertain and have wider spillovers, the response will have to be much more ambitious.

The European Union as a Sovereign Global Player?

“The Brussels Effect” and European Sovereignty

Anu Bradford

Abstract *The Brussels Effect: How the European Union Rules the World* was Anu Bradford’s response to the prevailing narrative of the inevitable weakness and decline of Europe—the idea that somehow Europe’s best days are over, and that it is no longer able to exert influence on the global stage. Bradford disputes that narrative and argues that the European Union exerts continuing global influence through its regulations, which enhance European sovereignty and elevates its role globally. In addition to illustrating the manifestations and relevance of this aspect of European sovereignty, Bradford outlines a set of challenges that Europe needs to tackle in addition to thrive and succeed in an increasingly volatile world.

The Brussels Effect: *How the European Union Rules the World*[1] was a response to the prevailing narrative of the inevitable weakness and decline of Europe–the idea that somehow Europe’s best days are over, and that it is no longer able to exert influence on the global stage. That is not, however, the Europe observed daily in researching and teaching.

A few examples may be given of the powerful Europe that can be seen from the United States. If one thinks about some of the most influential US digital companies–Microsoft, Apple, Meta or Google–these companies use a single global privacy

[1] Anu Bradford, *The Brussels Effect: How the European Union Rules the World* (Oxford University Press 2020).

Text based on transcript of a keynote speech delivered by Anu Bradford at the 30th Anniversary Congress of the Academy of European Law Trier *European Sovereignty: The Legal Dimension – A Union in Control of its own Destiny*.

Henry L. Moses Distinguished Professor of Law and International Organization at Columbia Law School.

The speech was delivered at a Congress session analysing the European Union as a sovereign global player. The text has been slightly edited for clarity.

A. Bradford (✉)
New York City, USA
e-mail: abradf@law.columbia.edu

G. Barrett et al. (eds.), *European Sovereignty*,
https://doi.org/10.1007/978-3-031-71851-9_13

policy, which is written in light of the GDPR.[2] Staying within that industry and again looking at leading American companies, such as Facebook and Twitter, these companies do not look to the First Amendment of the US Constitution when they decide what constitutes hate speech that should be removed from their platforms, but rather use the European Union's definition of hate speech. However, it is not merely American companies that are affected by European law even when operating outside of Europe, nor is it just the digital economy that is shaped by European regulations: European law also defines how timber is harvested in Indonesia, how honey is produced in Brazil, what kind of pesticides African farmers use on their farms, what kind of facilities Chinese dairy factories install, and what kind of chemicals Japanese toy manufacturers use when producing toys. These are some of the examples of the Brussels Effect—a concept that refers to the European Union's unilateral ability to regulate the global marketplace.

The European Union is one of the largest and wealthiest consumer markets in the world and there are very few global companies that can afford not to trade in the European Union. In order to access the European market, these companies must abide by European regulations. That is not surprising, but often these companies voluntarily conclude that they are better off extending the European regulation across their global product range, or across their global conduct, because they want to avoid the cost of complying with multiple different regulatory regimes. By conforming to the most stringent regulation, which typically is the European regulation, these companies can access most markets. All the European Union needs to do, in order to exert that kind of regulatory power, is to regulate the Single Market. The market forces and the self-interest of the global companies do the rest. Arguably, this is a relevant form of power: regulatory power. It is an element of sovereignty, namely regulatory sovereignty. It matters because all of us everywhere feel the Brussels Effect every day. It affects the food we eat, the air we breathe, the products we produce and consume. This contributes to both the relevance and influence of the European Union.

It is worth considering why we observe the Brussels Effect, but not the Washington Effect, or the Beijing Effect. Small jurisdictions cannot exert global regulatory power. If Costa Rica decides to impose stringent environmental regulations, companies can simply abandon doing business in Costa Rica. But when the European Union imposes stringent regulations, it is very hard to write off a market this size. But this does not explain why we do not observe the Washington Effect or the Beijing Effect. These are also large markets, after all. However, it is not enough to have a large market. To exert global regulatory influence, it is also necessary to have the regulatory infrastructure and the legal institutions that allow the jurisdiction to unleash the power of those large markets and then convert that market size into tangible regulatory influence. That is what is found in Europe: the power that resides within the institutions in Brussels and Luxembourg is remarkable. Beijing, for instance, has not yet been able

[2] See Regulation (EU) 2016/679 of the European Parliament and of the Council of 27 April 2016 on the protection of natural persons with regard to the processing of personal data and on the free movement of such data, and repealing Directive 95/46/EC (General Data Protection Regulation) as amended. OJ L 119 (4.5.2016) 1.

to replicate it. It is busy building such regulatory capacity and may one day possess it, but if we look at why the European Union has exercised more power to date, it is because it also has strong regulatory institutions.

No doubt Washington also has capable regulatory institutions. Certainly, plenty of regulatory power resides in Washington. What is missing, though, is the political will to deploy that power. The Americans, roughly since the 1990s, have been quite unwilling to regulate, and this has been the case whether a Democrat or Republican has resided in the White House. It used to be that environmental regulations came from California, and thus from the United States. But the European Union has since taken the United States' place. When the United States voluntarily stepped away from regulation and left a vacuum, it was the Europeans who stepped in and assumed the role of the global regulator.

Let us consider whether the Brussels Effect is good or bad. In many ways, it is an advantage for Europe. It levels the playing field globally, ensuring that European companies are not disadvantaged in terms of their competitiveness when they compete on third markets in that the foreign companies also bear the cost of complying with European regulations. There is also a gain in terms of an increase in regulatory sovereignty. European regulations shape the global marketplace towards values defined as being important by Europeans. Hence European companies and individuals are not at the mercy of laws written by others: Europeans are the rule makers, not the rule takers, and this helps Union to be in control of its own destiny.

However, there are also some criticisms of the Brussels Effect. One is that regulation is costly and hinders innovation. If the Brussels Effect is taken seriously, then those costs are multiplied across the global marketplace, a point that will be returned to below. Another criticism heard very often in the United States is that it is American companies that are targeted. If one looks at, for example, digital regulation, it is always the big American companies that are pursued, and that this is therefore seen as protectionist regulation. At least until very recently that notion could be comfortably refuted. One could ask what European search engine the Commission and the Court were trying to protect when going after Google: for there is no European search engine. Moreover, if one asked who brought the initial complaint against Google, the answer was that it was another American company, Microsoft. Thus, it is often a case of American companies fighting a civil war in European territory because their own regulators and their own courts do not provide them with the kinds of remedies available in Europe. In that sense, it is hard to assert that these European regulations are anti-American. However, the tone of the discussion about protectionism is shifting–a point that this text will return to later as well.

A third criticism that arguably relates to the theme of sovereignty is the perception in many parts of the world that, through the Brussels Effect, Europeans are undermining the regulatory sovereignty of the others–in other words, that they are overriding the preferences of democratically-elected governments elsewhere, and compromising both the political autonomy of those governments and their ability to write rules for their own citizens. That is a question worth considering. Some developing countries assert that they cannot afford to care about privacy or the environment at the level at which Europe can afford to, yet are nonetheless also affected by these rules–rules that the European Union writes not just for itself, but for developing countries as well. Similarly, American companies that perceive that Europe is targeting their companies have complained about the lack of accountability and cited their inability to vote out European leaders if they do not approve of the laws they put in place–even if those laws affect them.

To respond to this criticism, the European Union can invoke the idea that Europe is a "benevolent hegemon." Thus, when the European Union dismantles a global cartel, there are many developing countries that benefit as well. These countries do not have competition authorities that could have done the same, yet willingly free ride on European enforcement of competition law. Similarly, climate change does need to be addressed, and it can be seen as beneficial for the world if the European regulations seeking to mitigate climate change become globalised. Perhaps the best argument for the Europeans is that the European Union is not regulating the global marketplace, but is merely regulating the Single Market. If a company like Facebook chooses to extend the European Union's GDPR standards across the world, that cannot be viewed as regulatory imperialism. It is merely the Europeans exercising regulatory sovereignty, which they have the sovereign right, even the obligation, to do. However, it ought nonetheless to be acknowledged that this can be controversial and it may be asked whether a discussion of regulatory sovereignty ought to consider the impact such regulation has on the sovereignty of others.

It is also worth reflecting on how much the world has changed in the years since *The Brussels Effect* was written, and how the Brussels Effect might have changed in the course of the world events that have happened in that time.

First, the world was hit by COVID-19. An intensifying trade and technology war began, leading to gradual decoupling of the digital economy between China and the US. Then, the Russian invasion in Ukraine took place. Given these major shocks to the global economy, is it still possible to talk about the Brussels Effect? How should we think about regulation in this new environment? First, it is clear that hard power is back. One can unambiguously state that there are several dimensions of power and European sovereignty where European Union regulatory power has little to offer. Europe cannot regulate Russia out of Ukraine, neither can those regulations bring peace or keep Europeans safe from a military invasion. What the Brussels Effect helps us to understand, however, is where Europe is strong, and where Europe needs to get stronger; where Europe can rely on the markets to shape the world towards European values, and where it needs to use other tools, be they diplomatic tools, financial investments, and even military investments. But the Brussels Effect should instil confidence in Europeans that Europe can be strong, that Europe can be a globally relevant superpower that cannot be ignored and that Europe can shape its own destiny and that of others.

A few examples may be offered of how the Brussels Effect and the sovereignty debate have evolved. Let us focus on the "digital sovereignty" dimension of the sovereignty debate as that is where regulation directly intersects with this debate. We may ask ourselves the question of how the Brussels Effect is evolving against the backdrop of the US-China technology war and the unravelling of the global supply chains.

A common view suggests that there is growing uncertainty about supply chains and less trust in trading partners, which emphasises the need for greater digital sovereignty. This has led to a temptation to leverage the Brussels Effect and European regulatory power towards industrial policy and broader geopolitical goals.

In Bradford's view, industrial policy and growing digital protectionism does not provide any fruitful path towards greater European digital sovereignty. Europeans may be overplaying their hand if they succumb to the temptation to turn the Brussels Effect into such an instrument. One can understand where this new policy direction is coming from. The US is more protectionist now. China has been all along. Everybody is subsidising their key technologies. Arguably, Europe cannot be left alone at the mercy of such subsidy races. This explains why some European leaders have proposed to convert competition law into a tool for industrial policy in order to nurture European champions, or advocated for the pursuit data localisation or greater provision of subsidies.

There is also a legitimate fear of technological dependencies: we need to learn something from our energy dependence on Russia. However, protectionism is not what stands out as a solution to those dependencies. Europe needs to hedge and ensure it is not overly dependent on a single supplier. But it cannot go it alone. Technological sovereignty, according to Bradford, is not fully feasible. For example, there is not a single jurisdiction that will be able to declare self-sufficiency when it comes to critical technologies such as semiconductors.

Let us also reflect the implications of the Brussels Effect in this era of growing techno-nativism. What does that tell us about converting regulation into a tool for industrial policy? The answer is that industrial-policy driven, protectionist regulations get exported as well. The Brussels Effect is arguably an effective tool for exporting good and bad regulations alike. If we convert merger control into a tool for industrial policy, we should be ready to witness what happens when European companies are trying to buy a Brazilian company. The Brazilians will now have a template on how to look at that transaction as well: they may also prefer nurturing national champions and reject any European attempts to acquire those companies.

So, what should one do if one wants to steer Europe away from protectionism? It is not that we need to give up on digital sovereignty: Bradford is in favour of the digital sovereignty agenda if it means enhancing European capabilities, as opposed to engaging in digital protectionism. Governments can have a role in the digital economy. If one looks at some of the most path-breaking technologies that have emanated from the United States, they have not just come from Silicon Valley, but also benefited from the support of Washington. That US government has long been an important backer of many of those influential technologies, even if they have not been picking the winners as such. If Europe wants to be truly digitally sovereign, this requires more than unleashing costly subsidy races or resorting to protectionism. It requires real investment in innovation, research and development, and commitment to building European capabilities. The conditions need to be created for European technology companies to succeed.

If one thinks about the current position of European technology companies, squeezed between the technological balance of the United States and China, the path towards digital sovereignty looks daunting. In 2021, Amazon alone eclipsed the entire German DAX index, which represents about 80 per cent of the market capitalisation listed in Germany. In the Forbes 2021 listing of the world's largest technology companies, there were only two European companies in the top twenty: SAP and Accenture. At the same time, there were thirteen American companies among the top twenty. European companies contribute less than four per cent to the market cap of the largest 70 platforms in the world. The questions may be posed of how Europe can change that, and why are there no European Googles, Microsofts, Metas or Apples. Some have contended that Europe is regulating too much and that is why it does not succeed. Arguably, regulation is not the problem.

This argument is different from saying that *all* regulation is good—for example protectionist regulation is harmful—but generally America has shown us what an unregulated digital marketplace looks like and that is not a model for Europe to follow. In fact, one should arguably be more worried about Europeans regulating too little or at least not enforcing their regulations effectively.

There has been much well-known criticism of Europe's inability to enforce the GDPR. It is very easy to single out, for instance, the example of the Irish Data Protection Agency, and point out how ineffective it has been. However, its task is a tall order, and the enforcement of the GDPR is challenging given the limited resources of the agency. For example, the year the Irish agency started enforcing GDPR, its annual budget was equivalent to the revenue that the largest US tech companies headquartered in Dublin were making every ten minutes. Enforcement remains a major challenge today and needs to be strengthened.

So, what should Europe do? First of all, Europe needs to remember what the root of its power stems from the Single Market. Yet today, the digital single market is both highly incomplete and fragmented. Technological innovations require scale, and European companies cannot build at scale in Europe due to this fragmentation. They need to internationalise much earlier than their American counterparts do. Thus the first item on the agenda should be that Europe not lose sight of the importance of completing the Digital Single Market.

Secondly, capital is needed to fund innovations. Europe urgently needs to complete the Capital Markets Union. European startups can raise early rounds of funding in Europe. But when it comes to more advanced rounds, they depend on American capital. The American venture capital market is much more developed than that of Europe. That arguably also needs to change. There are some encouraging signs that this will happen, but more work needs to be done.

The third to-do item is the cost of failure in Europe. Entrepreneurs need to be encouraged to take risks. When they fail, this should not be a "life sentence" but instead they should be given a second chance. In Europe, failure is often fatal, whereas in Silicon Valley it is a rite of passage. In the US, an entrepreneur after a bankruptcy will often raise more funds because now the funders will know that the person has the courage to try, and will want to fund them again. One OECD study has compared the personal cost of failure, looking at insolvency laws. The countries where those personal cost of failure were the lowest were the United States, Canada, and Turkey.[3] Where they were highest were the Czech Republic, Sweden, Portugal, and some other European countries. These costs deter risk-taking, which is crucial for disruptive innovations. Instead, we need to allow European entrepreneurs to take risks, which means we need to also allow them to fail at times.

The fourth action-item that Europe ought to remember is that it cannot build a 'Fortress Europe'. Europe needs to have a proactive immigration policy to make sure that it will attract the talent to help build European companies in Europe. In part, American technology companies have been so successful because they have been able to draw from the global talent pool and benefited tremendously from immigration. One needs only look at the founders of the biggest tech companies: Apple's founder Steve Jobs was the son of a Syrian immigrant; Jeff Bezos of Amazon is a second-generation Cuban immigrant. Google's co-founder Sergey Brin is Russian. The co-founder of Facebook, Eduardo Saverin, is Brazilian. Tesla's Elon Musk is South African. And these are not rare exceptions. Indeed, over fifty per cent of the over-billion-dollar startups in the US have an immigrant founder.

One path towards success in Europe is to embrace this kind of openness, to have the red carpet ready for talent from around the world to find its way to Europe. None of these proposed foundations of European technological capabilities involve industrial policy. At best, they can be seen as elements of an "open strategic autonomy."

Let us move to the final argument for rejecting protectionism, which is that the pursuit of sovereignty needs to come with an understanding that Europe cannot turn inwards. Sovereignty is much harder to pursue in a world that has rejected our values. How, then, can that world be shaped so that Europe can thrive there as a sovereign Europe? The pursuit of European sovereignty calls for clarity of what we stand for, how we want to shape the world and what we see Europe's role in that world to be.

Is the world around us friendly or hostile to the kind of values that a sovereign Europe wants to promote–to its freedom, its democracy, its fundamental rights, and the rule of law? These are Europe's bedrock and foundation. It is much harder to exercise European sovereignty in a world that is turning away from European values and that is more authoritarian. Freedom House—an American Think Tank focusing on researching and advocating for democracy—noted that 2021 saw the fifteenth consecutive year of decline in freedom around the world. In this year too, Freedom House calculated that only 20% of the world's population lives in countries that they classify as "free." The battle for technological sovereignty and the future of the digital economy is thus fundamentally and ultimately also a battle of values.

There are basically three different models for digital economy and society from which we can choose. There is the American market-driven model, there is the Chinese state-driven model, and then there is the European rights-driven model. Arguably, the battle between the American and European models is shaping to Europe's advantage. Europe's digital regulation model is doing well. The conversation is shifting in the United States in the direction of Europe. The two are not

---

[3] See Müge Adalet McGowen and Dan Andrews, *Design of Insolvency Regimes Across Countries* (Economics Department, OECD 2018).

meeting in the middle; instead, Americans are conceding that self-regulation is not enough, and markets alone cannot be trusted to govern technology. The question is whether that country's dysfunctional legislator can actually convert that shift in public sentiment into legislation to that effect.

Notwithstanding the major battles that Americans and Europeans have had in the past over data privacy versus surveillance, over digital taxation, or over anti-trust issues, we have now potentially reached a global deal on taxation. The Americans and Europeans have also reached a new agreement to resolve their long-standing row over data transfers, with the Biden administration agreeing on enhanced privacy safeguards that they believe would also survive *Schrems III*.[4]

A set of antitrust bills are now pending in in US Congress, including a bill that resembles the European Digital Markets Act.[5] The US government has also issued a Blueprint for an AI Bill of Rights.[6] These legislative and executive initiatives are gradually moving the US much more towards the kind of world that the European legislator has for long been pioneering. Europe and the United States share a Trade and Technology Council, which provides a more institutionalised avenue for conversation and cooperation.

One defining battle remains very much a challenge, however. This is the rise of digital authoritarianism as an alternative to the model that European digital sovereignty is trying to push for and defend. What is at stake here is really the future of liberal democracy. Even if the European model is doing well in the democratic world, the Chinese digital authoritarian model is doing very well in many other parts of the world.

In this battle, China has proven many of the Western assumptions wrong. First, China has shown to the world that the internet is neither inherently free nor inherently global. Both are subject to political choice, and China has exercised its choice to limit internet freedom. Secondly, although this is a painful concession to make, China has also shown to the world that innovation can thrive even when freedoms are restricted. Hence under its restrictive state-driven model, Chinese companies have, managed to be successful.

Thirdly, China has also proven that it has the ability to export its model across the world. It is building the Digital Silk Road, building digital infrastructures, and also exerting greater influence around the world.

---

[4] A request for a preliminary ruling has been made by the Oberster Gerichtshof (Austria) in Case C-446/21 *Schrems (Communication de données au grand public)* following on earlier decisions of the European Court of Justice in Case C-311/18 *Data Protection Commissioner v. Facebook Ireland Ltd. & Schrems* EU:C:2019:1145 (judgment of the Court of Justice (Grand Chamber) of 16 July 2020 (*Schrems II*)) and Case C-362/14 *Maximillian Schrems v Data Protection Commissioner* EU:C:2015:650 (judgment of the Court of Justice (Grand Chamber) of 6 October 2015 (*Schrems I*).

[5] Regulation (EU) 2022/1925 of the European Parliament and of the Council of 14 September 2022 on contestable and fair markets in the digital sector and amending Directives (EU) 2019/1937 and (EU) 2020/1828 (Digital Markets Act) (OJ L 265, 12.10.2022, 1).

[6] See https://www.whitehouse.gov/ostp/ai-bill-of-rights/.

So, Europe has the Brussels Effect, while China has the Digital Silk Road, which sets the stage for a major battle between techno-democracies and techno-autocracies. The United States and Europe are looking to strengthen cooperation among a coalition of techno-democracies that will jointly provide an alternative to China, Russia, Saudi Arabia, and other techno-autocracies. This will be a hard but, many would argue, a necessary thing to do. However, there are many challenges in forming a coalition of techno-democracies, including the question of deciding who should be invited to the club. While countries such as China are clearly on the other side of the divide, what about countries such as India and Brazil? There are many important countries that straddle the divide between the authoritarian and democratic worlds. If they are rejected, they will find themselves more in China's orbit.

That is one challenge. The other is that if countries are compelled to choose between *e.g.*, the United States and China, many of them trade more with China, and thus, they may well choose China. There is also the question of whether the US and Europe are giving democracy a good name, given the current internal challenges to democracy both in the United States and in Europe. But ultimately, despite these difficulties, the stakes in this battle in the digital economy are high, and it is crucial how the Europeans to deploy their regulatory sovereignty towards success in this battle over the future of liberal democracy.

There are two ways for Europe to lose that battle. One is that it loses this horizontal battle to China, and that the Brussels Effect does ultimately lose out to the forces of the Digital Silk Road (or their version of the Beijing Effect). The second way in which Europe can lose the battle over democracy is by losing its vertical battle against technology companies. We have seen that Europeans can promulgate regulations–Americans cannot even do that–but can Europe enforce its regulations against these companies? Or, in practice, does the American market-driven model prevail if enforcement fails? Because ultimately, the question is what happens when Europe seeks to regulate a company like Google with the Digital Markets Act. This is not just a question of whether it is possible to unlock competition in the marketplace. What is also at stake is Europe's ability to show that there is a way for democracies to govern such technology companies. While Europe is betting against the Chinese state when the latter cracks down on its technology industry, the jury is out whether Europe and America can govern democratically technology companies. It would be a deeply disconcerting conclusion if Europe was forced to concede that it had not figured out a governance model–consistent with its other values–which ultimately will keep technology companies in check.

This is a battle that neither the United States nor the European Union can afford to lose. If a sovereign Europe cannot defend liberal democracy as the foundation for the digital economy and political life in Europe and elsewhere, the question is raised of what good that sovereignty does for us.

This chapter has outlined some challenges that Europe faces. However, this has been done from the standpoint that those who are the biggest champions of, and believers in, Europe also need to be its most honest critics, so that together they can help Europe overcome its difficulties and challenges. Hopefully, readers of this chapter will share Anu Bradford's ambition for, and confidence in, Europe and her deep hope that Europe will succeed–both for its own sake and for that of the wider world.

Democratic Organisation of European Sovereignty

The Relationship Between National Competences and European Union Competences with a Special Focus on the Field of Justice: A Romanian Perspective

Cătălin Predoiu

1 Introduction

This article is focused on a judiciary-related topic that has recently sparked many theoretical and practical debates: the relationship between national competences and EU competences in the field of justice.

In order to explore the multiple facets of this topic, it will first analyse the two main dimensions of European sovereignty: the sovereignty of the Union and the sovereignty of the Member States of the Union. It will then examine a concrete example of the relationship between national competences and EU competences, namely that in the justice area. It will then go on to explore the interplay between EU sovereignty and national sovereignties in the field of environmental protection with a special focus on criminal law mechanisms and, more particularly, on the introduction of the international crime of ecocide and of transnational eco-crimes. Finally, the essential strengths of complementarity and reciprocity between the sovereignty of the European Union and that of the EU Member States will be considered in the light of the current international context.

Minister of Internal Affairs and Deputy Prime Minister of Romania.

The author was Minister of Justice of Romania at the time of the 30th Anniversary Congress of ERA.

C. Predoiu (✉)
Bucharest, Romania
e-mail: office@predoiu.ro

G. Barrett et al. (eds.), *European Sovereignty*,
https://doi.org/10.1007/978-3-031-71851-9_14

2 The Metaphor of Janus: The 'Sovereignty of the Union' and the 'Sovereignty of the Member States of the Union'

There are a number of aspects which one much address with a view to setting the background for analysing the above-mentioned distribution of competences. In my view, there are two main dimensions of European sovereignty: the sovereignty *of* the Union and the sovereignty of the Member States *within* the Union. This dualism reflects also the intertwined relationship between EU interests and national interests of the Member States.

The interplay between these two dimensions has come under intense public scrutiny over the past few years and is increasingly becoming one of the 'hottest' topics on the public agenda in some member states of the EU. To give just one practical example of the intertwined relationship between national sovereignty and EU sovereignty, national interests and EU interests, I will briefly refer to one of the central topics on the current Romanian public agenda.

Although Romania is one of the newest Member States, having joined the EU only in 2007, we have proved ourselves a reliable partner and a staunch supporter of EU core values and fundamental projects. Romanians have always had a strong pro-European stance, a point confirmed again by a September 2022 survey, which showed that 70% of Romanians were in favour of remaining in the EU. Conversely, 61% of Romanians are also supporters of national sovereignty. This represents strong sociological proof that the two facets of European sovereignty do not exclude each other in the hearts and minds of the Romanian people.

This is why the relationship between the two facets of sovereignty–sovereignty *of the Union* and sovereignty *within the Union*–has to be carefully nurtured so as to adequately, and in timely fashion, relieve the inevitable tensions between the two and to consolidate their undeniable complementarity. For instance, the lifting of the Cooperation and Verification Mechanism (CVM) for Romania[1] in relation to the judiciary and the continuation of Romania's path under the Rule of Law Mechanism (just like any other European Union Member State) as well as its accession to Schengen are currently among the main strategic national objectives of Romania. At the same time, these objectives are inherent aspects of full European Union integration, just as much as the Union's core Article 2 TEU values, such as the rule of law, liberty and freedom of movement.

Starting from this concrete example, let us consider once again two closely interlinked facets–another hallmark of the complementarity between national sovereignty and European Union sovereignty. This intertwined relationship has the potential to enhance the level of progress in various areas, including justice, in turn consolidating the rights of every citizen, ultimately boiling down to the personal sovereignty of every individual. This is because we cannot speak in a true democracy about national

[1] The Co-operation and Verification Mechanism for Romania was lifted in September 2023 by Commission Decision (EU) 2023/1786 of 15 September 2023 repealing Decision 2006/928/EC establishing a mechanism for cooperation and verification of progress in Romania to address specific benchmarks in the areas of judicial reform and the fight against corruption.

or European Union sovereignty without this involving individual freedom. In turn, this generates the necessity to permanently connect the European Union's valuable policies to the cultural roots and strategic interests of Member States, as well as to the fundamental democratic base of any State and of the Union, which consists of the will of the nations concerned, of the people and of the individual.

Continuing to expand on the Janus metaphor, it may be argued that the relationship between European Union sovereignty and national sovereignties is structured through a legal space which includes 27 sovereign states (and 27 corresponding national constitutional systems guarded by national constitutional courts) and one specific supranational organisation–the European Union. Over the past few years, many reputable commentators have referred to this 'common European constitutional space'.[2]

3 The Relationship Between National Competences and European Union Competences in the Field of Justice

Having discussed the complementarity between national sovereignty and European Union sovereignty, it is now necessary to consider two concrete manifestations of the relationship between national competences and European Union competences. These concern two essential areas: first, the field of justice, and secondly, the field of environmental protection.

The relationship between national and European Union competences in the justice area has undergone significant developments over decades, raising complex issues, such as the primacy of European Law. Romania has been no stranger to this process. It had the possibility to experience at first hand several of these developments, given that the comprehensive reform of Romania's national judiciary was interconnected with wider European Union evolutions in the field of justice. For instance, at the end of 2022, Romania finalised a very complex legislative process with the adoption of new Justice Laws. This legislation will provide for essential prerequisites for the further modernisation of our judiciary, especially the completion of the process of giving the judiciary, through the Superior Council of Magistrates and the High Court of Cassation and Justice, the necessary tools (including budgetary and financial ones) for the self–governance of the judiciary based on the cornerstone principle of independence. The public debates and subsequently parliamentary discussions on these draft laws have raised interesting European Union law issues, such as the interpretation of the primacy principle in areas related to the application of the decisions of the Constitutional Court in the light of the Romanian Constitution and of relevant

[2] See Egils Levits, "On primacy, common constitutional traditions, and national identity in the common European constitutional space", a paper presented at the international conference *EUnited in diversity: between common constitutional traditions and national identities*, held at Riga, Latvia (2–3 September 2021). Conference proceedings are available online at <https://curia.europa.eu/jcms/upload/docs/application/pdf/2022-06/eunited_in_diversity_-_riga_september_2021_-_conference_proceedings.pdf> (accessed 20 January 2023).

European Court of Justice case-law. In the end, a balanced approach was undertaken regarding this issue, with the Parliament acknowledging in these laws the primacy of European Union law in accordance with the national Constitution, the Treaty on the European Union (TEU) and the Treaty on the Functioning of the European Union (TFEU).

The time-frame of "decades" merits emphasis, because these developments started many years ago. The most recent fundamental shift in competences in the judicial field began at the level of primary law, with the entry into force of the Lisbon Treaty in 2009. This significantly increased European Union competences in the field of justice, while also extending the jurisdiction of the European Court of Justice in this area. Subsequently, it also led to a reconfiguration of European Union secondary law in the justice area, including by virtue of the multiplication of the number of instruments adopted and of the addressing of specific topics.

In jurisprudential terms, the core European Court of Justice case-law on the independence of the judiciary began with the 2006 landmark judgment delivered in the *Wilson* case.[3] This case concerned the interpretation of certain provisions of the Lawyers Right of Establishment Directive 98/5 concerning, *inter alia*, the concept of a remedy before a court or tribunal in accordance with the provisions of domestic law for the purposes of this particular free movement directive. In its Grand Chamber judgment, the European Court of Justice coined several important requirements relating to the concept of "effective judicial protection" which must be provided by an "independent and impartial court". However, the Court had actually started developing these criteria in a series of Article 267 preliminary rulings decades ago, beginning with essential cases, such as the 1966 judgment in *Vaassen-Göbbels*,[4] the 1987 judgment in *Pretore di Salò*[5] and the 1997 judgment in *Dorsch Consult*.[6]

On the other hand, if a national court or tribunal fulfils all of the conditions under Article 267, then nothing in the domestic law of their Member State of origin (whether this be national legislation, even of a constitutional order, or the jurisprudence of top courts in that country, such as the Supreme Court or the Constitutional Court, or the stage of the proceedings) can prevent it from referring a preliminary question to the European Court of Justice. This thesis, however, also stems from consolidated Court of Justice case-law dating back to *Costa v ENEL*,[7] *Simmenthal*[8] and *Rheinmühlen*[9] (all of which judgments were delivered in the sixth and seventh decades of the previous century) and the *Melloni* judgment of 2013.[10]

---

[3] Case C-506/04 *Wilson* EU:C:2006:587 (judgment of 19 September 2006).

[4] Case 61/65 *Vaassen-Goebbels* EU:C:1966:39 (judgment of 30 June 1966).

[5] Case 14/86 *Pretore di Salò* EU:C:1987:275 (judgment of 11 June 1987).

[6] Case C-54/96 *Dorsch Consult* EU:C:1997:413 (judgment of 17 September 1997).

[7] Case 6/64 *Costa v ENEL* EU:C:1964:66 (judgment of 15 July 1964).

[8] Case 106/77 *Amministrazione delle finanze dello Stato v Simmenthal* EU:C:1978:49 (judgment of 9 March 1978).

[9] Case 146/73 *Rheinmühlen Düsseldorf* EU:C:1974:12 (judgment of 12 February 1974).

[10] Case C-399/11 *Melloni* EU:C:2013:107 (judgment of 26 February 2013).

Subsequently, in the *CILFIT II* judgment of 2021,[11] the European Court of Justice clarified its historic *CILFIT* case-law regarding the three situations in which national courts or tribunals of last instance are not subject to the obligation to make a reference for a preliminary ruling, namely, where: (a) the question is irrelevant for the resolution of the dispute; (b) the provision of European Union law in question has already been interpreted by the Court; or (c) the correct interpretation of European Union law is so obvious as to leave no scope for any reasonable doubt.[12]

These examples illustrate the model of sovereignty based on the primacy of European Union law. This model does not exclude drawing upon the national sovereignty of individual Member States within the Union, something wonderfully reflected by various sources of European Union law. For instance, primary law (via Article 4, para 2 of the Treaty on the European Union) expressly mentions national identities of Member States, inherent in their fundamental structures, political and constitutional. The constitutional traditions common to the Member States are recognised as general principles of the Union's law by the Treaty on the Functioning of the European Union (pursuant to Article 6, para 3) and by consolidated European Court of Justice case-law. According to such case-law, it has been long settled that national judges are European judges. Their role in upholding the fundamental values of the Union, enshrined in Article 2 of the Treaty on the Functioning of the European Union, as well as the right to effective judicial protection, enshrined in Article 19 of the same Treaty, is paramount. The reference to national judges covers all levels and categories of domestic jurisdictions, including the Supreme Courts and the Constitutional Courts. All national judges become guardians of European Union law, given that, at some point in time, all domestic courts will handle cases the outcomes of which will depend on European Union rules. The national identities of Member States and the common constitutional traditions of Member States may be viewed as safeguards which aid in preventing conflicts or contradictions between the two dimensions of the common European constitutional space, namely the national systems and the supranational system.

4 The Relationship Between National Competences and European Union Competences in the Field of Environmental Protection

Rendering 'European sovereignty' and national sovereignty harmonious and, more broadly, creating harmony between international cooperation and global management of the planet, on the one hand, and national sovereignty, on the other hand, are important not only for the present, but more especially for the future. The complex interplay

---

[11] Case C-561/19 *Consorzio Italian Management* ECLI:EU:C:2021:799 (judgment of 6 October 2021).

[12] See Case 283/81, *CILFIT v Ministero della Sanità* ECLI:EU:C:1982:335 (judgment of 6 October 1982).

between various levels of sovereignty impacts not only upon the field of justice and on the judiciary, but also on a wide spectrum of domains which are essential for the security of individuals, such as environmental protection, and consequently, a healthy environment for the life of our citizens and the human habitat in general and furthermore, the security of planet earth.

Currently, the protection of the environment by legal means, especially by criminal law and administrative law, is based in principle on national laws, based on the sovereignty of every state and is commonly accepted nowadays as being incomplete. As one author has put it, "economic globalisation is the origin of the globalisation of environmental criminality",[13] and environmental protection is nowadays incomplete as the difficulty (as the same author has noted) "actually lies in the difficulty of reconciling state sovereignty, economic globalisation and the global ecosystem".[14]

Being a 'global public good', the environment can be efficiently managed and governed exclusively at global level.[15] It may be added that the efficiency of the protection and restoration of the environment by legal means is subject to the same principle. Seen in this perspective, such challenges create a natural tension between global problems and national sovereignty. The key to solving such tensions is thus cooperation between national sovereignties or, in the case of supranational regional structures, such as the European Union, harmonising the approach of 'European sovereignty' and national sovereignties. This is the way in which Europe alone, united and democratic, has managed to organise proper transversal protection via the criminal law both at the level of the European Union, as well as at the level of the Council of Europe.

Insofar as concerns developments at European Union level, an EU Directive concerning the protection of the environment through criminal law, adopted in 2008, stipulated the criminalisation of serious violations of 72 environmental pieces of legislation in the environmental field and required effective, proportionate and dissuasive sanctions.[16] This Directive was assessed in 2020 by the Commission as having not generated sufficient effect on the ground, considering the very low number of environmental crime cases that had been successfully investigated and prosecuted. Thus, in December 2021, the Commission adopted a Proposal for Better Protection of the Environment by Means of Criminal Law,[17] which was meant to replace the 2008 Directive and aimed to make protection of the environment more effective by

[13] Rosmerlin Estupinan–Silva, "La lutte contre la criminalite environnementale au sein des Etats" in *Des écocrimes à l'écocide—Le droit penal au secours de l'environnement*, page 31. (Translation by editors).

[14] *Ibid.*, p. 32. (Translation by editors).

[15] Pascal Beauvais, *"Les limites de l'internalisation du droit pénal de l'environment"* in Laurent Neyret (ed.), *Des écocrimes à l'écocide—Le droit pénal au secours de l'environnement* (Bruylant, 2015) *at* p. 5.

[16] Directive 2008/99/EC of the European Parliament and of the Council of 19 November 2008 on the protection of the environment through criminal law (OJ L 328, 6.12.2008). See *ibid.*, pp. 8, 13.

[17] Proposal for a Directive of the European Parliament and of the Council on the protection of the environment through criminal law and replacing Directive 2008/99/EC (COM/2021/851 final) (15 December 2021).

obliging Member States to adopt legislation establishing minimum rules concerning the definition of criminal offences and sanctions in order to fight against environmental crimes. This Proposal was subsequently adopted as Directive (EU) 2024/1203 on the protection of the environment through criminal law.

As regards developments at the level of the Council of Europe, the Convention on the Protection of the Environment through Criminal Law (adopted in Strasbourg in November 1998) was a significant event in the development of environmental criminal law, as it was the first international convention to criminalise acts causing or likely to cause environmental damage.

Recent years have witnessed an increase in the efforts of transforming the protection of the environment from a narrow national domain into a transversal universal one. A large panel of legal experts proposed two proper transversal instruments in the form of a Draft Convention on Eco crimes and a draft Convention on the Crime of Ecocide, also referred to as "the missing 5th crime against peace."[18]

In conclusion, the way in which the harmonisation of 'European sovereignty' and the national sovereignty of the EU Member States has been brought into harmony could prove a positive, inspiring example for the world, including as regards prospects for a legal environment viewed through strong transversal legal instruments.

5 Looking both Ways: Complementarity and Reciprocity Between the Sovereignty of the European Union and the Individual Sovereignties of European Union Member States

As mentioned in the introduction, the aim of this chapter has been to explore the various legal dimensions of European Union sovereignty. The chapter was also envisaged as dealing, *inter alia,* with the way in which the future of this sovereignty might either shape itself or become shaped against the backdrop of numerous political, strategic, economic, social and cultural challenges.

I would like to conclude by setting forth some personal observations on the way in which this writer would envisage future developments in this area (a topic in relation to which some may take a different view). The distribution of competences between the European Union and its Member States in the field of justice is undoubtedly an intricate question, the evolution of which depends on a whole range of factors. As all are aware, law evolves together with the society to which it applies–a natural and permanent evolution which makes it almost impossible to predict precisely what will follow. However, it is this writer's belief that the principles that have been forged over decades and that are currently enshrined both in the Treaties and in European

---

[18] Anja Gauger, Mai Pouye Rabatel-Fernel, Louise Kulbicki, Damien Short and Polly Higgins, *Ecocide is the missing 5th Crime Against Peace* (2012, Report of the Human Rights Consortium, School of Advanced Study, University of London) available online at <https://sas-space.sas.ac.uk/4686/1/Ecocide_is_the_missing_5th_Crime_Against_Peace.pdf> (accessed 26 January 2023).

Court of Justice case-law are sufficiently solid and effective to provide excellent scaffolding for any future developments. These principles, some of which have been briefly referred to in this chapter, represent the core essence of European Union law. They not only underline our mutual trust, but also have the capacity to accommodate national diversities and nourish an integrated legal system, the main purpose of which is to function as a vehicle of our future development–both the development of the Union itself and the intertwined development of Member States within the Union.

6 Conclusion

It is sought to conclude by returning to the main point of the introduction to this chapter, namely the fact that the two facets of 'European sovereignty'–the sovereignty *of* the Union and the sovereignty of the Member States *within* the Union–are essentially governed by complementarity and reciprocity, and not by competitiveness or mutual exclusion. A selfish and one-sided approach to this issue will only lead to tensions both between the Union and the Member States and between Member States. Furthermore, a short-term approach will lead to a less clear future. This is precisely why discussion and debate have continued and will continue on this important issue. We need to build national interests and national sovereignty while keeping in mind the sovereignty of the European Union. Moreover, notwithstanding the fact that some or a few may argue differently, it is of the utmost importance to pool efforts and resources to consolidate 'European Union sovereignty', while always bearing in mind–and accommodating through dialogue and loyal cooperation–the national interests of every European Union Member State.

This complementarity makes us stronger together and better equipped to deal with the challenges of the future, irrespective of whether these are strategic, political, economic, social, cultural or even concerned with security.

Although it is a difficult goal for politicians in every European Union country, it is, nonetheless their task to harmonise these interests in the best way for all Member States by striving to find that 'perfect common denominator' which will undoubtedly form the basis for more extensive development, as well as a brighter and safer future. As a great man once said in a different context, "we choose to do other things, not because they are easy, but because they are hard."[19]

The experience of the present times proves that the best thing that EU Member States have going for them in these times of war is the existence of the Union itself, as well as that of NATO.

[19] John F. Kennedy, in an address given at Rice University, Texas, 12 September, 1962.

7 Final Reflections

Over a year has passed since the thirtieth anniversary of the Academy of European Law, a year that has undoubtedly proved complex and challenging, but has also been filled with various political and institutional developments and accomplishments both at national and at European Union level.

Regarding the concrete issues falling within the scope of this chapter, one such development was the shutting down of the Cooperation and Verification Mechanism occurred in September 2023. For sixteen years, the Cooperation and Verification Mechanism proved to be an important and useful mechanism for Romania, an appropriate one to appear on the historical stage when it was set up, and one that fully attained its initial purpose. These were sixteen years of undeniable progress and substantial reforms which modernised the Romanian judiciary and brought it well up to the highest European standards. With constant political and cross-institutional commitment, as well as with the valuable support of the judiciary itself and also of a strong civil society, Romania has always remained determined to move along the path towards progress and reform. The progress made along this path illustrates two points about sovereignty. First, the excellent results attained would not have been possible either without Romania, in all its institutional and civil expressions (including the executive, the legislature and the judicial power, civil society, the media and the people themselves), or without the tremendous support of the European Commission and the loyal cooperation of the other EU Member States. Secondly, there is no denying that there will always be room for fine-tuning such endeavours, because, on the one hand, assessing the impact of certain measures requires the passage of a certain period of time in order for definitive conclusions on their efficacy to be reached. On the other hand, the judicial system itself is meant to adapt to socio-economic developments in the country: and fine–tuning is a naturally-occurring process in all states throughout the EU. Moreover, on March, 31st 2024, Romania acceded to the Schengen air and maritime area, with solid prospects of acceding to the Schengen land area in the near future.

Another issue touched upon in this chapter that has seen positive developments over the past year consists of Romania's new Justice Laws, which entered into force in December 2022. These laws are an essential wheel in the mechanism of Romania's national justice system and–in a similar vein to the Cooperation and Verification Mechanism–are a wonderful example of the way in which the relationship between national competences and EU competences in the field of justice has evolved in the past decades, including when viewed through the lens of European Court of Justice case-law. For ultimately, the purpose of all our endeavours, at both national and EU levels, is the securing of the well-being of our peoples against a background founded on essential values and principles such as the observance of fundamental rights and freedoms, legal certainty and predictability and the rule of law.

A Federal Future for the European Union?

Christine Landfried

Abstract The European Union is not fit for the challenges of the twenty-first century. The many crises of the last decades have shown that European policies need more democratic legitimacy and more effectiveness. In this article it is argued that the gap between the growing political power of the EU and its low democratic legitimacy can be explained by the mechanisms of European governance. These mechanisms favour executive and judicial power to the detriment of parliamentary and societal power. Low democratic legitimacy, in turn, has a negative impact on the effectiveness of European policies. The argument will be developed in three steps. First, the mechanisms of European politics and their consequences for European democracy are described. Secondly, the normative criteria for reforms are developed. And thirdly, a concrete roadmap how to reach a more democratic and more effective EU by combining the Conference on the Future of Europe with a new Convention is outlined. The goal should be a EU that is not a federal state, but a supranational organisation with strong federal structures anchored in its Member States, shaped by the effective participation of citizens and able to transform cultural, economic and political differences into an overall unit.

1 Introduction

The crises of the last decades–from the Euro crisis and Brexit to the COVID-19 pandemic as well as the electoral successes of populist political parties in many Member States–have clearly shown that the European Union is not well equipped to deal with the challenges of the twenty-first century. And now, as if that was not enough, the European Union is confronted with Russia's war of aggression against Ukraine, and a war in the Middle East as the consequence of the terrorist attack by Hamas against Israel. In the new geopolitical situation, the weaknesses of the

---

Professor Emerita of Political Science, University of Hamburg.

C. Landfried (✉)
Hamburg, Germany
e-mail: christine.landfried@uni-hamburg.de

G. Barrett et al. (eds.), *European Sovereignty*,
https://doi.org/10.1007/978-3-031-71851-9_15

European Union are becoming especially obvious. Thus, the appeal of the French President Emmanuel Macron from 2017 for a strong European Union is more relevant than ever: "The Europe of today is too weak, too slow, too inefficient, but Europe alone can enable us to take action in the world, in the face of the big contemporary challenges."[1] Only Europe could "guarantee genuine sovereignty or our ability to exist in today's world to defend our values and interests."[2] In Macron's view we need a sovereign European Union in order to defend the European idea of relating freedom, human rights and justice, and to have not only a market economy, but also social justice. The "route which ensures our future" in the context of globalisation means, according to him, "a sovereign, united and democratic Europe".[3]

European sovereignty in the sense of Macron means that the European Union is strong and capable of acting. It does not mean that the European Union should become a state having the power to define its own competencies: Macron's understanding has nothing to do with Jean Bodin's definition of sovereignty as being the concentration of all public power within a state territory in the hands of the sovereign.[4] According to Bodin, the sovereign has the authority to unilaterally set law.[5] Sovereignty relates to a nation state and cannot be shared. However, the development of international law has led to a restriction of national sovereignty by the principles of the Charter of the United Nations and the prevalence of human rights. Sovereignty has been transformed from an exclusive right of state power at the disposal of the sovereign to a participatory and interactive right of nation states to be included in the international community thereby profiting from the advantages of the global infrastructure.[6]

The European Union is an actor representing the new meaning of shared sovereignty at the regional level. This supranational organisation is characterised by the "coexistence of public power of different public agents and the existence of functionally-separated legal orders in the same territory as one model of the territorial partition of power"[7] and can rightly be called a "federal community of law".[8] As the contributions to the Thirty Year Congress of the Academy of European Law on European sovereignty demonstrated, the Member States of the European Union have transferred many competences to the European Union in more and more areas. Yet,

---

[1] Emmanuel Macron, *Initiative pour l'Europe—Discours d'Emmanuel Macron pour une Europe souveraine, unie, démocratique*, Paris, 26 September 2017 (translated by the *service de presse de la Présidence de la République*) at 4.

[2] *Ibid*, 4.

[3] *Ibid.*

[4] Christine Landfried, "Einigkeit, Recht, Stärke", *Frankfurter Allgemeine Zeitung,* 23 December 2017, 12.

[5] Ulrich K. Preuß, "Souveränität—Zwischenbemerkungen zu einem Schlüsselbegriff des Politischen", in Tine Stein, Hubertus Buchstein and Claus Offe (eds.), *Souveränität, Recht, Moral. Die Grundlagen politischer Gemeinschaft*, (Campus 2007), 314.

[6] *Ibid*, 324.

[7] Peter-Christian Müller-Graff, "A Federal European Union of Law" in Carlos Francisco Molina del Pozo (ed.), *Hacia la construcción de un verdadero proyecto federal para la Unión Europea*, (A Coruña 2022), 217.

[8] *Ibid.*

there is not sufficient "strategic sovereignty" (topic 1 of the Congress), "budgetary sovereignty" (topic 2), or "digital sovereignty" (topic 3).

With my contribution I want to explore why the European Union is, in the words of Macron, "too weak, too slow, too inefficient" and whether a federal future within the defined new meaning of the term is a promising way to build a stronger and more democratic European Union–"in control of its own destiny". It is my hypothesis that the gap between the growing political power of the European Union and its low democratic legitimacy can be explained by the mechanisms of European governance. These mechanisms favour executive and judicial power to the detriment of parliamentary and societal power. The low democratic legitimacy of European policies, in turn, has a negative impact for the effectiveness of these policies.

The argument will be developed in three steps. First, the mechanisms of European governance and their consequences for European democracy will be analysed. Secondly, the normative criteria with which we can judge future reforms will be described. Thirdly, the necessary reforms allowing for a more democratic, more just and more sovereign (in the sense of a stronger) European Union will be outlined on the basis of these criteria. In conclusion, a roadmap will be proposed for realising these reforms.

2 The Mechanisms of European Governance

The analysis of the deficits of European governance is based on two normative premises. On the one hand, a strong European Union that is capable of acting depends upon legitimacy by procedures and by results, by the input and output of politics. Legitimacy by political output alone, often claimed to be enough for the European Union, does not work. Justice being in the centre of democracy–Rainer Forst defines democracy as the practice of justice[9]–can only be attained if free and equal citizens are able to participate in deciding who is shaping, and in which way, the structures of production and distribution of goods.[10] On the other hand, the legitimacy of European politics cannot be derived exclusively via the Member States. The European Union has far-reaching competences and influences everyday life of citizens in 27 Member States. This is why the European Union needs democratic structures of its own. The political power of this supranational organisation in order to be adequately justified requires structures that enable citizens to make their voices heard effectively.[11]

So far, such democratic structures do not exist in the European Union to a sufficient degree. This has to do with a specific form of European constitutionalism.

[9] Rainer Forst, *Normativität und Macht* (Suhrkamp 2015), 221.

[10] *Ibid*, 216.

[11] *Ibid*, 231: "Eine demokratische ist eine diskursiv gerechtfertigte Herrschaft, und das heißt eine solche, in der Rechtfertigungsstrukturen bestehen, die dem Maß der ausgeübten Herrschaft adäquat sind. Das erweitert die Frage demokratischer Herrschaft schon begrifflich über nationale Grenzen hinaus, je nachdem, in welche Herrschaftsbeziehungen ein Staat eingebettet ist".

Constitutions are a framework for politics and define the basic structure and principles for political decision-making. "What has been decided in the constitution is not the object but the premise of political decisions."[12] It is the task of politics to transform the constitutional principles into concrete policies and to use the space for interpretation when new challenges have to be met. Thus, "constitutions provide a durable structure for change."[13]

In the European Union, the treaties have become a quasi-constitution by virtue of two decisions of the European Court of Justice—the 1963 judgment in *Van Gend en Loos* and that in *Costa v. ENEL* in 1964. Since then, European law has been directly effective in Member States and European law has primacy over national law. However, while the European Court of Justice interprets the treaties "in a constitutional mode",[14] the treaties nonetheless differ from a constitution. In the European treaties, there are many provisions concerning concrete policies that would usually not be constitutional law but ordinary law. To deal with these treaties as if they were a constitution means, to use Dieter Grimm's term, an "over-constitutionalisation".[15] The effect has been a process of European integration not so much shaped by politics but by judicial interpretation. The European Court of Justice by interpreting the treaties and the Commission by implementing the treaties, decided questions with far-reaching political implications, circumventing public debates, parliaments and governments.

This mechanism of European governance has not only reduced democratic legitimacy in the European Union, but also influenced the substance of European politics. As the European Court of Justice has interpreted the treaties in a market-friendly way and interpreted the free movement of goods, persons, services and capital as being anti-regulation provisions,[16] the trend towards deregulation of the economy and privatisation of public services has been strengthened. This adjustment to the market has made it impossible for the European Union to effectively counteract the negative sides of globalisation like growing economic inequality and to regulate the power of private global actors in the interest of the European common good. Therefore, the question of Gertrude Lübbe-Wolff, whether the European Union doesn't offer an especially profitable field for speculation by transnational financial players, makes sense.[17]

This can be translated as follows: "Democratic governance is discursively justified governance and that means governance in which structures of justification exist that are adequate to the extent of power exercised. This expands the question of democratic governance conceptually beyond national borders, depending on the power relations in which a state is embedded".

[12] Dieter Grimm, "The Democratic Costs of Constitutionalization—The European Case" in Dieter Grimm, *The Constitution of European Democracy* (Oxford University Press 2017), 86.

[13] *Ibid*, 88.

[14] *Ibid*,91.

[15] *Ibid*, 97.

[16] *Ibid*, 94.

[17] Gertrude Lübbe-Wolff, "Die Zukunft der europäischen Verfassung" in Ulrike Davy and Gertrude Lübbe-Wolff (eds.) *Verfassung: Geschichte, Gegenwart, Zukunft. Autorenkolloquium mit Dieter Grimm* (Nomos 2018), 150.

In addition to the mechanism of an "over-constitutionalisation", we observe another characteristic of European governance that affects democratic legitimacy. When confronted with a crisis, the Commission and national executives often introduce new rules for governing without a public debate and without the influence of parliaments. For example, the Commission gained a lot of power during the Euro crisis.[18] Crisis management started in 2011 with five regulations and one directive (the so-called 'Six Pack') enabling the Commission to influence the budgetary policies of national parliaments. It is the Commission that translates the economic principles of the European Council into concrete instructions for the Member States, and it is also the Commission that advises the Council when it comes to assessing budgetary policies of Member States.[19]

On the basis of this evaluation, the Commission develops concrete guidelines for each Member State and parliaments have to adjust to these guidelines before they adopt their budget. The European Parliament sits in the auditorium and can only watch what is happening. All that MEPs can do is to initiate an economic dialogue with the President of the European Council or of the Euro group. Thus, the Commission became an important actor in shaping the budgetary policies of Member States during the Euro crisis. National parliaments lost power. Once the crisis was over, the measures were maintained. The new distribution of power turned out to be permanent.

The same happened with the "Next Generation EU" programme, which was initiated to fight the economic consequences of the COVID-19 pandemic. For the first time, the European Union has taken on debt on the capital market for which all Member States are jointly liable. The Commission places bonds on the capital markets and Member States guarantee these European bonds in proportion to their share of the European Union budget. A sum of up to 750 billion euro will be spent on programmes to counteract the social and economic consequences of the pandemic. These considerable financial resources will be spent primarily for climate protection and digitalisation. Modernisation projects have priority. In practical terms, "Next Generation EU" is the beginning of a European Fiscal Union.

"Next Generation EU" makes a lot of sense. Yet there is no basis in the treaties for such a programme. This is why politicians have claimed that it was an exception created for reasons of crisis management. But, once again, the exception seems likely to become the rule. The President of the Commission, Ursula von der Leyen, has proposed to take "Next Generation EU" as the model for organising the recovery plan for Ukraine. The mechanism is clear: political elites modify European governance by ad-hoc-measures. Thus, they can avoid difficult debates in public. They do not want to choose the risky path of a Convention and prefer changing the mode of governance through the back door of crisis management. The alternative is not between having

---

[18] For a detailed analysis of the Euro crisis, see Christine Landfried, *Das politische Europa. Differenz als Potential der Europäischen Union* (3rd (updated) edition, Nomos 2020), 153–186.

[19] See Regulation (EU) No 1175/2011 of the European Parliament and of the Council of 16 November 2011 amending Council Regulation (EC) No 1466/97 on the strengthening of the surveillance of budgetary positions and the surveillance and coordination of economic policies (OJ L 306 (23 November 2011)).

treaty changes or not. The alternative is between changing the treaties in a non-transparent, hidden way or in a transparent, democratic way.

The above-described mechanisms of European governance are not enhancing democracy. Yet a supranational organisation as powerful as the European Union needs democratic legitimacy in order to make effective use of its competencies. This means that reforms are overdue. What are the criteria that such reforms should fulfil?

3 The Criteria for Judging Reforms

First of all, reflecting rather than suppressing the European Union's transformation from a Single Market to a political order is of the utmost importance.[20] The changes of the last decades must be made conscious and ideas about Europe's future must be discussed in public in order to find a new consensus on the principles and rules of European governance. Such reflection has to include the role of the European Union as an international actor. A new balance between participating in the organisations of the multilateral order, on the one hand, and a certain degree of independence in strategic areas like energy and health, on the other, has to be a criterion for judging reforms.

Secondly, a reconsideration of Europe's social model and the values of justice and solidarity is necessary. According to Article 3 TEU, the European Union aims for a social market economy. But there is a huge gap between this goal and the reality. Since the 1970s, democratic governments in European countries and the United States have reacted to the process of globalisation by deregulating the economy. The European Union has not been an exception and indeed has strengthened this trend instead of being a protecting power in the process of globalisation.[21] Its decisions in favour of deregulation have given globalisation a certain direction shaped by an unequal distribution of goods, services, capital, technical and scientific achievements. Thomas Piketty has convincingly shown that once the rate of return on capital is "significantly above the growth rate for an extended period of time", then "the risk of divergence in the distribution of wealth is very high".[22] This mechanism has to be seen in relation to the unequal distribution of capital ownership.[23] Growing economic inequality (especially inequality of wealth) and social insecurity for ever larger segments of the population have not come out of the blue. Rather, democratically-elected governments have established, with their policies, structures that have systematically limited the capacity of societies to act and to learn. It will be difficult to change these structures.

---

[20] See for these criteria Christine Landfried, *op. cit.* (n.18), 299–302.

[21] Gertrude Lübbe-Wolff, "Ein Narrativ für die Europäische Union", *Frankfurter Allgemeine Zeitung* 6 January 2018, 9.

[22] Thomas Piketty, *Capital in the twenty-first century* (The Belknap Press of Harvard University Press 2014), 25.

[23] *Ibid*, 244 ff.

As a way out of this, political elites have chosen to downplay the problems. But a necessary condition for reforms will be putting the problems onto the table.

Thirdly, a criterion for judging reforms is the reduction of the gap between the comprehensive competencies of the European Union und the weak democratic legitimacy of European politics. The European Union is a representative democracy (Article 10 para 1 TEU). Representation means that the bond between representatives and represented is the foundation of the binding validity of politics.[24] Citizens must have the chance to engage in exchanges with elected representatives and to make their ideas and interests heard. Conflicts in such debates should not be avoided. And politicians, in turn, must consider these ideas, interests and conflicts in policy-making. What is "good politics" can only be found by the rationalising effect of public discourse.

Fourthly, and in connection with the last point, we need reforms that contribute to a reorganisation of European governance with a focus on the empowerment of citizens. Non-transparent reorganisations will not fulfil this condition, as we have experienced in the many crises of the last decades.

And fifthly, the regeneration of the European Union can only be successful if procedures of reflection, reconsideration, and reorganisation allow for representing the diversity of cultural, social and political difference, including the citizens throughout the process, having time for the exchange of opinions between represented and representatives, listening to the knowledge of experts and citizens and finally, allow for a thorough overhaul of European governance. Regeneration depends upon taking seriously the voice of citizens and caring about the results of the Conference on the Future of Europe.

---

[24] Ulrich K. Preuß, "Wo bleibt das Volk? Erwartungen an demokratische Repräsentation" in Margarete Fabricius-Brand and Bertram Börner (eds.), *4. Alternativer Juristinnen- und Juristentag* (Nomos 1996), 94.

3.1 The Conditions for a Democratic and Sovereign European Union

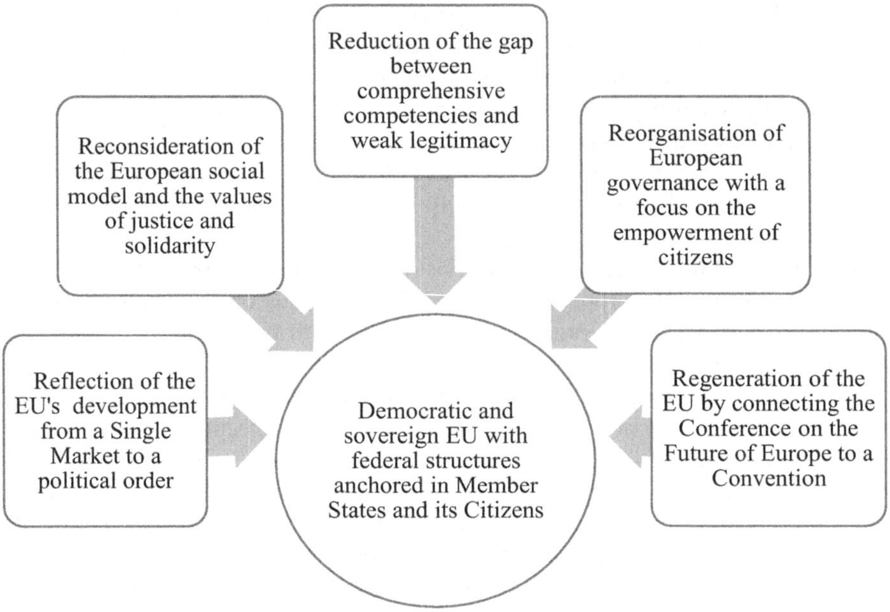

4 The Reforms for a Democratic and Sovereign European Union

Reforms must be embedded into a concept of the future European Union. Starting from the criteria I have developed, different paths are possible. Among the many scenarios discussed for the future European Union, its transformation into a federal state is according to Adrienne Héritier "implausible."[25] She argues that the main actors, the Member State governments, the European Council, the European Parliament, and the Commission have diverse preferences with regard to a European federal state. Yet, given that a reform of the treaties requires unanimity–or "a *de facto* large consensus"[26]–by the Member States in the European Council, a European federal state is unlikely to emerge.

Indeed, for the time being, a European federal state does not seem to be a realistic scenario. A federal state would mean that the Member States no longer transfer competences to the supranational level but that the European Union could decide about European competences in its own right. In a European federal state citizens

[25] Adrienne Héritier, *Quo Vadis, Europa? Five Paths, their Plausibility and Impact*, EUI Working Paper RSC 2021/49, 5.

[26] *Ibid*, 4–5.

would elect a federal parliament that then elects a European government. There would be a second chamber with representatives of Member States that participated in European legislation.[27]

I would propose taking a more differentiated view. The European Union could have strong federal elements without being a federal state. There are many intermediate stages between a union of states and a European federal state. Also, the main actors of the European Union cannot be reduced to the formal institutions but must include civil society, NGOs, citizens. And finally, the history of European integration demonstrates that the development usually was not linear but often took unexpected directions and turnoffs.

The European Union is not only unlikely to become a federal state, but also *should* not become a federal state in the near future, because the political will and important conditions for such a development—namely, a European identity and a lively European public sphere—so far do not exist to an adequate degree. Rather, the European Union should be a supranational organisation with strong federal structures, founded upon social justice, rule of law and democratic legitimacy matching European political power. In order to build up such a European Union and also to strengthen in the long run European identity and European public spheres, reforms cannot be postponed any more.

The following reforms that have been proposed by the Conference on the Future of Europe[28] not only have the potential to fulfil the conditions of a democratic and sovereign European Union (see diagram), but also demonstrate that randomly chosen citizens have communicative competence and can develop meaningful proposals for complex problems. To sum it up, the members of the Conference proposed, among other things, more autonomy in strategic sectors like digitalisation, energy and health, more democratic legitimacy by holding citizens' assemblies periodically, more justice by strengthening the social dimension, more transparency by giving understandable information about the European Union, and more effectiveness by deciding with qualified majority instead of unanimity in areas like the Common Foreign and Security Policy. Citizens underlined the necessity to implement values instead of just having them on paper. And finally, they pleaded for more openness to the necessary legal avenues, including treaty changes, in order to realise the proposals. This is why, according to the members of the Conference, the discussion about a European Constitution should be reopened and a Convention established. This clear position on the part of citizens in favour of a Convention is in sharp contrast to the approach of many politicians and scholars who prefer reforms that can be effected without changing the treaties.[29]

---

[27] *Ibid*, 2.

[28] For the 49 recommendations, see Conference on the Future of Europe, *Report on the Final Outcome* (European Parliament, Council of the EU, European Commission, Brussels, Strasbourg, May 2022).

[29] For a recent example see Christian Calliess, "Für eine bessere und größere EU", *Frankfurter Allgemeine Zeitung*, 13 July 2023, 6. Calliess makes convincing reform proposals, but emphasises that these reforms can be realised within the frame of the existing treaties.

5 Conclusion

It will be decisive that the political elites governing the European Union does not go on to reform the European Union by *ad-hoc*-measures of crisis management without any public debates. Rather, the elected elites must take the overdue decision to have a Convention in order to start a democratic and transparent process for finding a new consensus about the future political system of the European Union. Such a Convention could be built upon the impressive work of the Conference on the Future of Europe and draft the changes to the current treaties that are necessary for making the European Union fit for the twenty-first century. Including randomly chosen citizens and representatives of civil society into this process from the very beginning, would demonstrate that the people who are governed by the collectively binding rules should be the co-authors of these rules.[30]

Nobody can tell beforehand which concrete institutional framework would result from such a process of deliberation, communication, bargaining and finally deciding about the future rules of European governance. But one can indicate the direction that would make sense for a European Union in the twenty-first century. The European Union should not be a federal state, but rather a supranational organisation with strong federal structures, anchored in its Member States, shaped by the effective participation of citizens[31] and having the capacity to transform cultural, economic and political differences between nation states into an overall unit.[32]

---

[30] Rainer Forst, *op. cit.* (n. 9), 23.

[31] Claus Leggewie, *Europa zuerst! Eine Unabhängigkeitserklärung* (Ullstein 2017), 129–130.

[32] Ernst-Wolfgang Böckenförde, "Kommentar zu Ulrich K. Preuß 'Auf der Suche nach Europas Verfassung'" in (1999) 17 *Transit* 177: "Ausgangspunkt...muss die Einsicht sein, dass EG (und EU)... eine genuin föderale Struktur erhalten müssen. Diese Struktur muss föderal im Sinne eines politischen Föderalismus sein, der auf den politisch organisierten Völkern aufbaut, um von ihnen her eine übergreifende Einheit zu bilden".

This may be translated as "The starting point... must be the insight that the EC (and EU)... must receive a genuinely federal structure. This structure must be federal in the sense of a political federalism that builds on the politically organised peoples in order to form an overarching unity".

Author Index

G. Barrett et al. (eds.), *European Sovereignty*,
https://doi.org/10.1007/978-3-031-71851-9

The manufacturer's authorised representative in the EU is Springer Nature Customer Service Centre GmbH, Europaplatz 3, 69115 Heidelberg, Germany. If you have any concerns regarding our products, please contact ProductSafety@springernature.com

Printed and bound by CPI Group (UK) Ltd, Croydon, CR0 4YY
30/09/2026
02225589-0006